W9-ABX-451

PRACTICAL
LANDSCAPING & LAWN CARE

DAVID A. WEBB

WITHDRAWN
FROM THE RODMAN PUBLIC LIBRARY

TAB TAB BOOKS Inc.

Blue Ridge Summit, PA 17214

RODMAN PUBLIC LIBRARY

635.9
W365
A-1

Also by the Author from TAB BOOKS Inc.

No. 1518 *Growing Fruits and Berries*

Dedicated
to Charles, Robert, Merry,
and my mother, Marion

FIRST EDITION

FIRST PRINTING

Copyright © 1985 by TAB BOOKS Inc.

Printed in the United States of America

Reproduction or publication of the content in any manner, without express
permission of the publisher, is prohibited. No liability is assumed with respect to
the use of the information herein.

Library of Congress Cataloging in Publication Data

Webb, David A.
Practical landscaping and lawn care.

Includes index.
1. Landscape gardening. 2. Lawns. I. Title.
SB473.W395   1985   635.9   85-4618
ISBN 0-8306-0818-4
ISBN 0-8306-1818-X (pbk.)

Cover photo by The O.M. Scott & Sons Company.

Contents

Part 2   Natural Fences

Part 3   Herbaceous Flowering Plants

Part 4   Lawns and Groundcovers

Part 5   Flowering Woody Ornamentals

Acknowledgments

I would like to thank the following people and organizations for the help they provided:

Ada V. Murr, Assistant to Marketing Services Manager, Start Brothers' Nurseries & Orchards Co., Louisiana, Missouri.

Ken Ball, Community Affairs Specialist, Denver Water Department, Denver, Colorado.

Associated Landscape Contractors of Colorado, Denver, Colorado.

Dr. David F. Karnosky, Director, New York Botanical Garden Institute of Urban Horticulture, Millbrook, New York.

Jeanette Lowe, Staff Horticulturist/Public Relations, W. Atlee Burpee Co., Warminster, Pennsylvania.

Marion Michaels of Black River Falls, Wisconsin.

Dr. Robert I. Webb of Chicago, Illinois.

Charles Webb of Chippewa Falls, Wisconsin.

Mary Borofka-Webb of Chippewa Falls, Wisconsin.

Star Przybilla of Whitehall, Wisconsin.

Paul & Alvalina Nandory of Black River Falls, Wisconsin.

Evelyn Tester, Public Library, Black River Falls, Wisconsin.

Elizabeth Spangler of Black River Falls, Wisconsin.

Doris Erhardt of Black River Falls, Wisconsin.

Introduction

Imagine the delight of a yard filled with fragrant flowering plants. You will probably want to enjoy and get full value of your landscape in all seasons with spring—flowering lilacs, dogwood, daffodils, and violets; summer—blossoming or fruiting species like climbing Boston ivy or heavenly blue morning glory; autumn—blooming mums and container-grown genetic dwarf fruits that can even be raised in city apartments; and dark twisting branches against the white winter snow. All of these add to the delight of your landscape, and some plants provide ornamental interest for more than one season. (Chapter 2 is devoted especially to seasonal landscaping.)

Practical Landscaping and Lawn Care emphasizes that planting has a purpose, and the proper selection of plants can be used to create many desired effects. The goal of a well-thought-out landscape plan has plants in harmonious relationship to each other for the pleasure and convenience of owner and visitors.

Some sample landscape plan diagrams are included throughout the book. You should select plants that are hardy to your region, adaptable to the soil and other conditions (such as urban pollution), and that will help create the desirable seasonal colors and other effects such as shade, privacy screening, fruits, etc.

Special attention is given to hardiness throughout the book. Sickly plants are neither pleasurable nor useful. Having a beautiful specimen die is not a happy experience.

Because pure water is becoming a scarce commodity, Chapter 4 deals with this problem. Other chapters deal with the dry conditions that accompany water problems and suggest ways to save money on your water bills.

Each chapter compares species of the same type (i.e., lawn trees) to help you choose wisely among them for plants that you like and that would do best in your yard.

Practical Landscaping and Lawn Care is especially designed for people who might not be able to afford to hire greenskeepers, but want their yard to look as if they do have a staff.

Chapter 1

Plan Your Home Landscape

Successful landscaping starts with a plan, and you can avoid errors that might interfere with your final landscape design if you plan carefully (Fig. 1-1). For example, you will not want to block paths or driveways, obscure scenic views, hide windows, etc. Proper plant selection and placement is often critical; the final landscape, if it is to be appealing, must be more than just a mish-mash of individual plants. There must be a harmony of design and practicality of purpose in the shrubbery, trees, vines, and groundcovers that you put to use around your home.

The landscaping of your home requires you to consider many factors:

☐ Your site analysis. This includes soils, climate (Fig. 1-2), and the physical features of your property, both natural and man-made.
    ☐ Your home's architectural features.
    ☐ The neighborhood landscape character.
    ☐ Your lifestyle.
    ☐ Energy conservation.

☐ A central theme that best illustrates the effects you want to create.

SITE ANALYSIS

To develop the best design, you need a visual and physical analysis of your property that takes into account the existing conditions unique to your site. Draw up a list of existing conditions that have immediate or potential effects on the property. This list should include anything that is seen, heard, felt, or smelled. If you live next to a factory that produces unpleasant odors, one of your landscape goals should be to mask that odor. Certain strongly scented ornamental shrubbery will do the trick. Or you might want to hide an unsightly view with a tall hedge. You will discover that utility in landscape design depends upon how the selected plants can best meet your needs and be useful to you. A practical landscape can be measured by how successfully the landowner can modify or overcome site restrictions, as well as enhance and promote the property's good features.

1

Fig. 1-1. Successful landscaping starts with a plan.

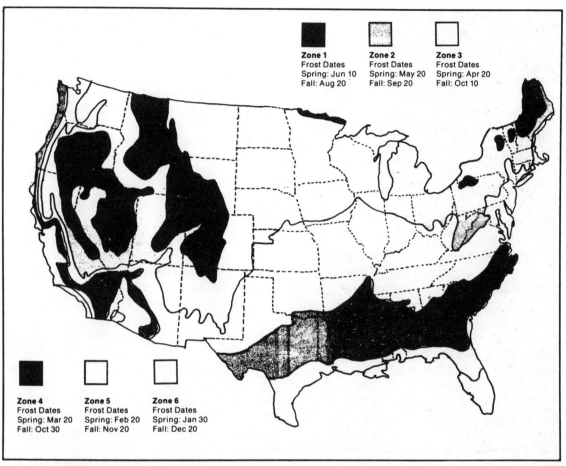

Fig. 1-2. Vegetable zone guide for climates.

The size and shape of the land, direction of the sun and winds, and the surrounding views of lakes, mountains, forests, parks, etc., all offer limitations and/or opportunities for landscape design. The land and buildings each express certain characteristics and offer various possibilities. You really have to get a feel for the land to fully understand what your site has to offer. Landscaping is an art.

Soils

Your property's soil is important because it must support both plants and man-made structures. Soil information is needed to determine what plants will grow best on the land or if changes must be made. Your county *agricultural extension service* will test your soil for a small fee. The soil can be tested for its *pH level* (acidity or alkalinity), natural fertility, and availability of trace elements or nutrients. (Note: throughout this book, the addition of peat moss and oakleaf mold is recommended. These organics can change the pH level, making soil more acidic. Test before and after adding them.)

Native plants already on your property can help you to identify the local environmental and soil conditions. Wild blueberries and pine trees can indicate acidic soil. Once you learn more about plants and their different habitat needs, you will become quite adept at judging the conditions of a site by the plants that grow there.

It is usually most important that your soil drains

3

well. Wet soils are detrimental to most plant growth. If poor drainage is a problem, you may have to have drainage tiles installed or the strategic burying of gravel before you plant. If difficulties persist, consult your county agricultural agent for assistance.

Sandy soils must have added ingredients to hold water and all soils will benefit from the addition of organic matter such as leaves, manure, or peat moss to them.

The soil needs of individual plant species vary, sometimes even within the same plant family. Check our individual soil requirements before setting out plants.

Climate

You obviously also have to take climate into account. No matter how much you admired your Georgia cousins' beautiful magnolia and peach trees, you will not want the grief of watching them die in the north.

Your Georgia relatives should resist the temptation to decorate their yard with rhubarb or other plants that may languish or die in climates with hot summers and warm winters.

Climate and weather affect plant life more than any other factors. Climate is the ultimate determinant of plant selection, so minimum winter temperatures are useful in determining both the northern and southern limits of plant *hardiness*. Plant hardiness is crucial. Resist the temptation to boost your ego by having the only southern magnolia or date tree in North Dakota. Any plant that is not sufficiently hardy for your area should not be planted. To do otherwise is to court disaster.

Your landscape will be affected by rainfall, frost-free periods, wind direction, and other features of your climate. Areas east of the Mississippi are usually humid. Areas to the west are usually quite dry. Artificial irrigation will be necessary in areas where natural rainfalls are too light to support plant life. In the north, the number of frost-free days per growing season can rule out certain ornamentals that may flourish in the south, which has a longer growing season.

Wind always affects temperature. A heavy wind can produce a *windchill factor*. The wind intensifies the temperatures, making cold winters even more severe by lowering temperatures considerably. During the summers, these same heavy winds can aggravate drought conditions and rapidly dehydrate plant life.

The changing direction of the sun from winter to summer creates a whole different set of sunlight and shade patterns on the land and buildings. Knowing where there is sunlight or shade at different hours helps solve planting problems and lets you plan for outdoor activity and living space as well.

Physical Features

Is your land sloping or flat? This characteristic of land is called *topography*. Aesthetically sloping land is most pleasing, but it may also produce *frost pockets* as cold air settles to the lower areas. A level or flat piece of land places fewer restrictions on planting, but flat land has less protection from the wind. Therefore, more climate-control elements such as windbreak trees are needed.

Your homesite may already have trees, shrubs, or other plants. Before deciding to include them in your landscape design, you must know what they are. Some may be desirable others not. Consider also the general quality or appearance of these existing plants. Will they interfere with the rest of your landscape design? What sunlight and shade patterns do they create?

It is also good to keep in mind that many of your own plantings may take several years to achieve the look and effect you want. Perhaps some of the present trees should be maintained for shade while your trees mature, and possibly longer. Nothing is uglier than a new house surrounded by a barren piece of land with a few twigs sticking out of the ground (your plantings) and a sea of mud or sand. Your children can play, or your friends can relax beneath a magnificent shade tree, be it oak, maple, willow, or other. Keeping existing shade trees and/or shrubs helps maintain the dignity of the scenery and provides a continuity for the neighbors.

The network of deep roots from existing adult trees and shrubs will help control any drainage problem of either too much or too little water. Your existing shrubs and trees will add oxygen to the air to counteract auto emissions, smoke, and other possible fumes in the neighborhood.

Although you have the legal right to remove every living green plant on your land (and even to bulldoze off several inches of topsoil), it is not the best policy, if you can possibly avoid it. This is the same rape of the land that contributes to mudslides, dustbowls, and the spreading deserts around the world.

Landscape Structures

Many people think they have to spend a great deal of money buying elaborate structures for their landscape. Such items as wooden decks, concrete patios, and wooden or chain-link fences are all right, but they are not usually necessary and may even detract from the beauty of your home.

There is something earthy and romantic about a simple path of rocks strewn along a trails. It is as effective as a concrete sidewalk, but looks more natural—as if the rocks had always been there. Another advantage is that it can be constructed for free if you are in or near an area where rocks are plentiful. All you have to do is collect the rocks.

If chain-link fences are popular in your neighborhood, you may decide to use one. To some people, however, chain links are reminiscent of schoolyards or prison compounds. A hedge will provide a living wall that is both more elegant and aesthetically satisfying. If you really love the look of a wooden fence, natural toned stained kinds are easier to maintain than painted fences and will blend in better with your landscape.

Gravel paths or driveways can be convenient, but they have certain drawbacks. Gravel is not very comfortable to walk on, and the little stones are very tempting to children to pick up and throw. If mud is a problem in your area, you might want to use a rock path or have your driveway paved.

Treated wood can also be used effectively for paths. It is especially appealing in areas where there are differences in ground elevation, as on hillsides. The woods helps retain the earth when used to create a natural stairway up the hill.

Brick paths are lovely. They can be informal—placed into the earth with grass growing between each brick, or they can be cemented in. The herringbone pattern is most popular, and natural earthtone-colored bricks are generally preferable to brightly painted bricks. Bright colors tend to attract attention, which is considered desirable in commercial places: most homeowners however, do not want their house to look like a "hot dog stand." Bricks taken from torn-down chimneys cannot be reused for fireplace purposes, but these used bricks, even when nicked or broken, make a handsome path. Save new bricks for your outdoor (or indoor) fireplace.

Size of Property

Your landscape plan will depend, in part, upon the size of your property. If you are fortunate enough to own a few acres, you will be able to do more and plan differently than if you own a mere city lot. A home on a small urban lot usually has much less space for plantings in the front yard or backyard than a suburban home.

You will want to decide whether to consult with landscape architects and other experts, which can be rather expensive. For most people, the practical approach is to design your own plan. Your plan should be as individual as you are. No two houses are exactly alike, even those built from identical plans, and neither are any two sites or families identical. Each home soon takes on the character of the people who live there, and your landscape plan must be realistic for the size of your property. Huge plants on a tiny parcel of land may look out of place.

YOUR HOME'S ARCHITECTURAL FEATURES

Nothing adds more to the value of a home than a good landscape, but it should be appropriate (Fig. 1-3). It should look as if it goes with the house, and the two do not compete with each other.

Your house's architectural features are important to your landscape theme. Many older Victorian homes required foundation plantings to hide ugly foundations; the ranch homes of today do not have this problem. Foundation planting are often used, but out of choice, not necessity. And it is possible to use plants in more creative ways.

Fig. 1-3. Your house's architectural features are important to your landscape theme.

A French provincial home calls for plants with certain traits that will complement the house's special features. Jackpine or other rugged trees and shrubs will not do the house justice. A refined house wants refined shrubbery. A log or mountain home, on the other hand, looks more natural with rugged, "woodsy" plants. It should not be surrounded with formal landscape plants. It would not look right and would ruin the *ambience* (feel) of the place.

The architectural style of your home may be the result of your voluntary choice, what you have inherited, or what you can afford. A practical landscape design should relate to the architectural lines and style of the house. Architecture, like landscaping, is to some degree a matter of personal preference. The trend is toward "organic" living and making the utilitarian-type home more romantic. Stone, brick, and masonry houses are the most organic, as are wood houses stained to earth tones; houses of painted wood or aluminum lap siding detract from the landscape.

Any home, no matter what the style, can be improved by proper landscaping. The secret is in understanding dimensions and lines, and in having a basic grasp of size relationships. It sounds complicated, but it is really quite simple. All it takes is common sense and a little practice to develop an "eye" for what should go where (Fig. 1-4).

THE NEIGHBORHOOD LANDSCAPE CHARACTER

It is usually wise to take the neighborhood landscape character into consideration when designing your own landscape plans. One criterion used to evaluate a community is the appearance of its homes and grounds. Your plans may not fit in with those of your neighbors, depending upon where you live. In many areas, you may find that your landscape is a source of constant concern to your neighbors.

It is best to avoid conflicts whenever possible, but you need not compromise to the point of mindless conformity. Look over your neighborhood and observe its landscape features. If everyone else is raising honeylocust trees, do you really want to grow pine? And if your neighbors pride themselves on their lawns, will they consider your wildflower garden a welcome sight or a weed patch?

Your landscape should be individual, and it should reflect the needs of your family, but remember the only real rights you have in life are those you fight for. The best way to get your neighbors to accept your landscape is to try to talk some of them into changing their own.

It is indeed monotonous to be in a neighborhood where everybody's place looks identical to the other—where even the same plants are used repetitiously. Anything that is considered too "different" may create unpleasant frictions, however. Sometimes you can create an unusual landscape that does not depart too radically from the rest of the neighborhood. Other times you may have to take a stand and fight for your freedom of expression. It

is worth considering. Certainly you will not want to find yourself in the position of the woman who came home to find that her neighbors had "helped" her by mowing off her grapevines!

YOUR LIFE STYLE

The success of a useful landscape plan is more assured when the project is well thought out and not forced onto a site. Your landscape should reflect your life style. Your needs and the time you will have to care for your shrubs must all be considered. Most people will not want to spend all of their free time doing yard work, so they will want to develop low-maintenance landscapes.

A key to planning the landscape for the people who will use it is to thoroughly understand their goals—what they need, what they want, and what they can afford.

Family characteristics, such as the number of family members, ages, and activities, should dictate

Fig. 1-4. One criterion used to evaluate a community is the appearance of its homes and grounds.

7

the type of landscape used. Children's play areas and outdoor recreation sites could be important. Hobbies and garden ventures, whether for fun or profit, need to be provided for in the best locations.

Will there be needs for storage, parking, and roadways? What about animals or pets? All of these things may be part of your life style. If you entertain at home, you will want more recreational space than if you never have guests—although it is wise for every yard to have some space reserved for outdoor recreational activities. Do not forget to consider your changing needs as years go by.

People with small children will want plants that are more durable and not so easily damaged as those chosen by people who live alone. People with arthritis will not want plants that require a great deal of pruning or maintenance work.

ENERGY CONSERVATION

Landscape your home with energy conservation in mind. To do so is most practical: strategically placed trees, shrubs, and vines can keep your house cooler in the summer and warmer in the winter (Fig. 1-5).

Trees help cool your yard and home in the summer with the shade they produce. Their leaves reflect and absorb solar radiation, thus lowering temperatures. The sun is high in the sky during the summer, and it heats yard areas on the south and west sides of buildings, so tall trees with a broad, dense canopy are desirable. These type trees produce the most shade and are called *shade trees*. Trees such as oaks and maples should be planted on the south and west sides of your house. Choose deciduous trees because they drop their leaves during the fall and allow the low winter sun to penetrate and warm the house. In warmer climates, where cooling is required on a year round basis, you will have a greater selection in your choice of trees.

Wall-climbing vines provide some shade on walls, windows, and porches. Even when plants do not directly provide shade, they help to moderate

Fig. 1-5. Strategically placed trees, shrubs, and vines can keep your house cool in the summer and warmer in the winter.

air temperatures by scattering and absorbing radiation.

Asphalt and concrete are especially common in cities. These surfaces heat up quickly during the day and lose heat quickly at night. Exposed soil has the same trait and also tends to dry out, pulverize, and turn into dust. Grass, flowers, vines, and other groundcovers are important for both beautifying and protecting the soil, as well as for maintaining more comfortable surface temperatures.

Trees help modify temperatures by a process called *transpiration*. This transpiration process cools the area around the tree in much the same way as perspiration cools our body. On a hot day, the leaves of a single isolated tree can release up to 100 gallons of water into the air. This is the equivalent of five room air conditioners.

Plants also help modify temperatures by forming *wind channels*. Breezes usually come from the south in summer. Trees and shrubs can be planted so that they increase the force of the wind and channel it in desired directions, such as toward windows.

Increased air flow occurs under a *canopy* of trees. A row of trees with high branches forms a "ceiling" underneath which the wind is traveling at greater velocity than elsewhere.

In winter, you can channel cold winds away from your home with *windbreaks*—a close row of trees or other tall shrubs placed to shield an area from heavy winds. The protection provided by windbreaks depends on such things as height, density, and branching habit. Plants create better windbreaks than man-made materials, because they diffuse some of the wind rather than just detouring it.

Maximum wind protection usually occurs at a distance of four to six times the height of the windbreak. If you have trees that grow 30 feet tall, plant them about 120 feet away from the house. Windbreaks that have some spaces in them for the wind to pass through are usually better than solid windbreaks. This is because solid windbreaks can create a strong current called *downwind*. Downwinds are those gusts that appear on the leeward side of the windbreaks.

The coldest winds come from the north; the strongest winds usually come from the west. Shelter plantings on these sides are most beneficial. Evergreen trees and shrubs usually provide more protection than deciduous plants, which are usually leafless in the winter.

Shrubs that are planted near, but not directly against, your house foundation can help to prevent the escape of heat from your home. The denser the planting, the greater the protection.

THEME

Every landscape should have a theme. Before you begin to develop the theme of your landscape and incorporate the effects you wish to create, you should understand some basic principles of landscape design.

Home landscapes differ according to family needs and preferences, but successful designs have certain underlying principles in common. Concepts such as unity, balance, accent, and proportion are all important.

Unity. When a landscape's predominant features have some visual characteristics in common, it is said to have *unity*. Plants that have similar shapes, colors, and textures can create unity, both on your property and within your neighborhood. This is also true of lawns, paving materials, and architectural designs. Repeating a design pattern, color, or texture in various locations helps create unity—like the stone of a barbecue pit being the same as that of the bird bath. Unless a landscape has a certain among of unity it will not look right. Chaotic yards stick out like a sore thumb.

Balance. *Balance* is achieved by the use of plants and landscape structures that have similar visual importance. With form, texture, color, and size you can direct attention to several areas of the yard or garden. Balance may be *symmetrical (formal),* in which each side of the yard is similar in pattern, almost like a mirror image. Or it can be *asymmetrical (informal),* in which each side may attract the same attention, but the greenery and spacing are very different in appearance.

Accent. *Accents* are necessary to create focal

points in your yard to which attention is immediately drawn. This helps to keep a design's unity and balance from becoming monotonous. A single contrast in color, texture, shape, or height will create a focal point. A gazebo, a bird bath, a majestic oak, or a hillside rock garden may be the focus around which all or part of your yard is centered. Many different plants can be selected to provide accents to your yard. When choosing plants that you wish to emphasize, try to keep in mind the four seasons; accent plants should not belong to only one short week of the spring or summer.

Proportion. *Proportion* refers to the size relationships among plants, structures, and open spaces. If a landscape is to be effective it must be in proportion. A 40-foot shade tree may look nice next to a high-rise building or in a large backyard, but is may be out of proportion if planted in the front yard of a small city lot. It could also shade out other plant life, such as flowers and grass.

In some situations, group plantings will compensate for plants that are too narrow to be impressive as individual shrubs. Some small shrubs are also most effective when planted in groups.

The space you have to work in is a limiting factor. Most people do not have an unlimited area. They can not start planting everything haphazardly. They must be sure to save room for their favorites. In selecting plants, it is best to list a first, second, and third choice. Remember, however, no plant is an island—each must fit into the whole picture.

Linear Design. The *linear* concept of design means that you are using lines to draw your plan. These lines may be straight or curved. Frequently patio, deck, and planting beds are laid out in straight lines that extend or parallel house and property lines. Equally successful and more natural designs can be created with curved lines.

Trafficways. Plants, buildings, and fences are used to divide a parcel of land into smaller living sections. These outdoor spaces should have separate identities to meet your area needs. They also should have *trafficways*—openings that leave room for passage from one area to another.

Maintenance Plan. The time to begin a maintenance plan for your yard is when the landscape is first designed. Maintenance does not have to be drudgery. Although many ambitious designs can make tons of work, most people today strive for a program of minimum maintenance.

THE FINAL DESIGN

Success or failure in producing a practical landscape often depends upon the planning stage. A landscape must look good 12 months of the year, not just in spring and summer. Also, how will it look in 4, 12, or 20 years? The picture you paint with your landscape is not a still life. Take time to coordinate your plantings; no amount of planting can overcome the lack of good organization.

You do not have to be a landscape architect or horticulturist to create a beautiful yard that will win you the praise and admiration of your friends and neighbors. All you need is an understanding of the basic principles of landscape design discussed above, a love of plants, and some common sense.

Design principles help you to map out what your landscape will look like before you begin planting—to help you spot possible errors and trouble spots, and save you money and wasted time and labor. The process of planning itself will make you better organized. Knowing what you want is the first step to attaining it.

Develop a Plan

Developing a plan is a fairly simple process, although it will require some time and thought. Each member of the family should have some input into the planning process so that the final plan best reflects the needs and desires of the entire family. Some compromises may have to be ironed out. For example, if Johnny likes to play basketball, he should let it be known that he wants a place to play. The way he will not be dribbling near your petunia bed. The greater the family member participation, the more likely the final landscape will meet the family needs and gain the cooperation desirable for upkeep.

A limited budget should not inhibit you from

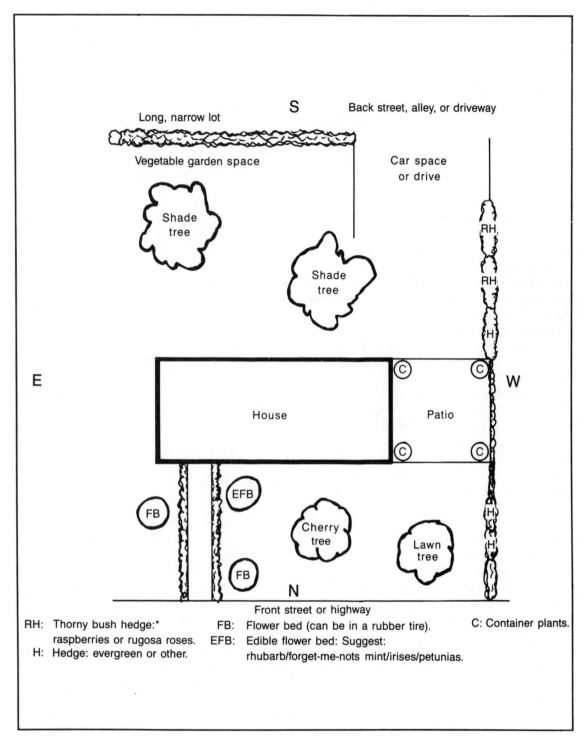

S

Long, narrow lot

Back street, alley, or driveway

Vegetable garden space

Car space or drive

Shade tree

Shade tree

RH

RH

H

E

C   C

W

House

Patio

C   C

EFB

FB

Cherry tree

Lawn tree

H

H

FB

N

Front street or highway

RH: Thorny bush hedge:*
raspberries or rugosa roses.
H: Hedge: evergreen or other.

FB: Flower bed (can be in a rubber tire).
EFB: Edible flower bed: Suggest:
rhubarb/forget-me-nots mint/irises/petunias.

C: Container plants.

Fig. 1-6. Landscape plan #1. Courtesy of Marion Michaels.

developing your plan. Rome was not built in a day. It is not crucial that you plant everything that you want all at one time. Concentrate on the basics, such as selecting trees and shrubs that will be focal points from which you develop your landscape. You can make additions of one or two desired shrubs each year, as your budget allows. Times change and so will the needs of your family. Your landscape should be flexible enough to incorporate these changes, so that it continually reflects your changing life style.

Moods in Landscaping

Plants create "moods" in a landscape. Trees and shrubs with pendulant or weeping branches savor an idyllic, tranquil mood. Conifers, such as spruce and pines, create a "woodsy" mood. There are an astonishing number of other mods that can be created by plant selection. All of these contribute to a landscape's character.

Landscapes usually are most effective when they display a central theme, although your yard can be divided up to express many themes. The effect(s) that you want to suggest or express, whether it be a stately, dignified look; a folksy, down-home country flair; or whatever you choose to express, will all be reflected in the plants you select.

Draw A Plan

A plan permits all parts of the landscape to be fitted together like parts to a puzzle. When carefully planned, the total landscape will present a complete and pleasing scenario.

A rough sketch is usually a suitable way to begin your plan. The sketch should include all buildings, walks, and driveways, as well as all existing trees and shrubs. It is not necessary that the sketch be drawn to exact scale, although a rough idea of the size of the area involved is vital. If you do draw to scale, remember to consider before you plant the *mature* size of the plant for each location. Otherwise you may overcrowd plants or space them so as to create undesirable gaps.

You can use any kind of paper you prefer to draw your rough draft. A plain sheet of white typewriter paper is sufficient. you will want to draw several rough drafts before you establish the final plan. Try to keep a perspective of what spaces are involved. Graph paper can be useful.

Your final design is the master plan. This will be your "blueprint" to your landscape. Understanding the principles of landscape design and plant composition will aid you in completing your project successfully (Fig. 1-6).

Chapter 2

Calendar of Change

It is important to remember when designing your landscape that the seasons are not static. Unless you live in the Deep South or California, it is to your advantage to plan your landscape to incorporate those changes. Plant for seasonal interest throughout the year. Bark and branch structure, foliage texture, and fruits are as important as flowers in making an attractive landscape.

It is only natural that large showy flowers are the first thing we look for in a landscape. Beauty is always pleasing to the eye, but for practical landscaping, it is wise to plant some species that will provide interesting features for those seasons when flowers are rare or absent altogether (Fig. 2-1).

BARK AND BRANCH STRUCTURE

The branching habits and bark of a tree or shrub can make the plant an attractive species, independent of any other qualities. The best example to illustrate the importance of bark is that of the white birch. These trees are usually grown in clumps of two or three and always make a sensational effect when planted in the home landscape.

A lesser-known species, the river birch, is quite lovely for the peeling nature of its sandy-brown bark. The shagbark hickory offers similar attraction due to its unusual peeling bark.

Some trees are noticeable for their smooth bark. The american hornbeam, with its musclelike trunk, is interesting to look at even when barren of leaves. Its trunk looks almost like the human biceps muscle.

A plant's branching structure can make it attractive. The Japanese maple has an arching branch structure that gives it an "oriental" look. Weeping willows are perhaps the most famous example of the effects that are created by a tree's branching habits.

SHAPES

Plants have different shapes and growth habits. Each shape or form is suited to some landscape uses better than to others. To understand where a plant will look its best, one has to consider the entire scenario. Sometimes a lovely shrub may look out

Fig. 2-1. Beauty is always pleasing to the eye.

of place when set in an area in which it does not belong. Always select your trees, vines, and shrubs for how they will fit into your landscape, not because it looked so pretty at so and so's. Some of the basic shapes are vertical, horizontal, pendulant, pyramidal, columnar, and rounded.

Vertical. Vertical forming shrubs and trees are best used sparingly as accent plants, or to provide height. They are usually quite tall and stand erect. They are most effective in those areas where taller plants are needed.

Horizontal. Horizontal plants are useful for providing width to a scene. They tend to create the impression of attaching structures or buildings to the ground. These plants are extremely popular, especially when set out beside the ranch style homes they complement so well. They tend to complement horizontal architectural lines in any building.

Pendulant. *Pendulant,* or weeping, plants are

best for accents. They may take up more space than many other landscape plants, and on small parcels of land it may not be practical to use them in any abundance. A weeping specimen always creates a focal point of attention.

Pyramidal. Trees and shrubs with *pyramidal* growth forms are also useful accent pieces. They add a dignified air to an estate, and they are quite practical for use as living fences to screen out unpleasant sights. They are also very effective when combined with rounded and horizontal plants.

Columnar. Those plants with *columnar* shapes are very useful for screens and windbreaks. They share many of the characteristics of pyramidal plants except these are narrower and can be grown closer together. Columnar specimens are ideal for entryways.

Rounded. Round shrubs are useful for creating large masses of greenery. They can be set in borders or placed as entry guards. They usually take up more space than narrower columnar types.

FOLIAGE

Leaves come in many forms; single and multiple-leafed species abound. Some leaves are smooth-edged, others are toothed, and some are deeply lobed. Some leaves have sharp tips, and others are rounded at the ends. Some leaves have two to three leaves together to form a leaflet; others have 30 or more. Other plants have needlelike leaves (the best example is the coniferous species).

Texture. The effect that is created by a plant's foliage is more than just the different types of shade cast. The size of a plant's leaves, twigs, and branches determine its *texture*. Fine-textured plants have small leaves and twigs. Coarse-textured plants have large leaves and twigs, and medium-textured plants are in between. Fine-textured plants are best suited to formal gardens, but you might want to select plants from among all three textures. Often the size of an area will determine which texture is most appropriate. A small space will seem larger when planted with fine-textured species rather than coarse-textured ones.

Coarse-textured plants are usually avoided in elegant settings. They are more often reserved for wooded areas and country homesteads. Some of them, however, bear large showy flowers, and for that reason they may be included in your landscape. The smaller leaves and those plants with leaflets (with many leaves on the same bract) offer a finer texture than do the large single-leaf plants, although the latter usually produce a deeper shade.

Some leaves are smooth and others are *pubescent* (have little hairs on them). Some leaves are glossy and others are dull. All leaves tend to reflect and scatter solar radiation, which helps to explain the *thermodynamics of shade* (leaves cooling effect).

Color. Color is another important aspect. Some leaves are light green, some are dark green, some have silvery undersides, and some leaves are not even green at all. There are leaves that are tipped with different colors; other leaves are shades of bronze, red, yellow, or purple. In many cases, the leaves of a tree or shrub can be just as pretty as its flowers—and in some cases more so.

The Sunburst cultivar of honeylocust is an example of a tree that is planted for the effect of its leaves, which look as if they are always in bloom because of the yellow edges and yellow new growth. The crimson maple is a popular shade tree that is commonly planted for its crimson-colored leaves throughout the summer. Some people like the effect it creates; others prefer the green form of the species.

Fall Color. When most people think of leaf color, they think of the autumnal displays of many deciduous plants that change their leaf color before they drop. Some plants are almost exclusively planted for their fall color display. The burning bush is an excellent example. Although it is a lovely specimen or summer hedge, its real time is in the fall when its leaves turn into a riot of color that adds spectacular beauty to the autumnal landscape.

The same is true of many other deciduous species. The maples are perhaps the most famous of the fall coloring plants. Whether used as shrubs or trees, the maple family will usually provide excellent fall colors. This is not true for all varieties of maple, however. Some, such as crimson maple, are grown more for their summer foliage and do not provide a brightly colored fall display. Japanese dwarf maples can be used in areas where a small tree is wanted.

Different varieties of maple have different fall leaf colors. Silver maple leaves turn bright yellow, sugar maple leaves turn bright orange or golden orange, and red maples have red fall leaves. Select cultivars such as October Glory, for best fall color display.

Decide which colors you want in your autumn landscape. Usually a mix of brightly colored trees is most impressive. Do not limit yourself to the maple family; many other deciduous trees and shrubs have fall color. Check with your nursery to select those you prefer.

Incidentally, one very utilitarian aspect of growing sugar maples is that after a few years you will be able to tap the spring sap for maple syrup and sugar. Check with your county agricultural extension before attempting this. They can provide you with the technique to tap maple sap with as little

15

injury to the tree as possible. Any time you tap your tree, it will leave a scar. For this reason, you might want to grow some trees in a separate area for syrup production and let your other trees be.

FRUITS

Many trees and shrubs produce fruits, but not all fruits are the kind we usually think of as *fruit*. Some fruits are best left for birds or ornamental display. They may be too sour or dry to eat, or be inedible because they contain various poisons that can make you ill or, in certain cases, kill you. (See later section on fruits and berries for choice edible fruits).

The firethorn bears bright red berries that are one of its most attractive features. It is a species that is grown solely for this pleasing fruiting display, much like some species are grown for their fall leaf color.

The European mountain ash produces orange-red berries in clusters. These fruits are edible and can be made into a jelly, but, they are not tasty raw. Birds like them, and the berries provide a pleasing contrast to their green foliage, which makes this one of the most handsome of the ornamental species of trees.

There are countless other examples where the fruit display is the primary reason for growing a plant. The Virginia creeper is a vine that bears blue colored berries in small clusters. Although the fruits here are not usually considered as important as the foliage, they do offer some interest in the seasonal landscape.

WINTER EFFECTS

It is practical when planting to consider setting out trees and shrubs for windbreaks against harsh winds as well as to provide summer shade. Remember, your landscape plants will cushion the elements. During northern winters, snow often accumulates, and the firs, pines, and spruces provide a contrast of green to the white landscape. If only deciduous trees are used in a location, the scene can become as drab as a black and white picture when covered with snow. In addition, many coniferous shrubs, when placed against the wind, act as natural snow catchers that help to keep snow off walks and driveways. Spruce are especially good at this. This can save much backache if you shovel by hand, and labor saved means more time for the other chores or activities of the winter season.

Usually, deciduous plants are not considered as particularly ornamental during winter—devoid of their leaves and all—but all deciduous trees and shrubs are not alike. Some are more snowy than others, with contorted, twisted branches that add character to a winter scene.

One advantage to using some deciduous plants in a landscape is that they will provide you with fallen leaves, which make good compost. Certainly, you will want to be sure to save your fallen autumn leaves in some way for use when spring comes.

FLOWERS

Do not forget to plant shrubs that will provide a floral display. There are species that bloom in spring, summer, and into the fall. By careful planting, you can always have something in bloom in your yard. Lilacs can provide you with spring flowers, and hydrangeas will provide flowers during those late summer and fall days when so few other shrubs are in bloom. Check with your nursery when selecting the species you want to see what their blooming season is (Fig. 2-2).

The showiest plants are those that produce large blossoms. A tree peony will produce blossoms among the largest of any temperate zone ornamental—beautiful, fragrant blooms that will delight the eye and nose. Some plants have small flowers, but the flowers are borne in clusters or are so numerous that they produce a spectacular display, even though the individual flowers are actually quite tiny.

Remember when setting them out that most flowering trees and shrubs perform better under full sunlight, protected from heavy winds, and kept well-watered and fertilized. It will not pay to plant a flowering tree or shrub only to neglect it. A sickly looking plant with flowers is not going to add to your

Fig. 2-2. Do not forget to plant shrubs that will provide a floral display.

garden. Flowering plants take more maintenance work than nonflowering shrubs, but, when in full bloom, you are likely to receive satisfaction and pride in your accomplishment!

Chapter 3

Landscaping an Urban Lot

The urban environment presents special problems (Fig. 3-1). Many municipalities regulate what can and can not be planted in an area. *Zoning and local ordinances* must be obeyed. Practical landscaping in the city involves knowing and following the various rules and regulations. You should be sure to check with your city tree commission before planting any trees or shrubs.

DEED RESTRICTIONS

It is a wise practice to review your deed before you make any alterations to your property. Some deeds restrict the removal of trees. If you were planning on cutting down that old elm to make way for a garden, you may be in for a surprise. Usually, deed restrictions are a problem only if you are buying the land on contract and do not actually own the land. There may also be such restrictions in your mortgage agreement, but that is not too common.

Needless to say, *tenants* should not alter the landscape of their dwelling. That is the responsibility of the landlord. You do not have the authority to make improvements without your landlord's consent. Any improvements you do make may end up *costing you,* should your landlord decide to raise your rent or sue you. Even if you are good friends with your landlord, money matters can destroy the best of friendships and real estate often changes hands. You may end up very unhappy. Another problem is that in buildings that are shared, as most rentals are, your life style may not match that of other residents. Friction may occur if you plant a flower bed and the renter's kids next door play in them. The cardinal rule for renters is: if you do not own the place, do not take on responsibilities that belong to the owner.

If you are a long-time tenant, know the landlord well and/or personally, and have a strong desire to have your own rosebush, be sure to check with the landlord first—and be sure to get a clearance.

AIR POLLUTION

One of the hazards of city life is air pollution. Not only does it affect people, it can adversely affect the

Fig. 3-1. Bath, England. An example of urban landscaping. Photo by Marion Michaels.

health of your plants as well. Air pollution usually does not originate from a single source, but is the result of a combination of chemicals. Cars produce gases as a byproduct of their internal combustion engines. Gases such as oxides of nitrogen, carbon monoxide, hydrocarbons, and lead compounds are among their emissions. Industrial factories contribute hydrogen fluoride, sulfur dioxide, and more hydrocarbons. Electric generators, refuse burning, and home heating stoves or furnaces all emit tons of smoke into the air. The combined pollutants mix with stagnant air to create a condition known as *smog.*

The two pollutants that damage plants most are produced by the chemical action of sunlight on smog. These pollutants are *ozone* and *PAN (peroxacetyl nitrate).* Ozone and PAN are called *photochemical smog.*

Pollution damage occurs more often in the spring and fall than in any other season because dur-ing those seasons, stationary levels of warm and cold air block the movement of the gases in the atmosphere. When this occurs, the smog, which is heavier than air, settles down and damages plants.

Symptoms and Causes

Here are some of the common symptoms of air pollution and the pollutants that are the most likely culprits.

Ozone and PAN. Produce streaked, spotted, and bleached foliage; can stunt growth and cause early leaf drop.

Nitrogen Dioxide. Causes white or tan irregularly occurring lesions near leaf margins.

Sulfur Dioxide. Causes bleached spots to appear between leaf veins and can stunt plant growth.

Hydrogen Fluoride. Causes dwarfed plants; sometimes it bleaches leaf margins and tips.

Ethylene. Causes twisted and withered leaves and early flower drop.

If you have any difficulty in identifying pollution damage, you should contact your county agricultural agent for assistance.

Smog Tolerant Plants

Some plants are better able to tolerate smog than others, especially photochemical smog. You may want to consider this smog resistance factor when planning your landscape. The following is a list of smog-resistant genus types: Acacia, Aralia, Arbutus (This genus is rare. It is a wild plant protected by law in most states but may be available at a few nurseries.) Buxus (boxwood), Camellia, Cedrus, Cistus, Cotoneaster, Cupressus (cyprus), Fraxinus (ash), Ginkgo (maidenhair tree), Prunus, Pittosporum, Pyracantha (fire thorn), Quercus (oak), Spirea, Syringa (lilac), Viburnum, and Yucca.

Although you are not likely to select or possibly even find the once prolific wild *arbutus* with its delicate flowers, there are many others of this group that you will find both practical and easy to grow.

Boxwood planted closely provides a fine hedge for bordering your yard or accenting parts of it. (See Chapters 5, 6, and 7 for more on hedges).

The camellia has large, showy white flowers that are very fragrant. They attract the bees that are so necessary for pollinating your fruit trees or garden. It is an excellent choice to use in front of your house if you live in an area where camellias are hardy. (See Chapter 22, Camellias and Gardenias.)

Smog Sensitive Plants

Some plants are very sensitive to photochemical smog and are not recommended for planting in large urban areas where air pollution is common. These include the following: Acer (maple), Alnus (alder), Calycanthus (Carolina allspice), Ficus (fig), Gleditsia (locust), Hibiscus, Juglans (walnut), Mentha (mint), Petunia, Persea (avocado), Pinus, Platanus (sycamore), Rhododendron, Robinia, Salix (willow), Salvia, and Ulmus (elm). (Many of these plants are further described in subsequent chapters, should you wish to know more about an individual species.)

Also, different degrees of sensitivity to smog occurs within each species of plant; some will be more resistant than others. For example, blue, purple, and red petunias are more resistant to smog than are the white varieties. Size can also be a factor in determining resistance. It appears that small-flowered petunias, the multiflora varieties, are much more resistant than the grandiflora, or large-flowered varieties. Plants that have small leaves are less susceptible than large-leaved plants.

The age of the plant and stage of its development is also a factor. The stage of plant development is quite critical to air pollution damage. Recently matured leaves are much more susceptible to damage than are the very young or old leaves. Rapidly growing plants are more likely to suffer than are slow growing species. There is no way to increase your plant's resistance, so select only those shrubs, vines, and trees that can tolerate smog conditions, particularly photochemical smog.

There are some things you can do, however, to minimize the effects of pollution damage. Reduce the amount of nitrogen fertilizer and the frequency of watering. High levels of water and nitrogen stimulate growth. This young, succulent growth is very susceptible to pollution damage. By reducing the number of times you water and feed your plant, you can reduce the amount of damage.

It will not be practical to cover your plants to protect them from the effects of air pollution. The only practical solution is to dig them up and replace them with shrubs that are better suited to the urban environment.

SALT INJURY

Unfortunately, air pollution is only one of the man-made problems city dwellers face. Another problem is salt injury. Salt is used on city walks, roads, and driveways. The problem occurs in spring when the accumulated salt runs off into the landscape at toxic levels, killing lawns, shrubs, vines, and even trees. A constant stream of salt spray from city streets on your shrubbery will cause noticeable injury and may even lead to plant death (Fig. 3-2).

Do not use salt on your sidewalks and

Fig. 3-2. Do not use salt on your sidewalks and driveways; use sand instead. Note distance of tender shrubs from drive.

driveways. Use sand instead. The sand will never injure your shrubs. If there is too much salt spray from city street traffic (and it does not seem likely or even desirable to change city road policy regarding your street), you may want to put up a fence to protect your yard. A fence is not always feasible, but it will go a great way toward shielding your plants from deadly salt.

The most practical thing is to plant only those trees and shrubs that are somewhat tolerant of salty conditions. No plant can tolerate too much salt, but some will tolerate more than others. These should be among the selections you make. You can plant these salt-tolerant species in the front yard, where they are more likely to be exposed to salt from street traffic, and plant your less tolerant species in the backyard.

STREET AND GARDEN LIGHTS

Plants are *photosensitive*, which means they react to light. Both sunlight and artificial lighting can affect plant growth. Many people do not realize this: they install lights for their garden that may make an attractive nighttime display, but the constant lighting is likely to alter plant growth.

Artificial lighting has certain characteristics that fall into four general categories: high-pressure sodium, mercury, incandescent, and fluorescent.

High-pressure Sodium. This type of artificial light gives off a pale yellow glow and is the only kind of man-made lighting that does not alter plant growth. It also will not attract insects.

Mercury. Mercury lights are available in pale blue or pale pink light. Both alter plant growth, the pale blue slightly less than the pale pink variety. Both also attract insects. Both mercury and high-pressure sodium lamps require special installation. They can not be used in ordinary light sockets and fixtures.

Incandescent. These lamps are the kind

used most in homes. They come in as frosted white bulbs or yellow, and in flood lamps or regular bulbs. The frosted lamp produces a white light; the ordinary bulbs a yellow light. White-frosted incandescent lamps are the kind most often used in the garden. They are usually preferred to the amber-colored lamps, which dull the colors of flowers and foliage. One disadvantage is that the white-frosted lamps attract insects, whereas the amber-colored lamps do not. Both types of incandescents will cause plants to continue growing if left on too long.

Fluorescent. Fluorescent lights alter plant growth. They are often used as aquarium and indoor garden lights to stimulate plant growth because they most nearly duplicate natural sunlight. "Grow Lights" are pink-tinted fluorescent lights.

There is probably not much you can do about fluorescent street lights, unless you lobby the city street commission to have high-pressure sodium street lights put in—otherwise, you'll just have to accept things as they are.

There are several kinds of lamps that can be used to light gardens. All of these emit blue light, except for high-pressure sodium and amber or yellow ceramic-coated incandescent lamps. Remember blue light attracts insects. Also, incandescent lights of all kinds will alter plant growth when used for too many hours each day.

If you wish to light your garden, you may want to limit lighting periods and how long the yard should be lit each evening. If you are using incandescent lights, use them only in the early evening. Keeping lights on later than 10 p.m. may cause the plants to continue to grow later in the season, postponing flowering. Serious cold damage can occur if plants continue to grow late into the fall.

POOR GROWING CONDITIONS

Plants are often damaged because of the poor growing conditions common to the urban environment. Some conditions show up as obvious symptoms of disorder.

Tan and white spots and leaves and *wilting* usually indicates an air pollution problem. (Review air pollution segment earlier in chapter.) Once pollu-

tion is identified, the proper steps can be taken to deal with the problem. Often this may mean growing a more resistant plant in place of the existing one.

Leaves that wilt, change color to a greyish-green, and fall prematurely usually indicate drought stress. The plant is not getting enough water to meet its needs. Drought problems are most frequent on sandy soils, but can also occur on clay soils during long dry spells when the soil bakes into almost bricklike consistency. Soils can be improved by the addition of organic matter, composts, leaves, and peat moss. The plants should be watered to restore them to vigor and carefully watched to see that they do not go into a relapse.

Green slime accumulating on soil or containers, indicates poor water drainage. It can also indicate too much water, fertilizer accumulation, and a very acid soil. To solve this problem, water less frequently. Stop fertilizing the plant. Dig up some of the soil, being careful not to injure the plant. Replace it with ordinary soil. Dust the area with lime to lower acidity (except in the case of blueberries, azaleas, or other acid-loving plants).

Twisted leaves and flowers that fall prematurely may indicate herbicide or pesticide damage. Perhaps it is drifting in from your neighbor's yard, or it is coming from those lawn fertilizer mixes that also contain weed killers. Try to avoid such mixes whenever possible. Once the plant has received the damage, prune to remove all abnormal growth. There is no chemical treatment to help plants overcome the damage they sustain from herbicides or other pesticides. Only time can help plants to return to normal growth.

Whitish coating on the soil surface usually indicates overfertilization, it is a physical symptom of the build up of soluble salts. The saline buildup will cause the plant's root hairs to wither and die. To correct the situation, remove the crust of the soil, if possible. Avoid disturbing the plant roots. Add fresh soil and water thoroughly to *leach* or wash away all of the excess fertilizer. Do not fertilize again for the rest of the season. Try using composted manure instead of commercial fertilizers. Bags of composted manure are available in several sizes at garden stores.

There are many problems that the urban environment offers to plants. If in doubt about any particular disorder, call or visit your county agricultural extension agent. In large cities, the city tree commission may also be able to help. The first step to solving any plant problem lies in the correct identification of the problem. Once the problem is identified, the solution is usually available.

HAZARDS OF CITY LIFE

There are other hazards to urban plant life. Many surfaces radiate heat, and the walls of buildings set up "canyons" that can cause sudden changes in air flow. Plants growing in sunny areas are especially susceptible to damage under these conditions. The heat can build up to harmful levels, and drying winds can dehydrate plants or injure them in other ways (such as prematurely blowing off petals, blossoms, or even knocking down an entire plant).

There are some protective measures you can take. Observe those areas where plants wilt rapidly and screen them from strong drafts and direct sunlight. Screens can be of many types of materials; those that blend into the garden setting are best. Sometimes hedges or bushes can be used for screening. At other times, that may not be practical. Arrange screens so that they permit some airflow, or the area will lack air circulation causing overheating problems to develop. Figure 3-3 shows a suburban English garden.

Be careful not to overwater plants. If they are under heat stress because of an unusually hot spell in the weather, however, it may be a good idea to turn on the garden sprinkler to a fine mist for the

Fig. 3-3. Bath, England. An example of suburban landscapes. Photo by Marion Michaels.

hottest parts of the day. That will provide some cooling. Do not leave the sprinkler on all day. If a plant is under a constant mist, it may be subject to attack by fungi and other disease organisms that thrive in wet environments. Also, such constant sprinkling will run up your water bill.

Some people try to reduce heat stress by spraying their plants with an *antitranspirant* spray, of which there are many commercially available. This is not recommended for beginners, because the temptation may be to drown plants in the stuff. It is more practical to simply turn on the sprinkler for a couple of hours.

Another problem urban gardeners face is dirt. Plants are soon covered with soot, dust, and dirt. This grime dulls the foliage and keeps plants from performing at their best. It is not always practical to hose plants down each day. If you are not careful, you can flood the soil and damage plant roots, as well as injure leaves, flowers, and other tender areas. Instead, try giving your plants a "bath" once a week (Fig. 3-4). Use a bucket of water. Take a bar of a gentle soap (such as Ivory) and work up a lather in the water. Do not use harsh soaps, deodorant soaps, or detergents. They may strip the plant of the natural wax coating that protects it. Remember, your plants are very tender, like children. You never bathe your kids in laundry detergent or bleach water. Do not bathe your plants in such substances. Gently sprinkle the sudsy solution over the plant, taking care to cover as many areas as possible. A sprinkling can help. If you have a particularly large shrub, you may have to make up two or three batches of soapy water. The dirt will start to dissolve. Then take the garden hose, set it on the mist level, and wash away the remnants of soap and dirt. Clean plants are healthy plants, but do not bathe your plants more than once a week.

DOGS AND NEIGHBORHOOD PETS

A frequent problem in the home urban and suburban landscape is that of trying to keep dogs (either your own or a neighbor's) and other neighborhood pets from tearing up your landscape shrubbery. You can train your own pets or keep them tied up on a leash, but there are limits to what steps you can take against neighbor pets without alienating neighbors or getting into trouble with the Society for the Prevention of Cruelty to Animals.

In some neighborhoods, especially in urban areas, there are pet ordinances that specify the regulations concerning pets and owner's responsibilities. Even in these areas, it is best to try to keep the peace with neighbors by taking precautionary measures to protect your landscape.

To keep your landscape from being of interest to wandering dogs, cats, and other pets, there are a few simple things you can do:

☐ Do not leave pet food outside all day or night. If you have a pet, feed it at a regular time. Take in dishes and leftover food for the next meal. Food left out will be a sure invitation to area animals and wildlife.

☐ Keep trash cans covered with a tight lid. Do not overfill trash cans. If you do not have enough room in your trash cans to hold all of your garbage without overfill, buy some new containers to take care of the overflow. If dogs are tipping over your garbage cans and breaking open plastic bags, you may have to keep your garbage inside (house, garage, or shed) until trash pickup day, or put it out the night before in those areas where trash is picked up early in the morning.

☐ Keep trash receptacles washed out and clean when not in use. Cans with an odor will attract dogs and other animals more than cans that are clean.

☐ Do not feed neighborhood animals (and that includes squirrels). If they come over for a visit, shoo them away. If you feed them, or are friendly, they may make your home a regular "vacation spa," and be over all the time to beg for goodies from you. Call the police or dog pound if you see packs of stray dogs.

☐ If you are having serious problems with a neighbor's pet, tell your neighbor. Ask that they restrain their pet's unwanted intrusions into your yard. Most people will be understanding if they are approached in a friendly way. Do not wait until it builds up into a war.

☐ Insure expensive shrubs.

Fig. 3-4. Clean plants are healthy plants, but do not bathe your plants more than once a week. Shasta daisies courtesy W. Atlee Burpee Co.

☐ Fence off areas or plants that you want safeguarded.

If your neighbor has a very friendly dog that has "adopted" you for everything but mealtime because his own family is never around, you may wish to train that dog in your own yard/shrub rules.

There are various scent-off chemical sprays commercially available that are supposed to repel pets. Reliance upon such sprays is unrealistic: they may be effective against a neighbor's pet, but are not necessarily going to repel your own pet—a dog is very loyal.

If the problem is your own pet, train it. Also provide some area of your yard for the pet to play in and do not landscape that play area. If the problem is a neighbor's pet (and you do not own a pet), you can fence in your entire yard or talk to your neighbor into fencing his.

In the case of a dog digging up a lawn, the only way to stop this is to either train the dog or keep the dog off the lawn. Dogs often dig for a warmer home, for treasures, or to capture small animals like gophers or moles. Dogs often dig holes to bury large bones. They will be less likely to do this if they are fed inside or not overfed. Your dog can be trained to not dig in the front lawn or near your favorite shrubs.

If your fur-coated dog would prefer to have a shelter where he could be kept warm with body heat, he may dig for that purpose. You may want to erect some sort of lean-to in an inconspicuous part of your yard, generous with dry, fallen leaves to snuggle in. You might also consider a place on your porch.

In any event, you can train your dog about digging by not allowing it. Rewarding your dog for good behavior—with softly spoken words and a loving caress—will help to accentuate the emphasis when you speak in harsh tones for bad behavior.

CONTAINER PLANTINGS

Container planting is perhaps most common in urban settings. Containers help to accommodate for lack of space, as well as offering some protection for the plants themselves. There are many kinds of containers: window boxes, planter boxes, tubs, hanging baskets, etc. They are made from all types of materials: plastic, metal, clay, wood, brick, stone, and more. Ordinary plywood and lumber are not recommended because they do not hold up well over time. Because they are plant materials, they tend to decompose when exposed to earth organisms. *Chemically treated woods,* that will resist decay are available.

To some extent, the containers chosen play an important role in complementing the plant. Exteriors can be covered or painted to blend into the surrounding patterns of the area. Containers that are "loud" and call attention to themselves or are ugly detract from the plant's dignity and should be avoided. Portable, ready-made containers are available. Unless you are a carpenter or a brick mason, it is practical to use a ready-made container. Making your own may be time-consuming and frustrating.

Prebuilt wooden planter boxes are readily available at most garden stores or home lumberyards. They come in a wide assortment of sizes, with a size to fit about any space. Some are ready-to-use (finished), and some you may have to assemble, stain, or paint. Stain is usually preferred to paint. It holds up better, requires less upkeep, and there are many colors from which to choose. Stain usually looks more "organic" than paint and is in keeping with the earth tone colors that are so popular today. A point to think about when selecting colors is that dark colors absorb heat and are best for shady areas, light colors reflect heat and are best for sunny areas.

Built-in planter boxes are often most favored by homeowners. If you construct permanent boxes of cement, brick, or stone, be sure to install drain pipes or place a layer of gravel within or beneath the box so that excess water can drain away. Although extremely sturdy and permanent, their weight can cause too much stress on balconies. Check the strength of a balcony before building a masonry planter. Built-in planters may be quite expensive to make, especially if you hire a specialist, although they are well worth the expense and/or effort in their beauty and utility.

Hanging baskets can be attractive containers in which to grow vines and other small trailing or flowering plants. They allow you to display plants where they can be viewed from all directions and to remove them to a safer location during extreme storm warnings, etc.

Baskets can be hung from any number of places, not just the roof. They can also be displayed along walls and entryways. When doing so, it is best to use a loop hook to hang them. These hooks are available at garden or hardware stores and are better than nails. First, they hold the basket more securely in place, and although they allow for some flexibility, there is little chance of the basket falling off the hook. Second, the hook design itself, which is available in brass, is more ornamental than a regular nail.

Many modern baskets are made of plastic. They have a flat bottom with a drainage area and often this tray is removable.

Older types were made from wire mesh lined with moss. The problem with this is that they drip water, are somewhat difficult to handle, and are best suited for porches. Sometimes people will use wicker or straw baskets for hanging. These work fine, provided that they are lined with something that will protect the basket and allow for proper drainage of excess water.

Some hanging baskets are clay pots secured in place by nylon or rope netting. These can be attractive, but they should not be placed in areas where there is traffic or a chance of children bumping into them. Clay pots are breakable—they also hurt if you bump your head on one.

Clay Pottery

Clay pottery is one of the oldest types of containers used for potted plants. They have both advantages and disadvantages. They last longer than plastic, unless broken, and they blend in well with most gardens. The major disadvantage is that they do break. Also, unless you make your own, they are more expensive than plastic pots. Another disadvantage is that they can become quite heavy when filled. If you plan on moving things around a lot,

it may be more practical to use a lighter pot. Many of the plastic pots come in colors vaguely resembling clay pots. (For large plants, it is best to not disturb them once they are set up. If you must move them, use a *plant dolly*. These wheeled platforms are available at many garden or hardware stores.)

You may encounter moss and algae growth on the outside of clay containers. Clay is like a rock, and it encourages such growth. You can buy disinfectant containing *quaternary ammonium* to control algae growth. Follow the instructions for use as directed by the manufacturer on the label.

You can also simply wash the growth off these containers as it occurs. You will have to be careful to not injure plants when cleaning pots. It may be necessary to clean pots on a regular basis during the growing season. A solution of household bleach can be effective, but be extremely careful to not get any bleach on plant tissues, because it will injure or even kill your plant.

Container Soils

What soils you put into growing containers will depend in part upon what type of plant you wish to grow. Azaleas and rhododendrons, for example, require very acid soil and will need a different medium than lilacs, which prefer lime soils. Check to find out the specific needs of your plant before fixing up the soil for it.

You will have many choices. You can use garden soil or create a homemade mix from peat moss and topsoil, or purchase a commercially prepared mix. The advantage of the commercial mix is that it will be sterile of harmful organisms and weeds. The main disadvantage is cost. Commercial mixes are expensive, especially when compared to your own garden soil, which is free for the taking. Most people mix their own media. That way they can save money and tailor-make batches for plants with diverse soil requirements.

Regardless of the type soil you use, be sure to prepare it properly. If you are not careful, you can create high water-holding situations. Remember, containers tend to hold water fairly well on their own, and poor drainage can kill plants. Peat moss, perlite, vermiculite, and other such additives help to aerate soils and make them light.

Conversely, a too light soil will not anchor plants properly. Poorly anchored plants may blow down in a heavy wind. A good mix is one that is well-drained, fertile, pliable, able to retain some moisture, and rich in humus. Usually adding composted cow manure to a mix will help keep it fertile.

To make your own mix, add two parts sand, one part topsoil, one part peat moss, and one part composted animal manure. Be sure to use only well-rotted manures, or they will injure the plants set in it. You may add vermiculite or perlite to lighten soils or improve aeration. Conversely, clay can be added to sandy soils in order to improve the water-holding capacity.

Chapter 4

Water Conservation Plantings

More than one-third of the yearly water bill for the average American home is spent on water used for garden and landscape plants and lawns (Fig. 4-1). This can add up to quite a sum of money in a year's time and is only one reason more and more people are becoming aware of the need for water conservation.

DROUGHTS, DRY SPELLS, AND SHORTAGES

In addition to the economics of conserving water, people often face no alternative. Dry spells from prolonged droughts, temporary water shortages, or unforeseen water cutoffs can leave a home stranded with little or no available water. At times, what water you may have is designated to purposes other than watering the landscape. The yard will not take a high priority when drinking water is scarce, and rates behind such uses as cooking, bathing, and washing.

Sometimes, chemical contaminants can disrupt a well. In fact, you never know when your water supply may be affected and become unusable. There is no reason to panic or become paranoid about water shortages, but it is a good idea to consider the possibility. Too often an abundant and cheap supply of water is taken for granted. This is especially true in the eastern half of the country. In Western states there is greater respect for water, because it comes a bit more dear.

PRACTICAL WATER USE

Wherever you live, it is practical to consider the best ways to use water most efficiently. There are many ways to put this valuable resource to wise use. Some factors you will need to consider include where plants are set out: soil; types of plants; and methods of lawn, shrub, and tree care.

Where Plants Are Set

Certain areas of your yard offer less water burdens on your ornamentals than other areas in that same yard. Plants grown in shady and semishady places lose much less water to evaporation than plants growing out under the hot sun all day.

Fig. 4-1. Over one-third of the yearly water bill for the average American home is spent on water for garden plants and lawns. Courtesy of Charles Webb & Mary Borofka-Webb.

Some gardeners advise against planting ornamentals too close to shade trees and other existing plants. They contend that the larger plants will compete with your newly set ornamentals for water and nutrients, and the result will be that your ornamentals will lose. This idea, however, is not necessarily true. It can work that way, but it often does not. A plant is usually offered greater protection against drought stress when grown in the company of other plants and trees. It may not stand much of a chance by itself in the sun, but when set out among other plants, the same plant can fare better. There is good reason for this: existing trees and shrubs help to hold moisture in the ground. Although they do compete for moisture, they also share their moisture supply with neighboring plants (Fig. 4-2).

In general, plants tend to be quite supportive of one another, and the idea of competition is overrated if not inaccurate. Cooperation is perhaps a better way to describe the habits of the plant kingdom. Of course, there are exceptions and extreme situations where individual plant survival may be at stake.

Never plant any shrub near a black walnut tree. Black walnuts produce chemicals that have a herbicidal effect on neighboring plants. Their natural herbicide is called *juglans*. It kills or seriously weakens all vegetation that comes in contact with it. Grass will not grow under a black walnut tree. Some plants are more susceptible to damage than others from juglans. The best place for your black walnuts is in the home woodlot, removed from your landscape plants. Black walnut trees should not be used for landscape purposes.

Because existing plants tend to help out new plants in most circumstances, it is essential when designing your landscape to leave some of the existing trees and shrubs in place, rather than wiping the area completely clean of vegetation. select those existing plants that best fit into the theme you have chosen. You can always remove them later, once your new plantings have become well established.

Shade may sometimes present a problem. Most ornamentals require full sun or a good part of a day's sun to grow and thrive. If heavy shade is a problem, trim branches to let the sunlight filter through to those spots where your newly set plants are growing. If it fits into your landscape theme, you may plant those types of ornamentals that are shade tolerant. By the careful removal of branches, however, you can usually reduce shade to the point where it will not be so intense as to disrupt your ornamentals' growth habits. Some shade, especially during the hot afternoon summer sun, can actually be helpful in keeping your plants from drought stress.

Watch the sun patterns in the area so that you know which limbs to trim to rid unwanted shade. A little effort expended here can save you much worry later on, and produce the desired results without extreme labor. People living in areas with high water tables are rarely affected by problems of drought unless plants are set upon a hill. Because the force of gravity is responsible for water flowing downhill, plants set upon windswept hilltops are likely to be more endangered from water stress than those set in other areas. In fact, any area where

winds are strong will present problems. Hot, dry winds increase the rate of water evaporation from plants' leaves and tissues. Prevent this water loss by planting windbreaks, or set plants out in an area where they will receive some protection from high winds. You may also bury extra humus, such as leaves, generously around your hilltop or hillside. Do not disturb the roots of your shrub. Dig holes around it and fill them with leaves, alternating with dirt. Then cover the top of the holes with dirt and pack it down well. The increased organic matter will increase the water holding capacity of the area and lessen drought problems.

In urban areas there is the problem of *heat reflection.* Asphalt, concrete, brick, and other structures all absorb heat, and they also reflect it. Plants that are too close to all these man-made structures will feel the heat and lose more water to evaporation than plants that are set back from these structures. Remember, there is relationship between temperature and plant respiration. The higher the

Fig. 4-2. In general, plants tend to be quite supportive of one another, and the idea of competition is overrated if not inaccurate.

temperatures, the more the plant *transpires* or loses moisture.

Soil

Probably one of the best ways to conserve water is to improve the water holding capacity of the soil. The best way to do this is to increase the organic matter content of the soil. Soils rich in organic matter hold water better than those soils with little organic matter in them. *Humus* (decaying organic matter) improves the soil in many ways. It is not enough that there is water in the soil. That water must be made available to the plant. Humus helps to make the water in soils available to the fine little root hairs or *feeder roots* that most plants have. It also increases the amount of moisture that soil will hold. Only about half of all water absorbed by a soil can be taken up by the plant. In humus-poor soils, much more of the water passes rapidly by the plants roots, making the amount of water absorption much less. When a soil is rich in organic matter, that ratio increases and much more water is made available for plant use.

There are many things that can be added to improve a soil. Manure, peat moss, and composts are among the best. Compost is the cheapest, because it can be made from rotted leaves, grass clippings, and remnant items such as potato or cucumber peelings.

Sometimes lime and other minerals can be added to a soil, depending upon whether you want to change the soil pH or not. In most soils that have poor water-holding capacity, the addition of garden lime will be beneficial.

Another way to improve soil is through use of a *green manure*. A green manure is a crop, such as Sudan grass, that is planted and turned under with a shovel or plow, after it has grown, to provide the soil with its organic matter. This decaying organic matter will greatly enrich the soil. Usually, a crop such as Sudan grass or a *legume* (bean-type plant) is grown for this purpose. Many times the crop can be cut during the growing season, as is the case with Sudan grass, and the clippings put into the compost pile.

Green manures are rarely used for landscape purposes. If you are just getting started, however, it will be an ideal way to get you off to a good start. Raise a fall crop of Sudan grass, clover, or any of the legumes. Plants early in the fall, during those warm summerlike days, so that the plant will have a chance to make a good stand. The tall succulent leaves of Sudan grass decompose quite readily when clipped. Till plants under in early spring, as soon as the ground can be worked.

Drought Tolerant Plants

One of the best ways to save money on water bills is to select only *drought tolerant* plants for your landscape. Some plants, by their very nature, consume less water than others. Others will spread their roots further and/or deeper to reach the moisture that they need. These plants are said to be drought tolerant or *drought resistant*. This simply means they have low water demands and can withstand occasional periods of drought. They all need some water, however. If you live in an area where summer dry spells are usual or where water shortages are frequent, you may wish to consider planting these drought tolerant species.

Again, it is important that you give reasonable care even to these plants. The main advantage that they offer is their low water demand (Fig. 4-3). In fact, some plants are so efficient that they can survive on natural rainfall alone. Most will benefit from some additional irrigation, however. In areas where there is little or no natural rainfall, some irrigation will almost be a necessity.

Drought tolerant plants include trees, shrubs, and even some grasses and groundcovers. It is entirely possible, and in some cases very practical, to plant an entire landscape with only these species. Check with your nursery to see what drought tolerant plants they offer. You may be surprised to learn that there are so many available—from blue fescue grass to the Siberian peashrub, (a good hedge plant) to Russian olive trees, and more!

Lawn Care

More water is used—and often wasted—on lawn

Fig. 4-3. Your ornamentals and trees require special care throughout the growing season. This carefully trained pine is an excellent example.

care than for any other purpose. This need not be so. There are sensible ways to water a lawn. Irrigate lawns during the night or early morning instead of during the afternoon. By avoiding the hot periods of the day, you will find that less water is lost through evaporation. Many people have their sprinklers on all day, especially during hot summer afternoons. They do not realize that to do so is inefficient. It is an actual waste of water, because over half the water may be lost to evaporation. In the not-too-distant future, as time-of-day use is incorporated more into electric and other utility bills, watering time may also be something to consider in the interest of economy.

To determine when to water your lawn, let your lawn decide. If the grass looks like it needs to be watered, irrigate. Do not let the number of days since watering, nor the neighbor's constant sprinkling, be your guide. Your neighbors may end up with lawn diseases if they keep their lawn under constant moisture. And have you seen their water bill?

Common sense is the best guide to tell you when your lawn needs watering. Of course, you should not go to the other extreme and allow your grass to turn yellow or brown before watering it. Look at your lawn: if it looks like it needs watering, water it—but wait until the cool of the evening or early morning.

Mowing. A practical way to conserve water on lawns is to not cut the grass as low as usual. Cut grass at a 2-inch level or no shorter than 1 1/2 inches. This will result in a substantial water savings. When grass is cut too low, it needs more water to survive and restore rapid growth. Your lawn will look more attractive and require less water when cut at this higher height. Also, try to avoid cutting grass at all during a prolonged dry spell. Conversely, a good time to cut is just before a rain.

Sprinklers. Sprinklings systems are the most common method used to water lawns. Some people have fancy underground systems and others simply use the garden hose for a thorough soaking.

A good soaking is probably better than a sprinkler system, but it may have some drawbacks. Too much pressure can uproot flowers or tear shrubs. Soak the lawn early in the morning so it has a good chance to be dry by evening. You will want to use your lawn, and wet lawns are more susceptible to injury from recreational activity than are dry lawns.

One problem with sprinklers is that some people keep them on all the time. This creates ideal conditions for fungus and other disease organisms. Ideally, a lawn should be allowed to dry completely between waterings.

Be careful not to flood your lawn. Soak the grass to the roots; do not create mud puddles or drown your ornamentals.

When using the overhead spray-type sprinkler, which is most common, remember to station it only in those areas where it will water the plants—not the sidewalk or paths. Some people waste water every day on their driveways and walks.

Another trick to remember is to schedule your watering so that you water different plants at different times. Water your lawn separately from your shrubs and trees. Sometimes they may tend to overlap, but as a rule it is more efficient to water the deep-rooted plants separately from the shallow-rooted plants.

Lime. The addition of garden lime is helpful to most lawns. Lime helps to conserve water. *Dolomitic limestone* is best, because it contains both calcium and magnesium. These elements will help keep your lawn a deep green. Garden lime tends to increase the water-holding capacity of the soil. Lawn grasses, like any green plant, also have a definite need for nitrogen. Animal urine falling naturally or gathered and mixed with water (two parts) is a beneficial source.

The care that you give your lawn will help in water conservation. Lawns that are properly mowed, fertile, and well-tended consume less water than those that are cut too close to the round and in need of constant repair. It takes more water to repair a lawn than to maintain it.

Shrub and Tree Care

Your ornamentals and trees require special care throughout the growing season. Because they are deeper rooted than your lawn, they will be able to withstand longer periods without water, but even they can suffer from drought stress. Depending upon size and other features, they may require a greater amount when they are watered.

Water. It is advisable to water trees and shrubs on a weekly basis until they are established. It is essential to water them regularly, throughout the first growing season, or they may not survive. Once established,they will benefit from weekly waterings. When watering shrubs, soak the ground thoroughly. Established plants have deep roots and water must reach them. Water the area under and around the *branch span* of the tree or shrub. Do not just water near the trunk. The roots of your plant will stretch out as wide as it branches, and the plant will grow best when it receives water that is fairly evenly distributed under its branch span.

Distribute water evenly. If you water only one side, it may cause your shrub to grow lopsided. Do not sprinkle around established plants. They need to be *deep-watered*. A light sprinkling can do more harm than good by encouraging plants to develop shallow roots.

Water should be applied to the base area under a plant. You can on occasion water the canopy (top) of trees or shrubs. Be careful to not use to much pressure when watering tops of plants. Otherwise you can knock leaves or fruits off. Never water the tops of plants during blossomtime. If you water a plant, do so in the early morning so that it has a chance to dry off by the latter part of the day. Do not keep shrubs under constant sprinkler irrigation, or it may encourage disease organisms to attack the plant's foliage.

During periods of drought, if you have a limited supply of water, you can cool trees by spraying their foliage with water. Plants will absorb some moisture through their leaves. If the plant is in really desperate shape, you may be able to stave off plant death through *foliar irrigation*. Then, pray for rain.

Drip Systems. Drip systems are probably the most efficient way to water plants, although they require a certain amount of labor to maintain. These systems work by allowing water to drip near the base of the plant. They can be designed to skip areas where nothing is planted. One advantage of the drip system is that much water that is normally lost to evaporation with the sprinkler method can be saved.

Although the drip system is an excellent one, during periods of extreme drought you may want to give everything a good soaking with the water hose to be sure that plant needs are being met.

Mulch. Use of a *mulch* around the base of trees and shrubs is very effective in reducing water demands and conserving soil moisture. Organic mulches are best. Place the mulch in a circle around the base of each plant. It should be no more than 2 inches thick (during the summer) and never touch the trunk of the plant itself. If the mulch is too thick, it can have the same effect as the thatched roofs in Old England: it will prevent natural rainfall from penetrating and reaching the plant's roots. This will only aggrevate drought problems.

If you suspect your mulch may be too thick, thin it out. Straw mulches are preferable to broadleafed mulches, which have a tendency to compact and prevent water filtration. One way to get around this is to shred your leaves. You can do this with a special commercially available machine or with your power lawnmower. Just run your power mower over a pile of leaves a few times. That should do the trick. Shredded leaves are an ideal mulch.

Keep mulches spread evenly around plants and watch your plants for any sign of drought stress (such as yellowing, or wilted leaves). Occasionally, you may wish to loosen your mulch if it starts to clump. A pitchfork works well.

Chapter 5
Deciduous Hedges

A good way to begin your landscape plan is by planting hedges (Fig. 5-1). Hedges serve several practical functions. They can be used to define your boundaries, provide privacy, and act as a "friendly fence"—a much less obvious barricade than the chain-link variety. Hedges have other advantages over other types of fencing as well. They are quite economical and, on a per foot basis, are cheaper than almost any other kind of fence you can erect. In addition, they are fairly easy to maintain. Unlike a wooden fence, hedges will never need painting or staining. They never rust, like metal fences can, and with proper care, they will improve in beauty through the years. British gardeners are noted for their use of hedges in many of the fine and exquisite gardens in that country.

Hedges serve more useful purposes than that of mere fencing. They can help to prevent soil erosion, and some types, such as the Siberian peashrub, can actually improve the soil in which it is planted. These plants have the rare ability to extract atmospheric nitrogen and incorporate it into the soil—

in short, they make their own fertilizer. There are hedges to attract songbirds and others, if left undisturbed, will become nesting places for wildlife.

TYPE OF FENCE

For most people, a fence along property lines is desirable. It will help to keep neighborhood youngsters out of your yard and offer some privacy, depending upon the fence. The type of fence you erect will depend upon many factors, including what kind of neighbors you have and how close you want to be to them. If the neighbors' kids are always playing in your backyard, or their dog likes to chase your cat, or they annoy you in other ways, you will want to have a good fence to keep out their intrusion. Barbed wire may be what you feel like erecting, but it could give your yard the appearance of a prison compound. Besides, your neighbors might get the idea that you do not like them. Even if that is precisely the case, it is best not to be too obvious. After all, you may need to ask a favor of them sometime. Life will be much more peaceful if you

Fig. 5-1. Begin your landscape plan by planting hedges. Courtesy of Marion Michaels.

are not feuding with your neighbors like the "Hatfields and McCoys."

If neighbors are a nuisance, a hedge can keep them out. There are some hedges, such as barberry, which are almost impenetrable. The multiflora rose is another fine hedge. All those lovely blossoms will likely meet with your neighbor's approval, and they will welcome the fragrant flowers. And all those "lovely" thorns will keep Junior and Fido in their own backyard!

Even if privacy is not a consideration in your landscape plans, it is still a good idea to outline your borders. That way you will know where your property line ends and your neighbor's begins. There is no point in buying expensive shrubbery for your neighbor's land.

If you are quite sociable and chat over the back fence, your hedge can be a conversation piece. Hybrid tea roses or dwarf lilac bushes can be quite stunning when in full bloom, and they will provide

you with cutflowers for your and your neighbor's home.

WHY A DECIDUOUS HEDGE?

Deciduous hedges offer a certain utilitarian advantage over evergreens. The leaves they lose each fall, when left to decay, will enrich the earth, but the main advantage of a deciduous hedge is the multiseasonal interest it offers. Evergreen hedges, which may be mostly conifers, usually create the same effect year-round. Although they may afford some color changes, they are not as spectacular as are those of deciduous hedges. With deciduous hedges, each season brings its own special show.

All deciduous hedges are not alike. While some, such as the burning bush, may come ablaze with full color, others are best planted for a different feature of interest and may bear little, if any fall color.

All deciduous hedges lose their leaves. Some,

however, hang onto them longer in winter and are almost never barren; others are left with only a silhouette of branches to outline their form against the cold winter snows. Although leafless branches are rarely dazzling, sometimes they can produce an interesting scene. A few varieties hold greater interest in that way than others. Those hedges that continue to hold fruits well into winter are perhaps most exciting. The brightly colored fruits add sparkle to a dull, gray wintry scene.

In spring, when the new leaves start to form, your hedges will quickly fill in, covering the framework of branches with a blanket of green. Evergreens remain much the same all year-round, but your deciduous hedges will change with each season and, like the changing seasons, create moods and reflect times that you will remember and enjoy in the years to come.

HOW HIGH SHOULD A HEDGE BE?

Generally speaking, there are only two things that limit the height of a hedge. The first is the natural height a plant attains at maturity. The second is the height at which you wish to maintain it by pruning. For outside borders, the heights you choose will be based on your particular life style. Tall hedges are excellent for privacy. Inside your yard, you may want to limit the size of your hedges. This is especially true for hedges that are used for edging pathways. There are a nice selection of dwarf hedges for this purpose, and almost any hedge can be maintained at a fairly low level.

Proper pruning is recommended. There are some hedges that are almost maintenance-free, such as Clavey's dwarf honeysuckle, but most hedges will benefit from a good pruning program. Prune to let the sun in to lower levels. This will increase plant density by encouraging twiggy growth. Allow bottom areas to have plenty of leaves. Plants such as lilacs are prone to develop a characteristic known as *leggy growth*. These will require heavy pruning to maintain them. Leggy growth occurs when the bottom areas are devoid of foliage, and the trunks are bare. Prune to allow more sunlight in to encourage leaf development in the lower extremeties. Proper pruning can also encourage bloom, and up to a point, larger blossoms (Fig. 5-2).

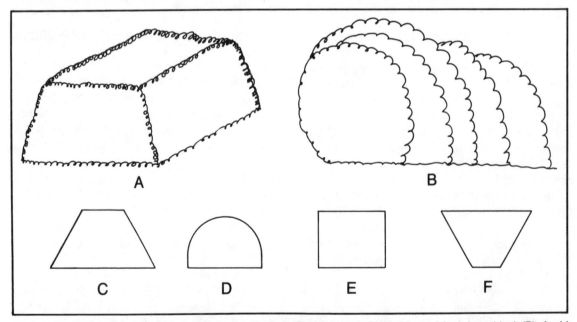

Fig. 5-2. Hedges can be sheared to formal shapes (A, C, D, E) or kept only lightly trimmed for informal look (B). Avoid shapes that leave top wider than bottom (F); not enough sunlight reaches lower branches and growth becomes leggy.

PLANTING A DECIDUOUS HEDGE

The correct time to plant hardy deciduous hedges is best determined by individual climatic conditions. As early as possible in the autumn and spring are the best times. This allows newly transplanted hedges to establish strong root systems before the first freeze or the hot, dry weather of summer.

Where winters are mild, some hardy varieties of hedges may be planted during spells of mild weather, if the soil is not frozen.

Late fall and winter plantings are less likely to be successful if you have heavy clay soil; conversely, a late fall planting in sandy, loose soil may do very well.

After you have decided what plants will make up your hedge and where it will go, the next step is to prepare the soil to accept the new plants. Do this preparatory work at least two to three weeks before you actually plant your hedge. (If you're using plants from a mail-order house, try to schedule your order for delivery accordingly.) This waiting period allows the soil to settle; never plant hedges in loose soil. To do so could cause the plants to settle too deeply into the soil and suffocate, lean out of line, or to allow water to slip past the roots (in the case of balled and burlapped specimens).

Begin your preparations by having the soil tested for pH value and fertility. Check the cultural requirements of the plants and determine what, if anything, must be done to correct the soil condition.

You will most likely want your hedge to run in a neat line. If you are planting along a property border or want a straight line hedgerow, measure in carefully from the border line or other parallel reference at intervals of several feet along the planned row. Mark the line with small sticks stuck in the ground. Mark the ends of the row with heavier stakes driven firmly into the earth. String a length of twine tautly between the stakes to give you a guideline. Lastly, "eyeball" along the string to be sure it is straight, taking into account irregularities in the lay of the soil.

If you are planting your hedge in a curved line, lay a garden hose or clothesline on the ground and move it around until you have the proper design. With a hoe, carefully scratch a shallow line along the ground, following the curves. This will serve as your guideline.

You can now begin to dig. If the hedge plants you have chosen need a substantial amount of room between individual plants, you must dig individual holes for each plant. To achieve accurate spacing, measure from the center of a hole to the center of the adjoining hole. Dig each hole deep enough to allow lots of room for roots to spread out. For average size hedge plants, a hole 2 feet deep and 2 to 3 feet wide is sufficient.

If you are planting denser hedges that require shorter spacing between individual specimens, you can dig a trench of the correct depth instead of holes.

Place the soil you remove in a wheelbarrow or other container. You will want to replace any infertile or hardened subsoil with good topsoil taken from another part of your yard. Do not allow the soil you dig out to lay on the grass; it will kill it.

Now is the time to correct the soil's pH level, consistency, and fertility. If the soil is too acid, add crushed limestone; if it is too basic, add peat moss, oakleaf mold, pine needles, or ferrous sulfate. Add well-rotted manure or compost to the soil to improve fertility and consistency. Work all these things well into the soil. You must not allow bare roots to come in direct contact with fertilizers, lime, or acidifiers.

Allow the soil to rest and settle for two to three weeks. If your bare-rooted mail-order plants have arrived before you are ready to plant, you will have to heel them in. Dig a shallow trench somewhere in your yard and lay the plants in on their sides. Cover the roots and lower stems with soil, leaving only the top branches and leaves exposed. Firm the soil over them. If you have purchased balled and burlapped plants or plants grown in containers, keep them in a cool shady place and keep their roots moist with occasional waterings.

You are now ready to plant. If you are planting bare-rooted plants, you must be sure that the roots are never allowed to dry out, even for a few minutes. Keep them wrapped or covered in wet burlap or newspaper until the plants are ready to set out.

Set each plant upright in its hole or in the trench, being careful to set it at the same depth as it grew. Do not plant hedges either deeper or more shallow than they originally grew; the uppermost roots should be covered by no more or less than 2 to 3 inches of soil.

Spread out the bare roots over a small mound of soil in the hole. (If the roots are badly tangled, soak them in water to help untangle them.) If the day is dry, you may want to mist the roots with water even as you set the plants in the ground. Begin to fill the hole by placing handsful of soil over the roots. Place a little soil in the hole, then firm it in place with your hands. Continue to do this until the hole is completely filled. Firming the soil as you fill the hole, rather than filling it in all at once and then firming, will allow the bare roots to set in more securely.

If you are planting balled and burlapped hedge plants, set the burlap covered root ball into the hole or trench, making sure the plant is at the same depth as it grew. When the plant is in proper position, cut the twine that holds the burlap and remove it. Carefully cut away and remove the burlap, being careful not to dislodge the plant. Be sure to remove any burlap that may be above ground; it will act as a wick and cause the plant to dry out. Don't worry if you can't pull out all the burlap—it will rot. Fill in the hole and firm the soil as above.

If you are planting container grown plants, you must remove the containers. If the plants are small enough, place one hand over the top of the soil with the main stem of the plant between your spread fingers. Invert the plant and container, supporting it with your hands. Rap the edge of the container sharply against a hard edge, like a table or fence post. The plant, with its ball of soil intact, will drop neatly into your hand.

If the container is too big to invert, cut it away with a knife, heavy shears, or tin snips. Be careful not to injure the plant stem or cut too many roots. Set the plant in the ground and firm in as above.

If you are planting in the spring, leave a shallow saucerlike depression around the base of each plant to collect rainfall. You need not do this when planting in late fall, but you may, especially if the weather is dry.

Once your hedge is planted, clean up the area by raking soil level and removing debris. Water your newly planted hedge thoroughly, soaking the ground to a depth of 8 to 9 inches. If your deciduous hedge plants are without leaves (dormant), they need not be watered unless the soil is rather dry.

You may want to prune back newly set dormant plants to about 6 inches. This will help to concentrate the plant's energy on producing heavy root growth, and promote denser growth at the base of the hedge. If the plants are in full leaf, however, it may be wiser to wait until they are dormant in the fall.

Water the hedge once a week, soaking the soil thoroughly. Temporary shade may be necessary if the weather gets very warm and leaves start to wilt. You can construct a shade screen from burlap or branches. This will help to prevent excessive transpiration (moisture loss) from leaves and twigs. Leave the shade in place for up to three weeks, or until plants show definite signs of recovery.

Pruning

Fast-growing privet hedges can be sheared three times a year; medium growing hedges, twice; and slow growers, once. A deciduous hedge should increase in height and width by only a few inches each season.

The best time to trim is in early summer or when the year's growth is completed. Flowering hedges should be clipped as soon as their flowers have dropped. Choose a humid, overcast day and clip in late afternoon or early morning when the air is coolest.

If you're faced with a hugely overgrown deciduous hedge, you can rejuvenate it in one of two ways.

First, in early spring, cut the hedge back right to the ground. It will look awful, but by early summer, new growth will begin to sprout from the stumps. Loosen the soil, fertilize with compost, and mulch to encourage growth.

Second, you can renovate an old open hedge by a technique known as *plashing*. Cut away all loose open side stems. With a sharp knife, cut part way through the center stems, enough to allow you to lay the stems flat along the ground, in the direction of the hedgerow. Peg these stems securely in contact to the soil. The old branches will survive if you have not cut them too deeply, and new shoots will grow up from them.

You can use this method to fill in gaps where, because of dense roots, you cannot insert a new plant.

SELECTING HEDGE PLANTS

The remainder of this chapter is devoted to a list of select deciduous hedge plants. Most of these plants can be grown in any part of the United States, with some exceptions. All are temperate zone ornamentals.

Alpine Current. The Alpine currant (*Ribes alpinum*) is one of the hardiest of the low-growing hedges. It can be kept trimmed from 1 1/2 to 4 feet to form a dense green hedge. These plants have a rounded form, but can be sheared to other shapes if desired. They make very neat and compact hedges and are ideal for formal garden display (Fig. 5-3).

Apline currant is comparable to boxwood because of its excellent color, fine texture, and low-growing stature. In many respects, it is superior to boxwood, and it certainly is hardier. This is a fine choice for northerners.

Alpine currants should be planted 12 to 18 inches apart within a row for a dense hedge. Some people set them slightly farther apart, but they should not be spaced so widely that unsightly gaps appear in the hedge.

The year after they are planted, Alpine currants should be cut back to encourage branching and growth at the base of the plant. Cut them back by about half or, if you prefer, by one-third.

It is vital that the plants be well-tended the first season they are set out. This is necessary to get them established. Once they develop their root system, they will be sturdier and able to withstand more adverse conditions. (This is true of all plants. First-year care is a critical factor to plant survival.) The characteristics, culture, and use of each plant is discussed. This listing is not exhaustive, but rather a selection of "tried-and-true" plants with which beginners will have good luck. Check with

Fig. 5-3. Alpine currant. Courtesy Denver Water Department, Xeriscape Conservation Garden.

your favorite nursery to see what varieties are available.

After the first year, plants should be maintained by a regular watering schedule—usually weekly—controlling weeds and tall grasses where necessary. Plants respond well to an application of manure in early spring. Be careful when using fresh manure so that it does not touch the plant itself.

There are many fine uses for this plant. It is ideal for northern growers who may have had trouble growing a quality hedge in the past. Although it produces fruits (small blue-black berries), they are inedible. This species is not the fruiting currant.

Amur River Privet. The Amur river privet (*Ligustrum amurensis*) is the privet to plant in the north, because it is hardier than many of the other species. These are the most popular hedges grown. They are almost evergreen in their characteristics, retaining their color and leaves for a long time into the winter.

This plant is well suited to urban areas. It grows under a wide range of conditions and soils, and it is best noted for its glossy, green foliage. This is a hedge you will encounter most frequently.

Amur river privet grows in sun or shade: in fact, it grows in almost any well-drained soil. Plants should be set out from 12 to 18 inches apart within a row. If you wish to grow a tall hedge, space plants a little farther apart. You can maintain Amur river privet at any height from 3 to 6 feet.

Newly set plants should be given careful consideration during the first season to help them become adjusted to their new environment. Water them thoroughly each week, more often during periods of dry weather. Control weeds and tall grasses. (A grass shears can cut grass without any chance of injury to your hedge; use a pair of scissors if grass shears are unavailable.)

In the spring of the second season, before the branches leaf out, cut them back. This will encourage the plants to branch out and produce growth at the base. If the plants are not cut back, they may not develop as fully toward the ground and the hedge will have a leggy look, which is undesirable.

Amur river privet hedges make a "friendly fence" and can be used wherever a hedge is desired. Frequently, they are used in foundation plantings or along the borders of property lines. In cities, they help people to keep off the grass. They grow rapidly and lavishly and require a certain amount of maintenance work to keep them looking their best.

Arrowood Viburnum. The Arrowood viburnum (*Viburnum dentatum*) is a tall growing shrub that can reach 12 feet or more in height. It has a graceful vase shape. This shrub produces white flowers during the early part of summer, and offers blue, inedible fruits later on. In the fall, the foliage colors to maroon. Arrowood viburnum takes up a certain amount of space in a yard. It is best to plant this shrub only in those areas where it will have plenty of room to grow.

Arrowood viburnum favors a rich, moist soil. It is very shade tolerant and seems to grow best in those areas where it can receive some shade. Keep the ground damp, but not wet. This plant may be adversely affected if it has to endure drought for any long period of time.

Remove weeds and tall grasses from around the base of the shrub; a summer mulch will help in this respect. Water plants by a thorough weekly soaking. Soak the area under the branch span at least once a week—more so during dry weather.

Arrowood viburnum makes an attractively tall hedge. It must be pruned to control size and maintain its graceful branching habit. Space plants about 3 feet apart in a row. This hedge is an excellent choice for a shady yard or to provide some privacy in a backyard.

Burning Bush. The burning bush (*Euonymus alata*) is planted for its sensational fall color. During the summer, it is handsome, but not spectacular. It is during the fall when you will notice the burning bush, aflame with pink-to-red coloring. You will never regret planting it once you see it in its autumn glory.

The burning bush can grow quite tall: under ideal conditions, it can reach 15 feet. Usually, it does not get that large, growing to only 8 feet or so. It has a spreading form.

If planting for individual specimens, set out between 5 and 6 feet apart. When planting for hedge use, a closer spacing is necessary—between 2 and 3 feet. You can maintain the height of your hedge by trimming. Left to grow naturally, it will become quite tall.

Control weeds, especially around newly set plants. The burning bush is a fairly hardy shrub.

Plant in full sun. It will not color up as well if it is set out under heavy shade. It favors a well-drained soil. The plant has corky, winged twigs, which give it an unusual silhouette when backdropped against winter snows.

The burning bush is very versatile and can be used in many areas. It is an excellent accent plant for fall gardens. It is impressive when set out beside entryways, and it is a sensational hedge, especially in the fall.

Autumn is the season for this shrub, just as spring is the season for many others. Remember this when planning your landscape theme: by strategic placement, you can have color throughout the growing season.

Cheyenne Privet. Cheyenne privet (*Ligustrum vulgare* var. *cheyenne*) can grow to 15 feet. Usually, it does not reach that height and is best controlled by pruning to create denser growth and a superior hedge. Cheyenne privet grows erect. It is one of the hardiest of the privets and especially suited to the dry areas of the Great Plains. It has white flowers followed by black fruits, but the foliage is the greatest feature of interest that this plant offers to the landscape.

Cheyenne privet grows well under urban conditions, where many other types of hedges may have difficulty. These plants grow well under adverse conditions and are highly tolerant of dry soils.

This is basically a hedge plant, although it can be grown for other purposes. It should be planted from 2 to 2 1/2 feet apart in well-drained soil, depending upon how tall you want your hedge to grow. If you space your plants too far apart, you may have gaps. If spaced too closely together, they may grow poorly.

Cheyenne privet favors sunny conditions, but will grow under shade. It can be planted anywhere that a hedge is desired. Individual specimens can be set out and trained for entryways, but "living fences" are the most effective use for these plants.

Clavey's Dwarf Honeysuckle. Clavey's dwarf honeysuckle (*Lonicera* x *xylosteroides*) is a very hardy hedge. It produces dense, foliar growth that makes it very effective as a screening plant. Plants grow up to 4 feet, but can be kept lower by trimming. It keeps its dark-green color late into the fall and requires less trimming than many other hedges.

Clavey's dwarf honeysuckle is somewhat fine-textured and has a round shape. It grows foliage from the top clear to the ground. It is very easy to grow, having virtually no disease or insect pests.

Plant Clavey's dwarf in any well-drained soil. It grows best in full sun. For a dense hedge, set plants 18 inches apart within a row. Trim plants at the top the year after planting, prior to their leafing out in the spring. This encourages plants to branch and develop growth at the base. (Hedges are most impressive when they produce a solid wall of green from top to bottom.)

Water plants on a weekly basis the first season to get them off to a good start—more often during periods of drought. Deep water the plants by soaking the areas around their roots. Do not just sprinkle them.

Clavey's dwarf honeysuckle makes a low, dense hedge and it is also popular for foundation plantings. Whenever your landscape needs require a quality hedge, try this one. It is one of the easiest-to-maintain hedges and an ideal choice for beginners.

Dwarf Burning Bush. The dwarf burning bush (*Euonymus alata* var. *compacta*) is a natural dwarf version of the popular burning bush. For most people, this is a better specimen than the standard size because it is easier to maintain and does not become as large. Although a dwarf, left to itself and under proper conditions, it can grow to 5 feet. Some trimming will be required unless you wish it to grow that tall.

This plant is also likely to go unnoticed throughout the summer, but come fall, it will be one of the focal points of your landscape. The color is a bright fire engine red. Dwarf burning bush has a spreading shape and bears pink and orange fruits, which will attract birds. The berries add some ornamental value to the plants but the famous fall foliage is their best feature.

The dwarf burning bush is tolerant of sun or shade, but it is at its best display when grown under full sun. The plants do not fully color up when grown under shady conditions. It favors a well-drained soil.

The dwarf burning bush can be used in the same locations as the standard burning bush and then some. It works better for smaller city lots and is easier to maintain than the standard variety.

Dwarf burning bush makes a nice hedge, or it can be used for specimen planting, or as accent plants in fall gardens. It is effective when lining walks and entry ways.

Emerald Mound Dwarf Honeysuckle. The emerald mound dwarf honeysuckle (*Lonicera* *x xylosteum var. nanum*) is somewhat similar to Clavey's dwarf, except that this lower-growing plant rarely exceeds 2 to 3 feet in height and has a mounded form. This plant makes an attractive low hedge or can be used for specimen plantings.

The emerald mound dwarf honeysuckle produces plants with dense growth and glossy green foliage. Its mound-shaped bushes require very little pruning to retain their attractive shape. This plant keeps its green leaf color until late in the fall. It has inedible red berries.

Plant in any well-drained soil. Full sun is best. For a dense hedge, plant 12 to 18 inches apart within a row. Keep weeds controlled and shrubs well-watered during their first season's growth. After that, water on a weekly basis and during periods of drought.

Only light trimming will be necessary to keep these plants looking their best. They are dwarfs, so they will not have to be pruned heavily to maintain size. They tend to form mounds naturally, so controlling their growth habits will require very little care.

These plants respond well to fertilizer. Apply manure in the spring. Spread the manure evenly around the base of the plant. Fresh manure should not touch the plant and should be covered with a few shovelsful of dirt to prevent gnats from breeding in it.

Emerald mound dwarf honeysuckle is practical for low-growing hedges, and is also attractive when set out on each side of an entryway. They make a nice wall of green for lining walks and driveways, and they are also very useful in keeping intruders out of flower gardens.

Japanese Barberry. The Japanese barberry (*Berberis thunbergii*) has thorns. It is a small plant, growing to 4 feet. It has a naturally mounded growth habit, produces red fruits and an orange fall color, and is an excellent hedge plant. The Japanese barberry is a low-growing shrub and makes a nice low hedge. It can be sheared to formal patterns or allowed to grow to its natural form. There are many excellent *cultivars* (cultivated varieties) of the Japanese barberry on the market. Each has certain advantageous characteristics.

Fig. 5-4. Red barberry. Courtesy Denver Water Department, Xeriscape Conservation Garden.

The cultivar *Crimson Pygmy* produces a low mound, smaller than the parent plant. It has red summer foliage and grows to 2 feet. It is most colorful when grown in full sun (Fig. 5-4).

Atropurpea is another cultivar. This plant is very much like the parent plant, except that it has reddish-purple summer foliage.

Japanese barberry likes full sun. The cultivars, especially, become more colorful when grown under full sun.

These are naturally low-growing shrubs and should be set 2 1/2 to 3 feet apart within a row for hedge use. If spaced too far apart, there are likely to be gaps in the hedge that will spoil its attractiveness.

These plants make a dense hedge and can be sheared to almost any shape. They are tolerant of dry soil. Grow in sun for best leaf color performance. Once established, Japanese barberry is fairly easy to maintain.

Use wherever a low hedge is desired; the dwarfs make excellent borders for entryways and driveways. They are also effective in keeping small animals out of your yard because of their thorns. Border your property alongside city sidewalks to keep people off your lawn. Select the cultivar that best suits your particular needs and preferences.

Manyflowered Cotoneaster. The manyflowered cotoneaster (*Cotoneaster multiflorus*) is a fairly tall and vigorous grower. It will reach from 10 to 12 feet in height. It has a mounded form, but takes quite a bit of room and cannot be recommended for small areas. This wide-spreading shrub bears white flowers in spring, followed by red fruits.

The manyflowered cotoneaster will make an impressive background for other landscape plants. It is especially useful in rural areas, or on farms where the space is available for such a large plant.

Manyflowered cotoneasters favor full sun. They should be planted on well drained soil. Space each plant in a hedgerow between 5 and 6 feet apart. The addition of lime to the soil will be beneficial.

Sometimes, you may find a pest or disease problem with these plants. Contact your county agricultural extension agent should such an event occur or be serious enough to warrant concern.

The most important thing you can provide these plants with is plenty of space in which to grow. If they are crammed together, their appearance will not be as effective as when they can spread out.

Use for tall borders. Plants can also be used as landscape specimens, especially for entryways. They should be set out in a sunny location along borders or wherever you want this hedge to grow.

Peking Cotoneaster. The Peking cotoneaster (*Cotoneaster acutifolius*) is a medium-growing shrub that can reach 5 feet, although it is usually kept trimmed below that height. It has an upright growth form and is a useful hedge plant. This shrub bears black, inedible berries during late summer. It is perhaps at its peak display in the autumn, when its leaves turn bright orange.

The Peking cotoneaster makes a good privacy screen. Although it may not totally screen out an unpleasant view, it will provide some privacy from busy streets or nearby neighbors. In the winter, it is barren of leaves, with only a few fruits clinging to it.

Be sure to add lime to the area when planting; Peking cotoneaster favors an alkaline soil. Once established, it is very tolerant of dry soils, but it must be kept well-watered the first season it is set out to give it a chance to adjust to its new environment.

Peking cotoneaster is perhaps the hardiest of all the cotoneasters. It is very tolerant of shade and grows best in those areas where it can receive at least partial shade. The fall color tends to be more maroon when grown under shady conditions and is a bright orange when the plant is set out in full sun.

Plant 3 to 4 feet apart, depending upon how tall you want your hedge to be. For a denser hedge, plant 3 feet apart within a row. Do not space plants much closer or they will be more troublesome to keep up.

The Peking cotoneaster can be placed anywhere that a tall, somewhat open-type hedge is desired. Because it grows well in shade, it can be set in areas where many other hedges would not grow as well.

Redbush Honeysuckle. Redbush honeysuckle (**Lonicera zabeli**) can be planted singly, but it makes a sensational hedge plant if you have the room for it. These plants grow up to 10 feet tall and almost as wide. They are covered with red flowers in the spring and bear red berries later on in the summer.

This shrub tends toward an open growth and spreading habit, producing a dense growth. Sometimes they grow too vigorously and are hard to maintain.

Redbush honeysuckle, sometimes called **Zabel honeysuckle**, is an ideal plant for urban areas, because it tolerates the stresses of city life. The only drawback is that many city lots are not really large enough to accommodate this shrub.

Redbush honeysuckle tolerates dry soil. It grows best in full sun, but does all right under partial shade conditions as well. Plant shrubs 2 1/2 to 3 feet apart within a row for a tight, dense hedge. If you want to produce a taller hedge, widen the distance between the plants to 4 feet. They will soon fill in.

This is a very hardy species and fairly easy to care for, although it will take some work to maintain it.

Redbush honeysuckle makes an effective windbreak and is useful as a tall screen. It can be grown as a single specimen where desired. A hedge of these plants will brighten your spring landscape with it red flowers and the summer with its colorful red berries.

Regel's Border Privet. Regel's border privet (*Ligustrum obtusifolium* var. *regelianum*) grows to about 6 feet if left to itself. It can be trimmed to keep it lower. Regel's border privet has a spreading growth habit. It is very hardy and produces white flowers in the spring, followed by a summer crop of blue-black, inedible berries. It remains green well into autumn, when it changes to a purple fall color.

Regel's border privet is one of the best. It is quite tolerant of dry soils and shade, and it makes a handsome green hedge that produces a dense growth. These hedges are easily sheared into formal shapes.

This is basically a hedge plant, but can be used as a decorative accent. When setting out plants, space them 2 to 2 1/2 feet apart in a row. You can space them farther apart, but this spacing gives you a nice dense hedge. For the densest hedge, it is best to not exceed 3 feet between each plant within the row.

Regel privet grows well under shade. Although established plants are very tolerant of dry soils, newly set plants deserve the utmost care. They must be watered on a regular weekly basis throughout their first growing season. During dry periods, extra water may be needed.

Regel privet can be used anywhere a formal hedge is desired. Its dense green growth is excellent for shaping into formal forms, and it is an excellent choice hedge for a "fancy" yard.

Siberian Peashrub. The Siberian Peashrub (*Caragana arborescens*) has an erect, oval form. As its name suggests, this species is very hardy. It is one of the hardiest hedges grown and one of the best for people who have poor, infertile soils. The Siberian Peashrub is a legume and capable of a process called *nitrogen fixation:* it can extract nitrogen from the air and use it for its growth. Thus, it tends to enrich any soil in which it grows. Of course, it needs care to become fully established, but it quickly becomes a rugged plant that can fend for itself under poor conditions and cold climates.

Although this plant bears yellow flowers in the spring, the blooms are so small and insignificant that they offer no landscape interest. The plant is best noted for its attractive green foliage. It has fine-textured leaves that take shearing well.

Siberian peashrub favors an alkaline soil; add lime to your soil when planting. Be careful to not overfertilize these plants with nitrogen fertilizers, because as soon as they are settled in, they can extract all the nitrogen they need from the air. If you give them too much nitrogen fertilizer, you may hamper their ability to extract nitrogen from the air, and you will be wasting money on unnecessary fertilizer.

This tall hedge reaches 10 feet, but it can be trimmed to 3 feet or maintained at whatever height you desire within that range. Set plants out 2 1/2 to 3 feet apart within a row for a dense hedge. Trim the tops of hedges back the spring after planting to encourage the production of branches and growth toward the base of the plants.

This shrub is very drought-resistant. During its first season, however, it must be kept well-watered to allow it to adjust to its new environment and develop greater stamina.

The Siberian peashrub is a fine hedge. It is practical for people who live in cold climates and who have poor, infertile soils—as well as for anyone who has almost given up the dream of ever growing hedges. Siberian peashrubs are a worthwhile investment for any landscape.

Spreading Cotoneaster. The spreading cotoneaster (*Cotoneaster divaricatus*) has a mound shape. It also grows fairly tall—to 8 feet—but can be kept lower by trimming. Spreading cotoneaster has fine-textured foliage and bears bright red fruits. It keeps its green leaf color until late in the fall, when the leaves turn to maroon before dropping off (Fig. 5-5).

This is perhaps the most attractive of the cotoneasters and can be sheared for formal plantings. It is not sufficiently winter hardy in the north however and will need a special site where it can

be protected from the elements to help it survive northern winters.

The spreading cotoneaster favors an alkaline soil; add plenty of garden lime to the planting site. It is very tolerant of dry soils and is a nice hedge plant for areas that experience routine summer droughts. Of course, during prolonged dry spells, these plants should be watered.

Spreading cotoneaster forms a mound, so that is the best way to train it to grow. It will involve less effort, and you will need only to prune plants to control their size or retain their desired shape. You can train them to grow in almost any shape you wish. (It is usually easiest to take care of a plant if you train it to grow according to its natural growth habit, however.)

These plants offer quite a bit of seasonal interest. Their red berries in late summer and fall contrast with their green leaves in a colorful display. When trained to formal plantings, these fine-textured shrubs make an impressive hedge.

Tallhedge. Tallhedge (*Rhamnus frangula* var.

Fig. 5-5. Spreading cotoneaster. Courtesy Denver Water Department, Xeriscape Conservation Garden.

columnaris) grows to a mature height of 12 feet. These hardy hedges are very rapid growers, sometimes producing 2 or more feet of growth in a single season. Plants are very narrow and columnar in shape, which gives them an extra "fancy" look. They require very little pruning to maintain their neat appearance.

Tallhedge is very tolerant of urban conditions and is an excellent hedge for city lots. Because it is so narrow, it can fit on small lots where other tall screening hedges cannot. It readily resists diseases and insects and is fairly easy to maintain.

Tallhedge grows best in full sun, but it will grow under partial shade. Do not plant under heavy shade. This species is not particularly fussy about soil, provided that it is well-drained. (Naturally, plants grow faster in fertile loam than on infertile soil.) Add peat moss to the planting site.

Because of its fast growth rate, these plants are heavy feeders. They should be fertilized throughout the growing season for best results. The addition of a timed-release fertilizer at planting time is most effective. Such pellets usually last for two seasons and do much to provide your hedges with the nitrogen and minor nutrients they need for fast growth. If you prefer the strictly organic route, manure can be added in the spring. Be careful not to apply fresh manure too close to the plant: if the manure touches it, it could burn plant tissue.

Provide plenty of water for your tallhedge plants throughout the growing season. Because of their fast growth, they require abundant supplies of water to meet their needs.

The best use of this species is for screening off unpleasant views or adding privacy to your yard. These plants can also be used as impressive single specimens for entryways.

Chapter 6

Evergreen Hedges

Evergreen hedges are ideal for formal landscapes where you want shape and color to remain constant throughout the year (Fig. 6-1). The very word "evergreen" almost instantly conjures up images of the many coniferous species that are so classified, but there are really two types of evergreens: conifers and broadleaf evergreens.

Not all conifers are evergreen. If that confuses matters, evergreens do not always stay green; many species turn an off-color, especially in cold climates. Some of the evergreens that are hardy enough to survive in the north may take on an almost deciduous nature when grown in warm climates.

Most broadleaf evergreens are not sufficiently winter hardy for the north. They are usually confined to warmer climates, where they thrive. If you live in a warm climate, such as Florida, you will have many broadleaf evergreens from which to choose for your landscape. Most of the conifers are hardy throughout the entire United States and are best for northern areas. The farther north you live, the hardier the plant species must be that you select.

There has been a popular explosion in the planting of evergreens, particularly conifers. These plants lend themselves well to the ranch style architecture so popular today. They are also suited to formal estates and provide an almost instant easy-to-care-for landscape.

PLANTING AND PRUNING

Hardy evergreen hedges may be set out slightly later in the spring and slightly earlier in the fall than deciduous hedges. Fall transplanting can be done as early as late August, as soon as the hottest weather is past. You may continue to plant evergreens until the ground freezes, but it's best not to set them so late that they have no time to develop new roots before the worst winter weather arrives.

The quick development of strong roots is very important, because evergreens transpire through their leaves all winter. This moisture loss must be made up for by the roots, or the hedge will scorch or die.

The best time to plant evergreens is in the spring, just when they begin to show new growth

Fig. 6-1. Canada hemlock hedge. Courtesy of Elizabeth Spangler.

or just before. Do not plant evergreens that are already displaying large new shoots; wait until fall.

After you've chosen which evergreen plants you will use and where your hedge will be, have the soil tested for pH value, consistency, and fertility. Many evergreens like a slightly acidic soil. Acidity can be increased by adding peat moss, pine needles, or ferrous sulfate. Check the cultural requirements of the species you are planting and alter the soil accordingly. All soil preparation should be done two to three weeks before actual planting to allow the soil time to settle and firm up.

For hints on laying out and planting your evergreen hedge, see Chapter 5, Planting a Deciduous Hedge. The same rules apply for evergreens, with a few exceptions and additions.

Evergreens should always be moved with a good ball of soil around their roots. Never buy or transplant bare-rooted evergreens (except for very small seedlings sometimes sold in bulk lots from forestry nurseries). Be especially careful not to let balled and burlapped or container grown evergreens dry out before planting. If you must plant bare-rooted plants, make sure their roots are never allow-

ed to dry out, even briefly. Mist them or keep them wrapped in wet burlap or newspaper. Plant them as soon as possible in moist soil.

When planting balled and burlapped specimens, be especially careful to remove any burlap that may stick out above ground. It will act as a wick and draw moisture away from the roots. Remove the burlap after the plant is set in its hole.

Remove container grown plants from their pots as described in Chapter 3, or cut them out, making sure not to damage the plants or remove too much soil from their roots.

Be sure that evergreen plants are set in the soil at the same depth at which they grew. No more or less than 2 to 3 inches of soil should cover the uppermost roots. To plant too deeply will cause the plant to suffocate; too shallow, and the plant's roots will dry out and die.

Set the plants gently into the trench or individual holes and firm the soil evenly around them. Leave a depression to collect rainwater around the base of each plant.

Evergreen plants should not be cut back at this time, unlike deciduous hedges. You can, however, snip off any stray tips and level off the top of the hedge.

Evergreens may be sprayed with an antitranspirant (antidessicant) before the hard winter weather sets in. This will prevent them from drying out and scorching over their first winter.

Evergreen hedges should be clipped once or twice a year, allowing them to make only a few inches increase in height and width each season. The best time to trim broadleaf evergreens is from mid-March through mid-July. You can reduce the height of established plants by shortening new stems by 6 to ten inches. Pinch off new shoots to encourage bushy lower branches on new plants.

From mid-May to mid-July, nip off any straggly new growth, but do not cut back branches or try to change the hedge's shape. Remove all spent blooms and tidy the hedge. Never prune after mid-July.

For needleleaf evergreens, prune from mid-April to mid-June. Cut new growth to shape as it appears, but before new wood forms. Pinch out the "candles" on upright pines to keep their shapes neat. You can shear evergreen needleleaf hedges from mid-June to mid-August, especially the new growth of vigorous hedges like yew and arborvitae. You can prune lightly from late October to freeze to repair and correct shape.

Water evergreen hedges thoroughly throughout dry spells and mist them occasionally to prevent their leaves from drying out during hot weather. Mulch and fertilize in late fall; feed in spring to encourage fuller growth.

Protect evergreen hedges from winter drying by spraying with antidessicant. Make sure that heavy wet snow does not lie on top of hedges and cause them to spread or break.

EVERGREEN HEDGE SPECIES

Evergreen hedges are planted for many of the same reasons any hedge is planted—plus a few more. The evergreen hedge will maintain a privacy screen year-round. It always looks neat; most evergreen hedges are easier to take care of than deciduous hedges, there is no litter from fallen leaves and no fruits.

Once planted, an evergreen hedge can provide your yard with many years of beauty.

The following is a selection of evergreens well suited to hedge use. Your nursery can provide you with a list of others. Plant only those species that will be hardy in your area.

American Arborvitae. American arborvitae (*Thuja occidentalis*) is an ideal evergreen hedge for the north or any area of the country. Its hardiness makes it especially welcome in northern states. Although it can grow very tall, up to 40 feet, it seldom gets that high when grown as a hedge. You can trim it to any height you desire, down to 3 feet.

This fine-textured species has delicate foliage that takes shearing well. It can be shaped into almost any form you desire; it creates a very formal landscape, so it may not be appropriate for everyone.

Arborvitae favors a fertile, moist soil. It does not tolerate dry soils and may turn off-color if subjected to drought stress. Water this hedge on a weekly basis to meet its needs. It is a very fast grower and newly set transplants will form a hedge for you within a very short period of time.

Shear the plants to train the hedge to grow the way you want it. When shearing hedges for formal rectangular shapes, trim the tops so that they slightly indent from the sides as they go up. This permits greater penetration of sunlight and helps to balance foliar growth. When hedges are trimmed in this matter, the base area has a better chance of filling in with leaves.

Arborvitae is for formal use only; it is too elegant to use in a casual landscape and will look out of place. (There is a globe arborvitae for people who want a round hedge.)

Arborvitae is somewhat demanding to maintain, but it is very rewarding to view. This hedge can be used to border property lines or as a screen. Wherever you use it, your property will increase in beauty and value from this fine selection.

Browni Yew. Browni yew (*Taxus browni*) grows to 6 feet in height and about half as wide. This species has a somewhat spreading habit. It forms a dense, compact bush that takes a shearing well.

The Browni yew is a natural dwarf, semiupright in its growth. It is very easy to control its growth and can be sheared into a square or ball shaped hedge as desired.

Browni yew grows well in sun or shade. It is not particularly fussy, but it does, however, tend to favor a slightly alkaline soil. Have your soil pH checked before planting. The addition of garden lime is an excellent way to "sweeten" acidic soils.

This species is very easy to maintain. Its dwarf size gives it a utilitarian advantage over many larger shrubs. Because it grows wide, this species can be grown in ball or rounded form, which some like better than the more common square hedge shape.

Water plants on a weekly basis. Soak the area near the base of the hedge. Keep weeds out of the area where the hedge is growing. Weeds only rob moisture and nutrients from an area and will spoil the aesthetic qualities of the hedge. Cut tall grasses.

This species is best suited for formal gardens. It takes shearing extremely well, always forming a neat, compact hedge. It is also useful for foundation plantings. Some people favor it for this use, because it never gets out of bounds and is easy to maintain.

Canada Hemlock. Canada hemlock (*Tsuga canadensis)* can form a tree reaching as high as 75 feet. It is one of the most beautiful conifers. It produces soft, feathery foliage that remains green throughout the year. The needlelike leaves of the hemlock are distinctly flattened, and they are shiny on the upper surface.

Canada hemlock grows best in moist soil. It has a low tolerance for drought, and it is best planted under shade. If it is planted in an area where it will receive full sun, it must be given plenty of water so that the soil does not dry out.

Canada hemlock is very winter hardy and can be grown anywhere in the United States south of the Arctic Circle. It also can be planted on the north side of the house, where other plants usually run into problems. These are rapid growers if given good soil and ample moisture.

One of the best uses for Canada hemlock is as a tall hedge. It will provide a curtain of green, feathery foliage on a year-round basis to screen out unpleasant views. The plants can be kept low by pruning.

Canada hemlock can be grown naturally (unsheared) for an informal look. If sheared, these plants are among the "aristocrats" of the plant kingdom, lending eloquence and grace to your yard. They can also be grown as trees, where such a tree is desired.

Eastern Red Cedar. Eastern red cedar (*Juniperus virginiana)* is not only a decorative conifer, but an excellent hedge plant as well. It grows to about 20 feet, but can be kept lower by trimming. It is extremely hardy. This plant has fine textured foliage that takes shearing well, which makes it ideal for a formal hedge because formal hedges usually require a great deal of trimming to shape them into the desired form.

During the winter, this species may take on a slightly brownish color. Its dark green foliage color will return when temperatures warm up again in spring.

The cultural requirements for eastern red cedar differs slightly according to use. Hedge plants should be set out closer together than specimen plants, and more trimming will be necessary to train the plant to hedge form, to restrict its height, and encourage the development of foliage on lower branches.

Eastern red cedar is drought-resistant. It tolerates dry soils extremely well and favors a sandy loam. It grows well in either sun or partial shade.

Your hedge plants will benefit from a regular maintenance program. This should include removing weeds, watering on a weekly basis, fertilizing plants in the spring, and—very importantly—pruning. The pruning or shearing of your hedge plants will keep them in the shape you want. If neglected, they can get too tall and lose some of their aesthetic appeal.

Do not plant this hedge near your apple, crabapple, or juneberry trees. It is an alternate host to a disease called *cedar apple rust,* which will afflict your fruit trees.

This evergreen looks good in almost any yard. It grows tall, so it is a good borderline hedge. If you plant it on your property's edge, the other side will need to be trimmed from time to time. This is an excellent privacy hedge.

Intermedia Yew. Intermedia yew (*Taxus intermedia*) is a dwarf species. It grows to a height of about 4 feet. It has a spreading open habit, but can be pruned to more formal shapes.

This species has bright green foliage. It shares the same fine texture as other yews and remains green all year-round. It is a fast grower and one of the more popular hedge species. Its rapid growth, combined with its dwarf size, makes it very easy to manage. It takes a shearing nicely.

Intermedia yew tends to favor slightly alkaline soils. Check your soil pH levels before planting. If it is necessary to change pH levels, all you will have to do is add garden lime until conditions are right. If in doubt, contact your county agricultural agent for assistance.

Plant in any well-drained site. It does well in sun or shade, so fit it into your landscape in whatever area you desire. This species is easier to maintain than many others. Even though it grows fast, its dwarf nature always keeps it in bounds—even when you forget to shear!

Intermedia yew is practical for most people and useful for many sites. It can serve as a foundation planting, provided that you keep it sheared low enough so that it does not block the views from windows. It is graceful when lining paths and to accent entryways. It looks neat along a driveway, or to fence off the backyard.

Irish Juniper. Irish juniper (*Juniperus communis* var. *hibernica*) grows to 15 feet in height, but can be kept lower by pruning. This species has a columnar growth habit. It produces dense, green foliage from the ground up and takes a shearing nicely.

Irish juniper is an aristocratic shrub, ideal for formal landscapes. The dark green, fine-textured foliage makes it a "classic" in any yard.

Irish juniper grows best in full sun. It likes a heavy, clay-type soil; if you have sandy soil, you should add plenty of peat moss or humus to help increase the water-holding capacity. This plant loves moisture, but not "wet feet." It should not be set out on poorly drained soils.

Water plants on a regular basis. It is always best to soak the area around the base of the plant when watering. Do not sprinkle, or you may not be meeting your plant's moisture needs. A summer mulch is helpful.

The Irish juniper can be used to create a wall between you and neighbors. Unless trimmed, it grows very tall and its dense growth makes it a valuable privacy screen.

This species can also be set out for specimen plantings—for entryways and at house corners to provide accents. Do not plant in front of windows, because it will quickly block the view. This species is ideal for the formal landscape; it is very impressive and will complement almost any home.

Irish Yew. Irish yew (*Taxus baccata* var. *fastigata*) can grow as high as 50 feet or more, but is almost never allowed to get that tall. This species is actually a tree, but it stands clipping well and can be trained as a hedge. It is most practical to grow as a hedge. The Irish yew is very long-lived.

This species has fine-textured foliage, dark green in color. The leaves are somewhat shiny on the upper surfaces and a dull, light shade of green on their undersides. Leaves are small and narrow.

The Irish yew favors a slightly alkaline soil. Add garden lime to the planting site. Before setting out this species, it is a good practice to have your soil pH tested for alkalinity.

The Irish yew grows equally well in sun or shade. It is not terribly particular about planting sites.

Water plants on a weekly basis. Weed the area adjacent to the base of the plants so that weeds do not crowd the hedge and compete for water and nutrients. Cut tall grasses. A grass shears should be used if you are cutting grass close to plants to avoid accidental injuries that can occur when power equipment is used.

Prune plants by trimming with a hedge shears. There are manual and electric shears available, so purchase the type that best suits your needs. You can shape these shrubs to grow in almost any form you wish, and they tend to grow more lush with each clipping.

The Irish yew is a very attractive, dense hedge.

It can be grown as a tall hedge for privacy or kept to a lower level. It is useful for lining walks, back yard garden areas, recreational play areas, as a good borderline plant for property lines, and as an evergreen fence to offer privacy from neighbors.

Korean Littleleaf Box. Korean littleleaf box (*Buxus microphylla* var. *koreana*) is a beautiful little hedge plant that has a multitude of uses. It is one of the few broadleaf evergreens that are hardy enough for the north. It is grown for its attractive green foliage.

The Korean littleleaf box takes shearing well and forms a small, but dense hedge. It can be shaped into almost any form and is best for formal use.

These plants are very tolerant of shade. They have a naturally rounded growth habit but can be sheared to other shapes. Shrubs rarely exceed 2 feet in height and can be kept even lower.

Plant 2 1/2 to 3 feet apart for a dense hedge. Keep plants well-watered; most broadleaf evergreens are not very tolerant of drought stress. Once established, these plants are very hardy. They will not need any trimming until after the first season. Some people make the mistake of pruning their hedges back before they have much of any growth on them, and thus set them back.

Korean littleleaf box is a very good hedge. It has fine-textured foliage and retains its leaves throughout the entire year. It is an excellent choice for formal gardens. This low-growing hedge can be used to line driveways and sidewalks and is also effective in backyard plantings, to line swimming pools, or outline flower gardens.

The Korean littleleaf box is one of the "standards of excellence" by which other hedges are judged in comparison.

Red Tip Photenia: The red tip photenia (*Photinia serrulata)* is an evergreen shrub that grows to a height of 7 feet. It can be kept lower by trimming. It is an exceptional hedge plant, because it makes dense growth. This tender evergreen has many features that will make an interesting landscape planting. In the spring, it bears flowers in showy white clusters. These are later followed by red fruits.

Perhaps the most noteworthly feature is the foliage of the new growth in spring and early summer; the new foliage is always a vivid red. Against the background of the older, green foliage, it appears to be tipped in red, which is where it gets its name.

The red tip photenia is not sufficiently winter hardy for the north. It is a broadleaf evergreen and best reserved for warmer climes. Areas with extremely cold winters should not grow this species.

The best leaf coloring usually appears under conditions of full sunlight, but this plant will grow in almost any area without much trouble.

The first year is the most important. It is during this time that your plants will adjust to their new environment, and special attention is necessary to help the plant to adapt.

Keep the area around the base well-weeded and free of tall grasses. No competing vegetation should be allowed to choke out the young plants. It is very important to keep all weeds pulled.

Water plants on a weekly basis. Once a week waterings are usually sufficient. If the weather is very hot and plants look extremely dry or show signs of drought stress, such as yellowing of leaves, water them.

The best use is for a hedge that will make an interesting display in the home landscape. These plants are also suited to specimen plantings where accent shrubs are needed.

Chapter 7

Hedges to Attract Songbirds

Have you ever visited a home where to venture outside was to be eaten alive by mosquitoes or dive-bombed by wasps? Correct landscape design can be used to control insect pests by improving drainage and soil conditions that attract them and by planting trees and shrubs that attract insect-eating birds. The loss of a few cherries or blueberries is well worth the price.

The most helpful birds are bluebirds, wrens, orioles, mockingbirds, and cardinals. There are many, many more helpful species including the whippoorwill, the bobwhite, and more! To learn more about songbirds, find a good book on the subject— one with photos in it to help you to identify the various species. Go to your local bookstore or library or write to :Audubon, 950 3rd Avenue, New York, NY 10022. They can refer you to your local chapter of the Audubon Society.

Find out and familiarize yourself with the kind of birds in your area so you will know how to attract the desired ones and protect your property from pest birds. For example, one bird you will definite-ly not want to attract is the house finch. In large numbers, they can do a great deal of damage to any fruit crops you might have.

SECRETS TO ATTRACTING BIRDS

The real secret of attracting songbirds is to provide an environment that will meet their needs. This includes housing or nesting places, water, and sources of food.

Housing

There are many types of housing that can be provided. Regular bird houses can be used to attract specific breeds of birds. A less expensive and perhaps more practical method is to plant shrubs that allow the birds to build nests in them. Usually, the best nesting shrubs are those with an open form of growth, where the birds will not be frequently disturbed. Formal hedges that are sheared into tight squares are of little use to birds looking for a home. Also, trimming the hedges can frighten birds off, especially if a gas or electric powered trimmer is used. Open shrubs permit room where birds can build their nests.

Water

Birds need readily available water. The simplest way to see that they receive the water they need is to set up a birdbath. Birdbaths do not have to be elaborate or expensive. There are plastic models available commercially that will fit the bill and look quite handsome in your yard. Fill them with small stones or sand to hold them steady. Be sure that during the summer your birdbath has plenty of water in it and change water from time to time. Clean water is nicer than dirty water. During the winter, especially if you live in an area with freezing temperatures, the birdbath should be empty of water. If it is a plastic model, it should be taken indoors and stored to protect it from the elements.

Food

Birds eat a wide variety of seeds, grains, berries, and bugs, so there is usually some food available to them in almost every yard. The more berry-producing plants you have, however, the more attractive you make your yard to birds. Sometimes people like to buy birdseed and set it out for birds; that's fine, but plants that produce their own "bird-food" will save you much money, produce a landscape that is inviting to your fine-feathered friends, and provide you with many hours of watching and listening pleasure.

(For tips on planting and pruning the following fruiting hedge plants, refer to Chapter 5.)

HEDGE SPECIES

Hedges offer one of the best attractions for birds, especially common garden songbirds such as the mourning dove, the song sparrow, and the robin. Ornamental hedges can provide beauty for your yard, shelter for bird nests, and a supply of fruit for birds (most of these fruits are not the luscious types that people enjoy, but there are exceptions).

Some songbirds like to build their nests close to the ground, in areas where they will not be disturbed. With the vanishing wilderness, your hedges may provide a home.

For the serious bird enthusiast, there are many things that can be done to lure birds to your yard, but one of the best ways is with the plants you select for your landscape. Naturally, some hedges are more attractive to birds than others. The following is a selection of some of the best hedge plants for attracting songbirds. Most of these plants have great ornamental value and are relatively easy to grow. Your county agricultural agent can provide you with a list of others that are suitable for your area.

Autumn Olive. Autumn olive (*Elaeagnus umbellata*) is a tall shrub that makes a good hedge plant. It grows to a height of 8 to 10 feet, sometimes taller, with a spreading form. The autumn olive has very fragrant flowers, and it bears red, edible fruits. The fruits are best used for making jelly, as they are not delectable when eaten off the shrub. Left on the shrub, the fruits serve as decorative accents and will attract songbirds to your garden.

If grown as individual specimens, set plants between 5 and 6 feet apart. When planting for hedge use, they should be spaced closer: between 2 and 3 feet apart within a row. This will form a tall hedge, so you may want to trim it to maintain the height you desire.

Autumn olives grow best when set in areas where they receive full sunlight. They are highly tolerant of poor, dry soil and will grow in places where another shrub might fail.

Weeds should be controlled, especially around young plants, so that they do not shade them out or compete for nutrients and water. A summer mulch is helpful, both in controlling weeds and conserving moisture.

Autumn olives produce twiggy growth. When the leaves have fallen, the barren twigs are quite expressive against the winter landscape. This plant is very attractive to songbirds, which like to eat the fruit and make nests in its branches.

Buffalo Berry. The buffalo berry (*Shepherdia argentea*) is a thorny, shrubby plant that grows to about 10 feet. It is native to the Great Plains. Buffalo berry plants have silvery leaves and bear scarlet berries that can be used for making jelly. American

Indians used them in their meat dishes, but there is no commercial market for these fruits today. Birds are attracted by the berries.

Buffalo berry plants can be trained to small-tree form, but are probably most useful when grown as a hedge. When training to tree form, it is simply a matter of pruning off the bottom branches and selecting one stem for a solitary trunk. The tree form can also be grown in a hedgerow for a somewhat more formal effect.

These are extremely hardy plants and very drought-resistant. They grow in almost any soil, but favor a fertile loam. The soil should be well-drained. The plants grow best in open sunlight, which is where they have the highest berry production. They also grow well in partial shade.

Culture for these plants is fairly easy. Once established, buffalo berries practically take care of themselves. You will want to prune them to maintain their growth habit and control size.

Buffalo berry plants are somewhat coarse in texture and not for the refined landscape. Their fruits can sometimes by considered a litter problem to people who pride themselves upon their immaculate lawns. They will attract songbirds, however, and you can use the fruits for jelly. If you want a practical hedge, you may wish to try this one.

Chokecherries. Chokecherries (*Padus virginiana*) can be grown as a tall hedge. They tend to have an open growth habit and be somewhat coarse in texture. This coarse texture makes them less than ideal for formal plantings and fancy landscapes, and the fruits may cause a litter problem.

Plants spread by suckers from their roots. To keep chokecherries in manageable rows, it will probably be necessary to prune out these suckers early each spring while plants are still dormant.

Chokecherries offer several features of seasonal interest for those who enjoy unusual deciduous shrubs. In spring, they are one of the first plants to bloom, producing a delightful display. The white grapelike clusters will fill your air with a sweet, heady perfume. Everyone who visits you will comment on the lovely fragrance.

Chokecherries are not for small yards. They can grow to a height of 12 feet of more and almost as wide. They will need pruning to maintain them as hedges. Even when planted for hedge use, they still need plenty of room. Consider them as a tall hedge with a very open form of growth. It is best to not plant chokecherries in formal gardens, nor too close to your property line. Your neighbors may not appreciate having the suckers springing up all over their yard, nor the litter of fruits on their lawn.

During the summer, when the plant is in fruit and panicles of berries change from red to purple, the shrubs are very attractive—and quite tempting. Do not give way to temptation, however, for you will be disappointed. These astringent fruits pucker your mouth, and you may even gag on them. If you want to eat chokecherries, make them into a jelly. You will not like them raw. (They do make a noteworthy jelly, especially when mixed with apple juice.)

Chokecherries do not have very spectacular fall color, but some of the fruits tend to cling on into the winter, which provides a snack for winter birds in search of food.

Chokecherries are worth growing if you have the space to grow them and time to maintain them. They are practical for many reasons: to attract, feed, and house birds; to provide homemade jelly; and for their blossom and fruit displays. Another nice feature about the chokecherry is that it is very hardy and can thrive through droughts and on sandy soils. They are a high maintenance plant, however, and will require a great deal of pruning to keep them in hedge form.

Compact European Cranberry Bush. The compact European cranberry bush (*Viburnum opulus* var. *compactum*) grows to about 4 feet in height. It can be kept lower by trimming. It is not a true cranberry, but gets its name from the edible, red berries that it bears in clusters. These berries make a tart jelly that resembles the taste of cranberries.

This plant has an attractive floral display of blossoms each spring, hanging in clusters on the bush. Later, berries develop. The berries are persistent and hang on the shrub for a long time. They are eaten by birds and can be picked for jelly. The berries appear as bright red clusters, making a very attractive ornamental display.

The compact European cranberry bush grows in sun or shade. It favors a rich moist soil and will not tolerate drought stress. Water your hedge on a regular weekly basis, more often during periods of dry weather.

It is necessary to prune these shrubs to encourage dense growth. Otherwise they will become leggy (have green foliage at the top and barren branches toward the bottom). Such a trait is unappealing. Pruning also helps to control size of the plants and shape them for hedge use. Another beneficial aspect of pruning is that it stimulates the production of new fruiting wood.

They produce an attractive hedge sure to appeal to birds.

Hedgerow Hawthorn. The hedgerow hawthorn (*Crataegus monogyna*) is the best hawthorn for hedge use. It is a natural dwarf and can be kept as low as you want (within reason) by trimming.

Hedgerow hawthorn blossoms during the spring and fruits during late summer and fall. The small fruits add to the ornamental value of the plant, because they contrast nicely against the green foliage. The fruits are also attractive to birds, which like to eat them.

The hedgerow hawthorn favors a heavy soil. It needs plenty of moisture for best growth. Hawthorns like a sunny location with good air circulation. Do not crowd this plant.

For best hedge growth, pruning is recommended. Prune to shape the plant and to encourage the development of bushy growth. Always prune to allow the sun to filter through to the undergrowth. This will help to keep foliage full. You can also prune to restrict height, should you so desire.

Hedgerow hawthorns have thorns, so be very careful when pruning or working near them. Wear a long-sleeved shirt or blouse and a thick pair of gloves so that you do not get scratched up too badly. Control weeds and tall grasses with a summer mulch.

This is an excellent hedge for attracting songbirds. They like to build nests in their branches. The thorns make it an effective barrier to keep out small animals that might attack birds (also any neighborhood children). It can be planted along property lines: its wicked thorns will keep out all intruders more effectively than any fence, except perhaps barbed wire or electric. The hawthorn is better looking and more practical for most people.

Nanking Cherry. The Nanking cherry (*Prunus tomentosa*) will provide multiseasonal interest in your landscape. In spring, it will be covered with white blossoms. During the summer, the plants will be a deep green and later bear fairly large red fruits of good eating quality. Although these fruits are attractive to birds, they are also quite flavorful. These tart cherries make excellent homemade pies, cobblers, and turnovers. It will be a temptation to harvest all the fruits for yourself, but save some for the birds, because songbirds love cherries. In the fall, the foliage will provide color before the leaves drop.

Nanking hedges offer a place for birds to build their nests, as well as fruits to feed them. The plants can be trimmed to rigid formal shapes, but produce more fruits where such pruning is minimal. Most often, Nanking cherries are grown close together to form a hedge with an open growth habit.

Bushes can grow to 6 feet. You may want to prune your hedges to keep them at a lower height or let it grow tall. It all depends upon what other functions you expect from your hedge. If privacy is desired, then the bushes should be allowed to grow tall.

Where you place your Nanking cherries is not especially important, unless you do not wish to share fruit with your neighbors. If you plant this hedge along your property line, the chances are that the people who live on the other side of the hedge will feel quite free to pick all the cherries that grow on their side of the hedge. If you do not wish this situation to occur, you probably should not plant the hedge on your common borders. Plant a different hedge there, one that will provide a tall screen or have thorns, such as one of the many flowering rose hedges available. Thorns will keep the neighborhood youngsters from cutting a path across your lawn to get into your fruit growing areas.

Russian Mulberry. The Russian mulberry (*Morus alba* var. *tartarica*) makes the hardiest of the mulberry hedges. It grows very tall and will grow into tree form if not kept trimmed.

To attract birds, you will want the female fruiting-type. The male of this species does not bear any fruits and is strictly for ornamental use. Birds love mulberries and so do most people. The fruits taste and resemble blackberries.

The mulberry flower is not ornamental, and the plant itself is somewhat coarse in texture. It can be sheared to almost any shape and fit into more formal plantings if you so desire.

Some people consider the fruit to be a litter problem, but usually it is not too bad because as soon as they ripen, you are likely to be out there among the birds eating these luscious fruits. They will stain clothing however, so do not go walking barefoot near your mulberry hedge.

Be sure to purchase only hedge-grade plants for use as hedges. The tree-grade plants will not be suitable. The hedges will rarely need to be pruned during the first season they are set out, but afterwards they will require pruning to train them to the growth patterns that you want them to establish. Prune to encourage branching and denser growth and to control size.

When pruning hedges to a formal shear, always make the tops somewhat indented at both sides. This will allow the sunlight to filter through and prevent the top part of the bush from shading out the undergrowth.

Mulberries are most productive when allowed to grow in their natural shape, rather than to a formal shear. A rounded top is one of the easiest ways to maintain the mulberry. Be wary when pruning not to cut out any more fruiting wood than is necessary to control the size or shape the plant; otherwise, you will reduce fruit production.

Russian Olive. The Russian olive (*Elaeagnus augustifolia*) has an open growth habit and will grow to tree size if plants are not carefully trained and maintained as hedges.

Russian olives, set closely together in a dense stand, form a thorny thicket. Such thickets are excellent barriers to unwelcome intruders and also provide an ideal nesting area for many songbirds.

The Russian olive is extremely hardy and drought-resistant. This plant belongs to the legume family (like peas and beans) and has the unique ability to extract nitrogen from the air and use it. Wherever these plants are grown, they will have the beneficial effect of improving the soil.

Russian olives bear a small, pale, olivelike fruit. These fruits are usually a silvery color and are quite prized by birds. The fruits are very hard, but can be made into a zesty jelly.

Plant only hedge-grade plants when setting out hedgerows. Do not order tree-grade plants with the idea of later turning them into hedges. The hedge-grade plants are younger and can be readily trained into hedge growth. Tree-grade plants are not suitable for hedges (unless you plan on a hedgerow of trees).

Russian olives will form a good hedge if the plants are spaced from 10 to 15 inches apart within a row. Prune the plants the first year after planting to encourage branching and prevent the growth of central trunks. After the first year, trim the hedge once or twice a year to keep it in the desired shape and size.

If you wish to attract songbirds to your home, the Russian olive is one of the best hedges to use. Its fruits are loved by many birds and other wildlife. Songbirds known to eat Russian olive fruits include the song sparrow, the robin, the bobwhite, the mockingbird, the mourning dove, the cardinal, the Eastern bluebird, the mountain bluebird, and many others.

Sargeant Crabapple. The Sargeant crabapple (*Malus sargentii)* is a flowering crab that grows in shrublike form. It has a spreading, open growth habit and bears tiny red fruits. These little crabapples are quite persistent and hold onto the tree well into winter. They are very attractive to birds.

The Sargeant crabapple bears a flurry of pink to white blossoms in spring, which cover the entire plant. It has an alternate bearing habit, so that it tends to bear fruit every other year. Its shrubby form makes it a low-grower, seldom reading over 8 feet in height, and when planted close in hedgerows, will rarely reach over 5 feet.

Birds like the fruits. They are also to build nests in this shrub with its open growth. It is an extremely ornamental plant, even when not in full bloom, with the characteristics that make for an attractive landscape addition.

Sargeant crabapples should be planted 3 to 4 feet apart within a row. Do not plant them closer, or you will have a more difficult time maintaining them. They tend to have an open growth habit and that is the best way to train them. They do not take well to formal shearing, although if you prune them while they are very young into rectangular or square shapes, they can be maintained that way.

Crabapples perform best when exposed to full sunlight. They should be set out in a prominent place in your yard, where their spring blossoms can beckon house guests to your landscape.

Crabapples are relatively easy to care for. The only pruning necessary will be to shape hedges, remove dead or diseased branches, or control size. (See Chapter 25, Flowering Crabapples, for more information about crabapple culture).

Chapter 8

Garden Shrubs

If you like to watch the surrounding environment evolve as the seasons progress, be sure to include deciduous shrubs in your landscape plans. By selecting shrubs that offer different seasonal interests—like fall color or fruits—you will be able to enjoy a landscape that reflects the best of each season.

Listed here are some of the easiest-to-grow deciduous shrubs. All are temperate-zone hardy and can be grown almost anywhere in the United States and parts of Canada.

Some plants may interest you because of the splendor of their flowers, leaf texture, fruits, or bark. You will appreciate the practical value of other plants that do not require vast amounts of your precious (and limited) time just to keep them alive, let alone blooming. For complete instructions on how to plant deciduous shrubs, refer to Chapter 5, Deciduous Hedges. For tips on proper pruning, see Fig. 8-1.

Billiard spirea, for example, is a shrubby plant that is almost weedlike in many of its characteristics: it has coarse leaves and small flower clusters, but it also grows like a weed! It will attract butterflies to your garden, and it really fits in well with the natural, wildflower-type gardens so popular today. As you become acquainted with these easy-to-grow species, you will discover that landscaping can be fun. Perhaps you can pick up some ideas for what you might like in your own yard.

Check with your favorite nursery to see what shrubs they offer. Be sure to select only plants that will grow in your area. If a plant is not sufficiently hardy when grown in a location, it may die, and dead plants are not attractive.

Alpine Spirea. The alpine or Daphne spirea (*Spiraea* x *bumalda* var. *alpina*) is a very hardy plant. It forms a low mound that rarely exceeds 10 inches in height. It is one of the lowest-growing spireas. Its pale pink flowers usually abound in July.

The alpine spirea is ideal for rock gardens, although some of the spirea are not as attractive as nursery ads would indicate. They often resemble weeds, and more than one visitor may look at them and frown. They should never be used in formal

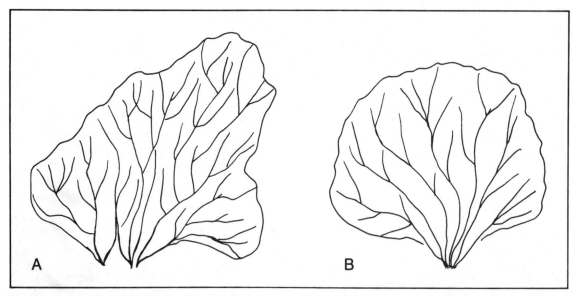

Fig. 8-1. Correct pruning of a deciduous shrub helps to keep it healthy and encourage attractive shape. (A) Shrub is uneven, lopsided, overgrown. Stems are too thick and tangled. (B) Proper pruning shapes shrub, removes excess and dead stems, thins to allow penetration of sunlight and air.

landscape, but they are well suited to rock gardens.

Plant alpine spirea in well-drained soil. These plants favor a sandy loam and need full sun to perform their best, so avoid shady locations.

Alpine spirea, like other members of the spirea family, is very drought resistant. This plant will hold up well to summer heat and dry weather. Because it grows so close to the ground, it is one of the hardiest species to plant.

Weeds and tall grasses must be controlled. They can be yanked out by hand most efficiently. If they are not controlled, the weeds and tall grasses may shade out your spirea and, in any case, will likely interfere with its floral display and aesthetic qualities.

This species is well suited to wildflower-type plantings and for naturalizing in sunny areas of your landscape. Their floral display is not as spectacular as many other ornamentals, but they are very hardy.

Whether you like them or not depends upon your personal preference. You may be enthusiastic about them, or you may not consider them worthy of a place in your garden.

American Highbush Cranberry. One plant that provides both beauty and edible berries for you

and birds in the American highbush cranberry. *Viburnum trilobum* grows to about 8 feet (Fig. 8-2). It has clusters of white flowers in the spring that layer upon the branches. Later, this plant bears clusters of red, edible berries. It gets its name from the taste of its berries, which, when made into jelly, taste something like cranberries. (It is not related to the true cranberry.)

Autumn color is sometimes an interesting feature with the highbush cranberry, but its red fruits steal the show. Birds are very attracted to this shrub and like to eat the fruits.

The American highbush cranberry likes a rich, moist soil. It does not do well on poor, infertile soils. It is very sensitive to drought and, when suffering stress from hot, dry weather, will rapidly decline in its ornamental value.

The American highbush cranberry requires pruning to control its size and to stimulate the growth of new fruiting wood. Plants that are left unpruned become leggy in appearance and produce less and less fruit. Pruning also encourages a denser growth.

The American highbush cranberry grows so large that it is best used as a specimen plant, unless

Fig. 8-2. Compact American cranberry. Courtesy Denver Water Department, Xeriscape Conservation Garden.

you have a large yard. There is a dwarf version that is more practical for people who have limited space and do not have the time to care for the larger shrub. Set this species out in a sunny area. Its seasonal changes will delight you. Do not forget—you can pick some of the berries to make jelly if you like.

Annabelle Hydrangea. The Annabelle hydrangea is good for those shady nooks in your backyard. *Hydrangea arborescens* var. *annabelle* is a low shrub, growing to about 3 1/2 feet. It has a dense growth habit and forms a compact plant. From mid- to late-summer, it bears large white clusters of flowers, which resemble snowballs.

Annabelle hydrangea favors shade and moist locations. Add plenty of peat moss to the planting site.

Control weeds, tall grasses, and other competing vegetation. A mulch will help conserve soil moisture, which is very important to this plant. It needs adequate water, especially during the time of flower formation and bloom. Water plants on a weekly basis by soaking the area under the branch span. During dry periods, and when the plant is in full bloom, it may be beneficial to add extra water. Touch the soil to see if its damp (not wet). If dry, it is time to water.

The blooms always occur on new wood: for the best blooms, prune back to the ground each spring. The shoots should be cut back to about 3 to 4 inches. The plant will then produce new shoots that will bear large flowerheads.

The Annabelle hydrangea is fairly easy to grow and an absolute must for any garden. It lends itself to formal plantings and can be used for foundation plantings as well.

Billiard Spirea. The Billiard spirea (*Spiraea* x *billiardi*), mentioned at the beginning of this chapter, is a small shrub with an erect growth habit. It rarely exceeds 4 feet. This sun-loving plant is in full blossom during July and August, when few other ornamentals are in bloom, and it adds a touch of color to late summer gardens. This shrub can be mixed with the other spirea species to add variety to your garden. The Billiard spirea bears pink flowers.

Always plant spirea in full sunlight. These plants do not enjoy shade and suffer even when planted in areas that are shaded half of the day. They also enjoy a well-drained soil. They must never be planted in muck soils or soils that are constantly wet.

Billiard spirea is very hardy and survive all seasons quite well. They are winter-hardy throughout the country, and they resist the dry weather of summer—a trait that makes them quite useful as landscape plants.

Use in borders with other bush-spirea for a colorful summer floral display. This plant bears its pink flowers on spikes, which hold themselves above the foliage, typical of other spireas.

This is a useful speciment plant, but it is best for easy-care landscapes, or those that have water shortages. Although its flowers attract butterflies, their beauty is a matter of opinion.

Compact Garden Spirea. The compact garden spirea (*Spiraea* x *arguta* var. *compacta*) is a small shrub with a mound form. It offers a display of white flowers in summer, borne on spikes that rise above the foliage. It has fine-textured leaves and a compact size, rarely exceeding 3 feet in height.

This is an ideal companion plant for the Froebel spirea, as the mix of colors makes an interesting garden display.

Garden spirea has the same cultural requirements as the Froebel spirea. This plant does well on poor soils and will bear flowers even when grown on infertile soil.

Garden spirea is an excellent shrub for foundation plantings. Its compact size allows you to use it in abundance if you wish. It makes an interesting pathliner for walks and driveways. It has a fine texture and retains its green color throughout the summer. It is especially attractive when set out among other varieties and species of spirea.

Cranberry Cotoneaster. From the name of the cranberry cotoneaster, you will not be surprised to learn that it has red, edible berries. *Cotoneaster apiculatus,* is a dwarf member of the cotoneaster family. It can grow up to 4 feet tall, but rarely gets that high. It is usually kept in a low mound by trimming.

The cranberry cotoneaster is noted for its dwarf

growth and its bright red berries. These berries are edible, but taste better cooked than raw. They are best used for making jelly. Their tart taste makes a cranberrylike jelly, from which the plant gets its name. (It is not related to the true cranberry.)

This shrub offers seasonal interest. In autumn, the leaves turn a bright red, which makes for a stunning fall color display. The bright red berries contrast with green leaves throughout much of the latter half of summer and persist into the fall. The berries are not as outstanding in the fall once the leaves turn color.

The cranberry cotoneaster favors a slightly alkaline soil. Add garden lime to the planting site. They grow best in full sun, and it is under full sunlight that they produce their best fruit and fall color displays. They will tolerate shade, but such areas are not ideal for them.

These plants seem to tolerate dry soils, but will not tolerate poorly drained soils.

Fruits can be picked for jelly or left for the birds to gather. The fruit is persistent, hangs onto the shrub, and does not cause much of a litter problem.

The cranberry cotoneaster is best set out for specimen plantings in sunny locations. It can be used to guard entryways or for foundation plantings. It is not practical for hedge use, because its growth habit is too open for most people's taste. It can be used for informal hedges, however.

Early Forsythia. The early forsythia seems to love city life, as it tolerates the urban environment very well. *Forsythia ovata* grows to 7 feet, in moundlike form, but is usually kept lower by pruning. This species is planted for its floral display in early spring. It produces smaller flowers than many other forsythia species, but it is among the earliest to bloom. For people who are weary of winter, the early forsythia brings them much closer to spring, or at least, so it seems.

The yellow flowers appear along the stems. You can cut off stems with flower buds and take them indoors. Set in water, the added warmth will cause them to open up in cutflower displays.

In many of the colder regions of the north, the flower buds may be injured or killed during extra cold winters. People who live in the north should contact their nursery for only hardy varieties that can thrive in their area.

Full sunlight is best; early forsythia will produce flowers in shade, but heavy shade should be avoided. Almost any well-drained soil will do. This plant is not too fussy about siting.

To encourage next spring's flowering it is the practice to prune plants after they have flowered for the season. Prune out the flowering wood. Balance your cuts so that the plants look neat and even, not butchered.

Protect the plants from birds during the late winter and early spring. A bird netting will do the trick. You will not have to keep your shrub covered in the summer.

There are a multitude of landscape uses for forsythia. They are effective hedges, border plants, or for specimens and will provide spring beauty for your landscape.

Fragrant Sumac. The fragrant sumac is a beautiful, fragrant plant, but do not eat the fruit. It's poison! *Rhus aromatica* grows in a mounded shrub of 4 feet (usually less but sometimes a little taller). Sumac is very hardy and has fine-textured foliage. Even the leaves of the fragrant sumac have a delightful scent. Red fruits appear later in the summer. (You will want to warn your family and guests that these are poisonous.) The shrub has an orange to maroon fall color.

Sumac are good ornamentals for poor, sandy soils. They require little care and are vigorous growers. Another species of interest to Westerners is the Rocky Mountain sumac (*Rhus cismontana*). This variety can be found growing in higher elevations (Fig. 8-3).

A sumac with unusual foliage is the tree leaf Sumac (*Rhus triloba*). These bushy plants bear leaves that resemble the large leaves of several deciduous trees, such as oak (Fig. 8-4).

The staghorn sumac (*Rhus typhina*), forms a wide-headed tree or large shrub. It is valued for its ornamental use. In autumn, its leaves turn yellow.

(Two species of sumac you will not want are *Rhus toxicodendron*, better known as *poison ivy*, and *Rhus radicans*, which is familiar to most people by its common name, *poison oak*)!

Fig. 8-3. Rocky Mountain sumac. Courtesy Denver Water Department, Xeriscape Conservation Garden.

Fig. 8-4. Tree leaf sumac. Courtesy Denver Water Department, Xeriscape Conservation Garden.

Sumac grows best in full sun, and it needs sun for its best display of fall color. It is one of the best species for providing fall colors in the home landscape. It is very drought-tolerant and is winter-hardy practically everywhere. Sumac grows in almost any type of soil; a sandy loam is best.

Control weeds and conserve moisture with a summer mulch around the base of the plants. These plants spread rapidly by underground shoots called *suckers*. You will have to prune the suckers down each spring to keep your sumac from becoming a thicket.

Sumac are mostly set out in sunny lawns for fall color. They are effective as single specimens (although they rapidly multiply) or when planted in groups of three. A good ornamental for those hard-to-grow-anything locations.

Froebel Spirea. If you would like to combine beauty with drought-resistence, the Froebel spirea is a plant you should consider. *Spiraea* x *bumalda* var. *froebeli* is a small shrub growing to about 4 feet in height, although it usually does not get that large. It has a rounded growth habit, forming an almost perfect, oval-shaped bush. This plant bears raspberry red flowers. The summer-flowering blossoms are borne on spikes that rise above the foliage. The bush remains green, even through dry weather during the summer.

In autumn, plants take on an orange to maroon fall color, so they are quite spectacular in the fall landscape (Fig. 8-5).

Plant in any good garden soil. Spring planting is best, but spirea can be planted in the fall in warmer regions of the country. Control weeds and tall grasses to keep them from crowding out your plants. Spirea are vigorous growers.

Plant in full sun. Never plant spirea in the shade, or it can adversely affect flower production. Also, shady areas tend to encourage the growth of mildew and other fungal diseases.

Spirea has excellent resistence to drought and tolerates dry soils. These plants are winter-hardy practically everywhere, but should be mulched in the far north and in areas where fluctuating temperatures produce heaving of the soil.

One of the nicest features about spirea is its

Fig. 8-5. Froebel spirea. Courtesy Denver Water Department, Xeriscape Conservation Garden.

resistence to heat and drought. This plant is ideal for water conservation, because it can survive almost entirely upon rainfall, except in the most arid regions where supplemental water is necessary.

Froebel spirea is an effective specimen plant or can be set out in small groups. It will grow in any sunny location in your yard.

Hybrid Forsythia. Forsythia is an excellent shrub for urban areas, because it withstands the environmental stress of city conditions very well. *Forsythia* x *intermedia* grows up to 9 feet in height. Forsythia is a rapid grower and forms a vase-shaped bush. It is planted for its springtime floral display of large, yellow flowers that appear in clusters along the branches. The clusters are usually so abundant that they cover the entire plant.

In colder areas of the country, some of the flower buds may be injured or killed during severe winters. One of the best cultivar selections is Lynnwood.

Forsythia favors full sun. It tolerates partial shade, but should have as much sunlight as possible for its best floral display. It is not particular about soil, provided that it is well-drained.

Forsythia produces the most flowers on the current season's wood. To get a bumper flower crop, it is best to prune out the wood after flowering. This will stimulate the plant to produce new flowering wood for next spring's display.

In many places, birds can present a problem. Some species of birds like to eat the flowerbuds before they open. Naturally, if the flowerbuds are removed, the shrub will not bloom. In such areas, it is advisable to protect the shrubs from birds by covering them with some kind of netting. Of course, if birds are too much of a problem, you may wish to consider planting a different shrub altogether.

This handsome vaselike bush is often used beside entryways. Although it does grow tall, it can be kept low. It is an effective hedge and practical for lining drives, walks, or along property lines.

Hypericum. Hypericum (*Hypericum elatum*) grows to about 4 feet in height. This summer-flowering shrub bears its blossoms all summer long and well into the fall. The flowers are single, large—about 2 inches across—and buttercup yellow. They have prominent golden stamens.

Hypericum produces a dense, compact bush, with attractive, green, ovular leaves. It bears oval, scarlet fruits.

Another species, *Hypericum frondosum*, is more dwarf. It grows only about 2 feet tall. It is an everblooming bush, producing flowers until frost. The blossoms are buttercup-yellow with prominent golden stamens. This plant produces a dense bush that is nearly round in form.

Hypericum tends to be evergreen in warmer climates. In the north, however, it may die back to the ground each winter. It will come up again in the spring and bloom in the summer. To keep this shrub at its best, be sure to water it well once a week—more often during dry weather. A spring application of manure is beneficial. If using fresh manure, do not set it too close to the plant, and cover it with a few shovelfuls of dirt to prevent gnats from breeding in it.

Although hypericum is quite hardy, a mulch is advised in areas with severe winters. Three to 4 inches of straw or composted leaves should do nicely. Remove the mulch after the weather has warmed up in the spring.

Hypericum is used to grace entryways or for foundation plantings. It is also an attractive specimen.

Japanese Dogwood. Japanese dogwood (*Cornus kousa*) is an excellent landscape shrub. It grows to about 10 feet in height. Pinkish-white bracts appear in early spring. (Bracts are colorful, petal-like leaves that surround the plant. Another plant with this feature, for example, is the poinsettia.)

Japanese dogwood is one of the best shrubs for springtime display, and is also ornamental during the summer, when it is a handsome green bush. In the autumn, the leaves change to bright scarlet color that sets the fall landscape aflame.

This shrub belongs to the dogwood family and shares many characteristics of the other dogwoods.

Japanese dogwood favors a semishady area. It needs some sunlight for best coloring in fall and floral display in spring; it tolerates shade quite well, but should not be set out in *heavy* shade.

Japanese dogwood likes a cool, moist soil. Add plenty of peat moss to the planting site. For best results, keep the area around the base of the plant damp (not wet) to the touch. Mulch plants. Plenty of organic matter makes for vigorous plants, and a spring application of manure is beneficial. Spread the manure evenly around the plant in a circle under the branch span. Do not touch the plant with fresh manure. Cover fresh manure with a few shovelsful of dirt to prevent gnats from breeding in it. Composted manure can be applied anytime up to July first. Do not apply fertilizer after July first. The shrub needs the latter part of the summer and fall to harden-off and prepare for winter months ahead.

Japanese dogwood is a good shrub for specimen or foundation plantings. Do not plant this shrub under a window, because it will grow too tall and block your view. These very decorative plants are always premium-priced at nurseries.

Mock Orange. When the mock orange is in full bloom, it will be the centerpiece of your garden. *Philadelphus* x *virginalis* grows to about 8 feet in height. It is most loved for its fragrant, white springtime flowers in both single and double form, depending upon the cultivar. The foliage is somewhat coarse.

There are many cultivars available. Some of the best are Snowflake, which has double blossoms; Beauclerk, which rarely exceeds 6 feet and is strongly scented; and Bouquet Blanc, which has fragrant, double-white blooms.

Mock orange is not particular about sites, as long as the soil is well-drained. This shrub grows vigorously on virtually any good soil and grows in sun or shade.

Prune out the flowering wood after the blooms have faded. This pruning will stimulate the production of new flowering wood for next year's blossoms. It may be necessary, on old plants, to cut them back to their base to renew them. This *renewal pruning* will stimulate the production of flowering wood so that you will have an abundant display of blossoms.

Mulch plants to conserve moisture and inhabit weed growth. An application of fertilizer in the spring is beneficial. Manure works nicely; place it in a circle around the base of the shrub without touching it. Add a shovelful of garden dirt over fresh manure. Composted manure can be applied anytime during the growing season but no fertilizer should be applied after July first.

Mock orange is mostly used as a specimen plant, but dwarf varieties offer opportunities for creative landscaping. One plant of the more fragrant variety will fill your yard with its springtime perfume.

PeeGee Hydrangea. A PeeGee hydrangea in full bloom is a show stopper. *Hydrangea paniculata* var. *grandiflora* is one of the loveliest of the flowering ornamental shrubs. It bears flowers at a time when most other flowering plants are not in bloom and never fails to delight the eye. It holds its faded blooms throughout much of the winter. The plant has an open growth habit and rather coarse foliage, but the flowers make it a real beauty.

PeeGee hydrangea grows to about 6 feet. It produces giant clusters of white to pink flowers during the late summer. These flower clusters are very persistent, fade to tan, and hang onto the shrub throughout the winter.

PeeGee hydrangea favors a moist, rich garden loam. Avoid sandy and dry soils. These plants are quite tolerant of poorly drained soils, but they will not tolerate drought. Add plenty of peat moss to the planting site.

A summer mulch should be applied to help conserve moisture and control weeds. Be careful that the mulch does not touch the plant itself and is no more than 1 or 2 inches thick. Otherwise, the mulch can prevent the plant from receiving natural rainfalls—sort of a "thatched-roof" effect.

Water these plants regularly, once each week, and give them extra attention when in bloom. They are heavy feeders and should be supplied with fertilizer for best results. A spring application of manure is beneficial. It using a commercial fertilizer, try a balanced formula such as 10-10-10, or one of the foliar sprays that go to work immediately after they are absorbed through the leaves.

Because of its size, the PeeGee hydrangea is largely restricted to specimen plantings, and, unless you have a big yard, that is their best use.

Potentilla. Potentilla (*Potentilla fructicosa*) is a compact shrub that grows to about 3 feet. It has delicate, fernlike foliage and is very fine-textured. This plant produces yellow, sometimes white flowers, depending upon the variety; a new cultivar has peach-colored blossoms. The flowers vary in size from small, 1-inch blooms to double that or larger. The plant is everblooming, in flower throughout most of the summer, and into the fall. Some varieties seem to be more free-flowering than others.

Potentilla comes bush form and vine form. These are different species in the same genus. Of the vine types, the cultivar Fire Dance is one of the most impressive. It has bicolored flowers of red and yellow that resemble flames.

Some of the best bush types are Day Dawn, which has peach-color blossoms; Klondike, which has golden flowers; and Mount Everest, which bears white blooms. There are of course, many other new cultivars on the market worth review. Check with your nursery to find out what kinds they offer (Fig. 8-6).

Potentilla favors full sun; it should have a maximum amount of sunlight to perform its best. It grows well in light, sandy soils, but plenty of peat moss should be added to the planting site because they are very thirsty plants. Because these plants are so everblooming, they should be given plenty of fertilizer in spring and throughout the growing season up until July first, when all feeding should cease. Keep plants well-watered when in bloom.

Potentillas really deserve greater use in the home landscape. Both the shrub and the trailing forms are very ornamental. These are excellent low-growing plants for foundation plantings or wherever you wish to add a touch of "class" to your yard.

Red Twig Dogwood. The red twig dogwood is very winter-hardy and can be grown in areas where many dogwood species are not hardy enough to grow. *Cornus alba* can grow to about 5 feet, but usually does not get that tall. Most often it grows to about 3 feet. It is grown solely for the bright red bark of its new growth.

The red twig dogwood has green leaves during the summer, which change color in the fall. They do not make a spectacular color display, however.

The red twig dogwood likes a moist soil, rich

Fig. 8-6. Golddrop potentilla. Courtesy Denver Water Department, Xeriscape Conservation Garden.

in organic matter. It will grow in other soils, but a woodsy soil is best. Add plenty of peat moss to the planting site.

Mulch during the summer with an organic mulch. Straw or composted leaves work well. The mulch should be placed fairly evenly around the plant. It should not be deeper than 1 to 2 inches. Do not permit your mulch to touch the shrub. If it does, it may prevent the bush from benefiting from natural rainfall.

To maintain the growth of the new wood (the most ornamental feature of these species), pruning will be necessary. Prune the shrub to its base each spring to keep the bush low. More importantly, this pruning stimulates the growth of new wood. The new wood twigs and bark are always the reddest.

Red twig dogwood makes a colorful hedge. It is of special attraction in winter, when its red bark contrasts with white snows. It is useful for lining pathways or can be used as single specimens.

This is a practical plant for those places where you want a shrub that provides a different accent than the usual spring or summer display.

Russian Sage. The Russian sage requires practically no care. *Perouskia atriplicifolia* grows to about 4 feet in height (sometimes taller; other times a little shorter). It is a grayish-green shrub with an open habit and fine-textured foliage (Fig. 8-7).

During late summer, it has pale, lilac-blue flowers that are borne on tall spikes. These spikes rise above the foliage and crown the plants, blooming at that time of year when few other plants are in blossom.

Russian sage favors full sun. It grows best on a sandy-loam and is very resistant to dry weather and poor soils. This plant is an excellent choice for people who live in the semiarid regions of the West. It demands very little attention, can be totally neglected and still survive, and it grows like a weed.

The grayish-green foliage of your Russian sage will contrast sharply with the dark green shrubs and lawns and makes an interesting display in your garden. If you have problem areas where it is difficult to get any form of life to grow, your sage should manage to make it, provided these problem areas are sunny.

It makes an excellent foundation plant, but should be kept sheared lower than 4 feet when used for this purpose. It can be grown as a hedge in dry areas or in places where water conservation is mandatory. It is also effective when set out as an entry plant on the edges of doorways or by the garage.

Santolina. Santolina can be totally neglected and still survive! Of course, it will benefit from some minimal care, such as control of weeds and watering during prolonged dry spells (Fig. 8-8). *Santolina chamaecyparissus* grows to about 2 1/2 feet in height. It is a compact bush. The foliage is almost silver

Fig. 8-7. Russian sage. Courtesy Denver Water Department, Xeriscape Conservation Garden.

Fig. 8-8. Santolina. Courtesy Denver Water Department, Xeriscape Conservation Garden.

in color and remains that way throughout the growing season.

Santolina flowers in the middle of the summer with little ball-shaped yellow flowers that are less than an inch across. These blooms grow on stalks that rise above the foliage. If you do not like the flowers, cut them off. It is a matter of personal preference.

Santolina favors full sun. It is extremely drought-resistant and a good plant for the semiarid regions of the West.

To maintain its shape, prune the plant after it has flowered. If the flowers are allowed to go to seed, they will use up much of the plant's energy and it will not look as attractive.

Remember, santolina foliage is silver. It will provide an accent wherever it is used in your yard, contrasting with the green shrubbery and lawns. It can be set wherever a dwarf bush is needed—along sunny garden paths or for foundation plantings in hot, dry climates. Santolina is very effective when used to border flowerbeds, because the foliage showcases the bright colors of your flowers.

Smokebush. You either love the smokebush, or you hate it. There seems to be no in between. It is an unusual sight, with its fluffy purple flowers (Fig. 8-9). *Cotinus coggygria* grows to a fairly large shrub of 10 feet in height. It can be kept lower by trimming. It can also be trained to a dwarf tree by pruning off the lower branches and allowing only one trunk.

The smokebush flowers during the summer. Its blossoms resemble puffs of smoke when in full bloom. They fade to pink and later turn brown.

This plant is noteworthy for its fall color. Its leaves turn red in autumn. The best cultivar for fall color is *Foliis purpureis*.

Plant in any well-drained soil. This shrub favors a good garden loam, but will tolerate a wide range of soil types (unless they are extreme). A summer mulch to prevent moisture loss to evaporation and to keep down weeds is practical. Weeds and tall grasses should be removed. Yank out weeds and keep tall grasses cut with a grass shears (or scissors if a grass shears is not available).

Prune to control size. Usually, people do not

want a 10-foot bush. When pruning to control size, remember to balance cuts so that they are fairly even all the way around the plant. Pruning has a stimulating effect upon growth sometimes. If you are not careful, you can cause an imbalance and destroy the symmetry of your bush.

This plant is very showy, but unfortunately, purple rarely goes with many colors. If you use this shrub, you may wish to plant one or two other purple-foliaged plants to balance your yard.

Snowmound Spirea. People with small yards appreciate the snowmound spirea for its nice compact growth. It never gets out of bounds. *Spiraea nipponica* is also sometimes called *dwarf bridal's wreath* because it resembles a small version of that plant. This dwarf bush grows in a mounded form to about 3 feet. It has arched, somewhat pendulant, branches that are very graceful. The shrub is covered with white blossoms when in bloom and is very showy. These bushes have blue-green foliage throughout much of the summer, and the dark leaf color contrasts well with the white blossoms (Fig. 8-10).

The snowmound spirea, which may also be called the *dwarf Japanese spirea*, favors full sunlight. It is a hardy plant.

Set it in fertile soil that is well supplied with organic matter. Add peat moss and composted manure to the planting site. This shrub often bears flowers the first summer it is set out, so go ahead and baby it. Water on a weekly basis, more often during dry spells. Do not sprinkle when you water. Water deeply, so that the plant's roots can absorb the moisture.

Control weeds and tall grasses. A summer mulch is beneficial. It will help to conserve the soil moisture and keep weeds down. The plant will need plenty of water, especially during flower formation and development because it uses much of its energy to produce flowers.

Fig. 8-9. Velvet cloak smoke bush. Stark Bro's Nurseries and Orchards Co.

Fig. 8-10. Snowmound spirea. Courtesy Denver Water Department, Xeriscape Conservation Garden.

Fertilize with a spring application of manure. Be careful to not get fresh manure too close, or it can injure the plant.

This plant is often used as a low-growing flowering hedge. It is useful for lining walks or driveways, especially because it grows so low that there is no danger of its blocking off visibility, as some taller plants do. It is an effective specimen for single planting or to accent the garden.

Vanhouette Spirea. Vanhouette spirea is a hardy, easy-to care for shrub. It is also an extremely showy plant when in full bloom. *Spiraea vanhouettei* grows to about 6 feet in height. It is a vase-shaped bush with pendulous arching branches. In late spring and early summer, these branches are loaded with clusters of white blossoms.

Vanhouette spirea is often called *bridal's wreath,* and it is sometimes sold under that label. Technically, this is a misnomer: it is actually a superior species, more graceful and easier to grow than true bridal wreath.

Vanhouette has fine-textured foliage and arching branches that look comely even when the plant is not in floral display.

Vanhouette spirea favors full sun, although it will grow under partial shade. It does well on all but problem soils.

Water plants on a regular weekly basis. The best way to avoid forgetting to do this is by setting aside one day of the week for watering chores. That way you can take care of all of your landscape plants at once. With or without a water conservation problem, a large yard can be divided into sections; water the northeast section Tuesdays, the southwest Wednesdays, etc.

Control weeds by hand removal. Use grass shears or scissors to cut tall grasses that may be too close to, or interfere with, your plants. A summer mulch can help conserve moisture. About 1 or 2 inches of straw or composted leaves is sufficient. Place it in a circle around the base of the shrub. Be sure the mulch does not touch the shrub itself.

Because it is a tall, large shrub, you may have room for only one. If you have a large yard, you will be able to plant several. You will never regret planting one of these. In full bloom, it is spectacular!

Weeping Forsythia. The weeping forsythia is a good shrub for urban gardeners, because it seems to do quite well under city conditions. *Forsythia suspensa* has a mound shape, noteworthy for its slender, drooping twigs and hanging branches. It is especially attractive in springtime, when yellow flowers appear along its branches, but it is graceful even when not in blossom.

Weeping forsythia may not be sufficiently winter hardy in many areas of the north. Flower buds may be injured or killed during severe winters. If you have any doubts about its hardiness and live in a borderline or marginally hardy area for this species, set your weeping forsythia in a somewhat sheltered location.

Plant where it can receive full sun; the more sun it gets, the better it will bloom. In marginally hardy areas, protect it from damaging winds and select a sunny, but more sheltered, location.

Prune out the flowering wood shortly after blossoms have faded. This will stimulate the growth of new flowering wood for next year's bloom.

Protect these shrubs from birds in the early spring, just before the flower buds open. Tie the netting down to make sure it is secure and that the birds do not go under it.

Water, weed, and tend your shrubs on a weekly schedule. The weeping forsythia looks great in almost any yard and is especially appealing in those yards with some other "weeping" bush or tree.

Some colors go well together, others clash, but the yellow floral display of the weeping forsythia should harmonize with any color scheme you have chosen for your spring landscape.

Wormwood. Wormwood grows like a weed on some of the saddest, poorest, sandiest soils you can imagine. *Artemisia absinthium* grows to about 3 feet in height. It is grown mostly for its attractive, silvery foliage, which forms a nice, neat, bushy plant. This species also bears ornamental yellow panicles of flowers on short stalks that rise above the foliage in early summer.

Fig. 8-11. Threadleaf wormwood. Courtesy Denver Water Department, Xeriscape Conservation Garden.

75

Another species of wormwood of interest is the threadleaf wormwood, (*Artemisia filifolia*), which is very valuable for dry climates, such as the semiarid regions of the West. This plant has long, very slender, threadlike leaves (Fig. 8-11).

Wormwood likes a sunny location, and it thrives on sandy soil. Wormwood is drought-resistant and will tolerate dry periods for longer time spans than most ornamentals. This plant needs very little attention.

Although wormwood is very hardy, it may benefit from a winter mulch in areas where fluctuating temperatures tend to heave plants out of the ground. A certain amount of winter mulch is not likely to hurt any plant, however, and may protect against unusually severe winters. Be sure to remove most of it in the spring, after the weather warms.

Wormwood is a fine-textured bush for decorating the home landscape. It is so easy to grow you may want to use it lavishly. Its silvery foliage makes an interesting contrast to the dark green of most other garden shrubbery.

Chapter 9

Decorative Conifers

When other vegetation appears dead and dull-colored and most other trees are leafless, the evergreens provide eternal green and stability in a constantly changing world (Fig. 9-1).

Evergreens come in two basic types, Broadleaf evergreens and conifers. (Incidentally, not all conifers are evergreen.)

The conifers are most practical. They can be grown with greater ease and in a wider range of areas and climates than the broadleaf evergreens. The most common conifers used in the landscape belong to the following families: arborvitae, hemlock, juniper, pine, fir, spruce, and yew. They come in numerous forms. Some are best as hedges; some as specimen plantings; others as trees.

Conifers strategically placed can lend an air of dignity to a home. They are frequently used for entrance plantings or to augment picture windows. Conifers retain their color year-round, remaining much the same whether it's spring, summer, fall, or winter. Most require very little care.

(For tips on planting decorative conifers, refer to Chapter 6, Evergreen Hedges.)

American Arborvitae. The American arborvitae is a fancy shrub best used in formal plantings. *Thuja occidentalis* is a very hardy species and a fast-grower. It can reach a height of 40 feet at maturity. It has light green, soft, scalelike leaves. This tree will tolerate partial shade, but should not be planted under heavy shade. It is very tolerant of wet soils (Fig. 9-2).

There are two cultivars you may wish to consider: *Fastigata* forms a pyramidal tree up to 25 feet in height. Its narrow, columnar shape lends it especially well to formal landscapes and to yards that do not have the space for large, spreading trees. It is very effective when used to frame entryways or to line walks.

Another cultivar, Techny, forms a smaller tree. This is one of the most popular of the arborvitae. It reaches about 20 feet at maturity and has a slow growth rate. It bears deep-green foliage year-round. It is a formal plant and can be used for entryways as well as to accent various areas of your yard.

Fig. 9-1. When other vegetation appears dead and dull-colored and most other trees are leafless, the evergreens provide that eternal green. Stability in a constantly changing world.

Fig. 9-2. The American arborvitae is a fancy shrub best used in formal plantings.

Arborvitae favors a rich, moist soil. It does not like dry soils and will turn off-color if it suffers from drought stress. Keep plants well-watered.

Mulch with composts, straw, or other available material. The plant takes a shearing well and can be trimmed to highly formal shapes. The care you give your arborvitae the first season will reflect in later years' growth, so go ahead and baby it.

Arborvitae has many uses, but it is most practical for formal landscapes. It is very dignified and tends to make a yard look as if "somebody rich lives there." Choose the variety that best suits your needs.

Ames Juniper. The Ames juniper (*Juniperus chinensis* var. *ames*) grows about 9 feet in height. It has a broad pyramidal shape with blue-green foliage.

Some cultivars of interest are: *Blaauw,* which grows only 4 feet tall. It is vase-shaped with grayish-blue foliage.

Hetzii juniper grows to 15 feet in height. Its branches ascent (grow upward). It has silvery-blue foliage.

Maneyi grows to about 6 feet. It has an upright and bushy growth habit and blue-gray foliage.

Old Gold grows to a height of 4 feet. It has a spreading, open growth habit. It is green with gold-tipped leaves.

Pfitzerana grows to 6 feet. It has a wide-spreading, almost horizontal growth habit. It has green foliage and does not produce fruits.

Pfitzerana Glauca is also called the *blue Pfitzer juniper,* because of its blue-gray foliage (Fig. 9-3).

Most junipers favor an alkaline soil. Soils should be tested for pH before planting. Garden lime can be added to planting sites to change the soil's pH.

The Plants are fine-textured and surprisingly tolerant of dry soil. They should not be subjected to drought, however. If the shrubs go for too long without enough water they will lose their vigor and aesthetic appeal. Drought-stricken shrubs are not something you will want in your landscape. It is essential to provide plants with enough water the first season they are set out.

The Maneyi cultivar makes an attractive hedge. Blaauw is good for decorating entrys. Hetzii can be useful as an accent in formal gardens, because it grows to 15 feet tall. The many other cultivars are useful for specimens or for those places where a juniper is wanted.

Black Hills Spruce. The Black Hills spruce is a decorative conifer for those who want the beauty and hardiness of a spruce, but do not have the space for a larger species. *Picea glauca* var *densata* grows to about 20 feet in height. An ideal tree for small yards, it has a dense, narrow form. It is a cultivar of the white spruce, with dark-green, almost black, foliage. This spruce maintains its color year-round.

The Black Hills spruce favors a sunny location. It is a slow growing tree that can fit into almost any nook or cranny in the yard. It is highly tolerant of dry soils and stands up well under drought conditions. Like all other landscape plants, however, it should not be allowed to suffer severe drought stress.

Keep plants well-watered. Water at least once a week, giving the area under the branch span a good soaking. Do not sprinkle. Keep tall weeds and grasses removed from around the tree. Grasses can

Fig. 9-3. Pfitzer juniper. Courtesy Denver Water Department, Xeriscape Conservation Garden.

be cut with a grass shears or an ordinary pair of scissors. Weeds are best removed by hand, and a mulch will help to control them.

Peat moss and other organic materials are greatly appreciated by these trees, so be generous in supplying them to the planting site.

Because it grows so slowly, the Black Hills spruce can adapt to various locations. It is a very hardy plant that will eventually become a small tree. It is ideal for people who live in northern areas, for woodland gardens, and to add color to the drab grays and whites of winter. It looks nice in formal landscapes, but is surprisingly at ease in casual landscapes, also.

For a grand sight in springtime, plant daffodils around the base of this tree, about 3 or 4 feet away.

Chinese Juniper. The Chinese juniper (*Juniperus chinensis*) grows to about 20 feet in height. It is slow to mature, with dark-green, fine-textured foliage and rather large inedible fruits.

There are many fine cultivars available for the home landscape. One of the best is *Mountbatten.* This selection has a narrow, columnar shape. It is an ideal plant for formal gardens or those with confined yards.

Chinese junipers are quite tolerant of drought. They also tolerate dry soils. They favor a sandy-loam soil and do not like "wet feet." Areas where water is left to stand on the ground for any prolonged period of time should be considered as unsuitable sites for this plant.

Chinese junipers like full sun. They grow best where they have access to a maximum amount of sunlight. Weed the area around your junipers and cut tall grasses. A scissors can be used if you do not have a grass shears. It is better not to use a power lawnmower too close to the plant to lessen the chance of accidental injury. Mulch during the summer to help keep weeds down.

Select the type of juniper that best meets your landscape needs. A columnar form, such as Mountbatten, can be squeezed onto lots where another specimen might not fit. Chinese junipers are a versatile plant for entrances, driveways, or garden areas.

Colorado Blue Spruce. The Colorado blue spruce is very tolerant of urban conditions and can be found in many city landscapes (Fig. 9-4). *Picea pungens* var. *glauca* is a slow-growing species reaching to 60 feet in height. This is the most popular spruce grown for ornamental purposes. The Colorado blue spruce has a formal pyramidal growth habit and always looks neat with its shiny, blue-green needles. The Colorado blue spruce is identical to the Colorado spruce, except for the color of its foliage. If you want a plain green tree, just plant the regular Colorado spruce (*Picea pungens*).

Colorado blue spruce trees are always sold at premium prices and are well worth the price when used appropriately in a landscape setting.

Colorado spruce favors a deep soil. It does not like dry soils. Use plenty of peat moss when setting out this plant. By giving the tree the best possible planting site, you will be sure to improve your chances for success.

Water the tree about once a week. Deep water around the base of the tree, do not just sprinkle. A good soaking will benefit the tree; a light sprinkling may not even sustain its existence.

Mulch with organic materials during the summer months to conserve soil moisture. As with any newly set plant, it is important to control weeds and tall grasses so that they do not interfere with the tree's growth.

The Colorado blue spruce has a multitude of uses in the home landscape. It is such a popular species that you need only take a drive to see how many other people have one. This tree is attractive in any season and maintains its bluish color throughout the year.

Creeping Juniper. The creeping juniper (*Juniperus horizontalis*) is a very popular species, especially among those with ranch homes. It complements the ground-hugging architectural lines of these homes; it grows about 1 foot in height and has a sprawling, horizontal growth. During the summer, it is dark green, but in winter it tends to turn brown.

The creeping juniper is a very hardy species

and, because it grows so low, can be grown safely in northern climates where other plants may not fare as well.

Some of the best cultivars are: *Wiltonii*, which only reaches 6 inches tall (Fig. 9-5). It is sometimes called *blue rug juniper,* because of its blue foliage and low horizontal growth.

Bar Harbor grows about 8 inches in height. It has a creeping growth habit and blue-green foliage throughout the growing season, which turns slate color during the winter (Fig. 9-6).

Blue Chip grows about 10 inches tall. It produces a mound of bluish foliage.

Douglasii or *Waukegan* juniper grows about 18 inches in height. It has a silver-blue color that turns purple in winter.

Hughes juniper grows about 12 inches in height. Its foliage grows in a radial fashion from the center of the plant, like the spokes of a wheel. It has silvery-blue foliage.

Plumosa or *Andorra juniper* is quite popular. It grows about 18 inches tall, with creeping radial growth. Like the Hughes juniper, its growth stems from the center of the plant outward, like the spokes of a wheel. It has gray-green foliage that turns purplish in the fall.

All junipers grow best in full sun. They like a good garden loam. Most are tolerant of dry soils, but not of poorly drained soils. Control weeds and tall grasses around plantings.

Keep animals away from your junipers. Dog urine can cause off-colors to appear on the foliage. Pets can also chew plants and destroy their aesthetic appeal.

Keep junipers away from fruit trees and bushes. Junipers are host to a disease called cedar apple rust. This disease will afflict your apple, crabapple, and juneberry trees.

Use these plants as they are best suited. Keep color harmony in mind when planting species that are of different hues. The overall effect of your landscape should be harmonious and not clash. Junipers are very versatile plants and can be put to many practical uses in your garden. They lend themselves best to formal landscape plans.

Dwarf Japanese Yew. Dwarf Japanese yew

Fig. 9-4. The Colorado blue spruce is very tolerant of urban conditions and can be found in many city landscapes.

Fig. 9-5. Wiltoni juniper. Courtesy Denver Water Department, Xeriscape Conservation Garden.

(*Taxus cuspidata* var. *nana*) is one of the most popular forms of yew. It creates a 4-foot mound of very dark, green foliage and dense growth. The undersides of the fine-textured leaves are a duller green than the uppersides, and it can be sheared quite closely.

Dwarf Japanese yew may not be fully hardy under some northern conditions. Check with your county agent if you have any doubts about its hardiness in your area. This shrub remains green

Fig. 9-6. Bar Harbor juniper grows about 8 inches in height.

throughout the year, but may go somewhat off-color during periods of drought or winter cold.

The dwarf Japanese yew likes an alkaline soil. Usually, the addition of barnyard lime to the planting site is helpful. The soil should not be allowed to become too dry. Water deeply around the base of the shrub once a week, more often during periods of dry weather. The plants must not sit in water, but they should not be allowed to suffer from drought stress or it will destroy their beauty. A drought-stricken plant is not a pretty sight to behold.

The dwarf Japanese yew favors a shady location where it can be shielded from hot summer afternoon suns. Place a mulch around the base of the plants to help conserve moisture and inhibit weed growth. The shrub may need further protection if planted in an area with severe winters.

This useful shrub can be sheared to form a dense, impressive hedge, or it can be left to grow in its natural mound form.

Eastern Red Cedar. Eastern red cedar (*Juniperus virginiana*) grows to about 20 feet in height. It is a very hardy species that can tolerate some of the coldest areas of the nation. It is an excellent landscape plant with its color, fine texture of leaves, and overall appearance. It is very formal and very popular.

Eastern red cedar tends to take on a slightly brownish winter color, but when the temperatures warm again in the spring, it quickly returns to normal green.

There are many cultivars of these species. Each offers certain traits that will work well with many different landscape plans. Some of the best are as follows: *Hillii* has gray-green foliage that turns purple in the winter. It does not bear any fruits.

Glauca has silver-gray foliage and a more informal growth habit. *Canaertii* has dark-green, tufted foliage. *Burkii* has fine-textured gray-green foliage.

Eastern red cedar favors a light, sandy soil. This species is very tolerant of dry soils and is quite drought-resistant.

Eastern red cedar does not require any special care, but it should be babied the first year it is set out. The real success to any landscape is a regular maintenance program. This includes removing weeds, cutting tall grasses, trimming dead, diseased, or unshapely branches, and watering.

Junipers are alternate hosts to a disease called cedar apple rust, so you will not want to plant junipers in the same yard where apple trees, juneberries, crabapples, and certain other fruits are grown. Select the best cultivar for your specific purpose. These plants have great versatility in the home landscape.

Korean Fir. Korean fir (*Abies koreana*) is a slow growing conifer that can reach an ultimate height of 40 to 50 feet. It is a needle-leaf evergreen that grows best on well-drained soil.

Plant in a slightly acid soil. This is a fairly hardy tree, but cannot be recommended for the far north, where it may suffer from winter injury.

The Korean fir has two enemies: dogs and iron chlorosis. To protect the tree from dogs, train your pet so that he or she does not bother your ornamentals. Of course, that could be easier said than done. Your dog, or your neighbor's dog, can do irreparable damage to your tree by chewing branches or urinating on it. You will have to do something about Fido, if you want to grow a Korean fir tree.

The second problem is iron chlorosis, a disorder caused by a change in soil pH, making it no longer acidic enough for the plant to absorb sufficient levels of the micronutrient iron it needs. One symptom is yellowing of leaves. You can restore the acidic levels of the soil's pH by adding ferrous sulfate, or aluminum sulfate to the soil. Follow the instructions on the manufacturer's package for use. There are also foliar fertilizers for acid-loving plants. These sprays are absorbed almost immediately and can restore a sickly plant to health in a very short time.

The Korean fir is best used in the formal landscape, because it lends itself well to aristocratic settings.

Lawson Cyprus. The Lawson cyprus (*Chamaecyparis lawsoniana*) is an interesting tree native to the Pacific Northwest. Although this tree can grow over 100 feet tall, most do not get that large. It is a slow grower.

Many cultivars have been developed for various desired traits. Usually only one cultivar is selected for a garden. The Lawson cyprus has fine-textured foliage, which stands shearing well. It is usually a deep forest-green depending upon the cultivar grown. It produces a rich, dense growth that makes a stunning effect when set in formal plantings.

There are many worthwhile cultivars of this species. Check your nursery to see which ones they offer. Some of the best are:

Columnairs has green foliage and a pyramidal growth habit—a very stately tree. *Erecta Aurea* has yellow foliage. This contrasts sharply with the usual green shrubbery in most yards. *Ellwoodii* is a round form, very slow-growing. Its foliage is a blue-green.

Lawson cyprus likes a woodsy soil. (These plants are not true cypress trees. True cypress trees are tropical plants.)

Prepare soil before planting by adding plenty of peat moss or other organic materials. As it decomposes, the organic matter will provide a source of nourishment for your plant. Mulch during the summer to control weeds and conserve soil moisture.

Use each cultivar for the purpose for which it is adapted. For example, a columnar variety makes a great plant for entryways or for lining drives. The Lawson cyprus is a very practical conifer for the home landscape.

Mugho Pine. The mugho pine is among the smallest of the pine species. It is somewhat unique as it grows very compactly, yet bears the familiar evergreen foliage that makes pines such popular trees (Fig. 9-7).

It is a low-growing mounded shrub that can reach up to 4 feet in height. It has typical needlelike pine leaves that retain their deep green color throughout the entire year. Mugho pine is very hardy—an excellent landscape plant for northern areas.

Like all pines, the mugho pine favors a slightly acid soil. It grows best on sandy loam. If grown on alkaline soils, it may suffer from *iron chlorosis*—its leaves turn yellow and the plant starts to die. Be sure to have your soil pH tested before planting so you

Fig. 9-7. Mugho pine. Courtesy Denver Water Department, Xeriscape Conservation Garden.

will be able to provide the proper acidic environment for your pine.

Mugho pine is quite tolerant of dry soils and summer droughts, but it will present a better appearance when kept well-watered. Plants that suffer from drought stress will have yellowed leaves and stunted growth. If stress is severe, especially during the first season, they may die.

Mugho pine favors sunshine and plenty of it. Although it grows under partial shade, it should not be planted under heavy shade.

Mugho pine is a small shrub and fits well into small yards. It can not be recommended for urban gardens, because it is very sensitive to air pollution. It should grow well in most other places, however.

This interesting little plant makes an effective specimen. It is useful for lining driveways, or setting beside entryways or garages.

Tammy Juniper. The tammy juniper (*Juniperus sabina* var. *tammy*) grows about 2 feet tall. It has a dense spreading growth habit, with bluish-green foliage (Fig. 9-8).

This species produces a fine landscape specimen with many of the features for which junipers are noted—fine texture and evergreen foliage.

Neat, compact, and low horizontal growth are traits this juniper offers. Tammy juniper tends to turn brown, or at least slightly off-color, during the winter.

As it warms up again in the spring, however, the plant should regain its dark, blue-green color. Another similar cultivar is *Buffalo*, which is a little taller and a darker green than Tammy (Fig. 9-9).

As with all low-growing plants, the bed where it is to be set should be prepared ahead of time. All weeds and competing grasses should be removed. Organic matter should be incorporated into the soil. This will provide the plant with a source of nutrients as the material decays. It will also help to improve the water-holding capacity of the soil.

Sunny location is favored. A semisunny spot is all right, but do not plant under heavy shade. Mulch plants during the summer. Prune any growth that is unsightly or that goes beyond the bounds of the area you have set aside for your shrub.

Tammy juniper can provide greenery in areas where grass can not grow. It is used for container plantings in some homes and will be an effective

Fig. 9-8. Tammy juniper. Courtesy Denver Water Department, Xeriscape Conservation Garden.

Fig. 9-9. Buffalo juniper. Courtesy Denver Water Department, Xeriscape Conservation Garden.

border plant when set along driveways, walks, or at the entry gate. It is ideal for formal landscapes.

Spreading Japanese Yew. The spreading Japanese yew adapts well to urban conditions and is great for city homes, where it successfully resists air pollutants and other urban stresses. *Taxus cuspidata* var. *expansa* has a spreading form and needs plenty of room to expand. Do not crowd other plants right up to it. It has dark, glossy-green foliage that remains green throughout most of the year. It is not fully hardy in some northern areas, and it may go somewhat off-color under adverse conditions, such as drought or severe cold.

Spreading Japanese yew favors a shady loca-

tion. It likes a chalky, alkaline soil, so be sure to add garden lime to the planting site. This plant also favors a moist soil. It will not tolerate dry soil; keep plants well-watered.

Like other yews, this shrub responds well to shearing. Although it has an open growth habit by nature, it can be shaped to suit your fancy. Control weeds and conserve soil moisture by placing a summer mulch around the base of the plant.

Birds are attracted to yew and should grace your landscape with their charm wherever yews are present. This shrub can be used as an open informal hedge and as an entryway planting. This is a popular species for easy-care, low-maintenance areas.

Chapter 10

Annuals and Biennials

If you would like a vegetable garden but don't have the room, edible plants can be easily incorporated into annual and biennial flowerbeds in a number of ways. Tomatoes, broccoli, and many varieties of lettuce work well with flowering annuals like marigolds and zinnias; and climbing vegetables like beans, peas, and melons can be trained to a trellis or fence alongside morning glories or biennial vines.

If you do have a producing vegetable garden, the inclusion of a few flowering annuals or biennials will add color, attract pollinating insects, and, in the case of marigolds, helps to repel harmful insects.

Tomatoes work especially well in flowerbeds because their lush foliage, bright yellow blossoms, and red fruits complement many annual flowers. The variety you choose, whether miniature cherry tomatoes or full size standards, depends entirely upon your personal tastes.

You may form round displays or use other shapes. It is best to set three or so tomato plants very near to one another, because it makes them sturdier and they will not usually require staking.

ANNUALS

Most flowering annuals require labor and attention to get them to grow and flower successfully. Annuals flower for only one season or part of a season and then die. For those who are interested in an easy-to-care-for "permanent" landscape, annuals are usually more work than they are worth. There are four exceptions that should be considered for any garden. They are the petunia, marigold, morning glory, and zinnia.

Each of these flowers has certain characteristics that make it a welcome addition to any landscape, and all are fairly easy to grow. Petunias, because of their everblooming habit, will provide your yard with a floral display all summer long. Morning glories can fill a blossom gap throughout the late summer and fall when so few other plants are in bloom. Marigolds actually repel some garden insect pests, and zinnias are so easy to grow that it is almost a sin not to plant any.

Planning is the key to success in growing flowers. Plan your flower garden before you plant.

Using information on size, draw a rough sketch of the various plants you intend to use on a sheet of paper. Most flowers favor full sunlight, so check the areas you have in mind for the amount of sun they receive. Any area that does not receive full sun for at least half a day will not be appropriate for growing annual flowers.

Plan for seasonal bloom. If possible, make sure that your landscape has a good balance of color whatever the season. (Of course, you will not have flower gardens in winter if you live in the north. Plant in masses. It is more effective to set out a particular type of flower in group displays, than to scatter individual flowers throughout the yard. They are also easier to take care of. Same-color plantings are usually more attractive than a mix of different colors. If you use different colors, try to establish some type of pattern for a more attractive display.

Do not be afraid to mix annuals, biennials, and perennials in the same flower bed. Know where each planting is, however, and arrange the plants according to height so that the bed will be well-balanced. Flowers blooming in sequence are usually more attractive than if they all bloom at the same time and are in direct competition with each other.

Decide on whether you want a formal or informal arrangement. In a formal arrangement, plants would be set out in straight lines, circles, square, or rectangular flower beds. Most people prefer an informal flower garden.

Remember not to set tall flowers in front of short ones if you are mixing species in a flower bed. Short plants are usually used for edging beds. Tall plants are normally placed at the rear and intermediate plants fill in the rest of the area. Different cultivars within the same species may vary in height. Check the information about a plant's height before you set it out. You will then be able to arrange it to its best advantage.

Decide on the purpose of your flower garden and whether or not you want it to consist of the same plants or a group of different plants. Remember that flowers are one of the first things that visitors will notice when they come to your home. If the flowers are drawing attention away from your other landscape plants you may want to decide whether the flowers are an asset or not (Fig. 10-1).

SEED OR TRANSPLANTS?

For morning glories, marigolds, and zinnias, seed is the usual route to take and the most practical. Just follow the instructions that come on the seed packet. When growing petunias, most people find it easier to work with plants already started. Petunia seed is very small and does not germinate as readily as do some other flower seeds. It is practical to purchase young transplants from a nursery.

The plants will give you a head start over the seeds. Although they cost a little more, there will be less waste and they will be in bloom long before your seedlings have much growth on them. Seeds are cheaper, but the transplants are worth the extra cost in time and labor saved.

Of course, you can start your own plants indoors. Many people do. That way they can grow their own transplants and have a jump on the growing season. If you do not want to go through all the work involved in starting your own plants, or do not have the time to do so, plan on buying petunia plants and sowing the other flower seeds outdoors when frost danger is past.

California Poppy. The California poppy (*Eschscholzia californica*) is an easy-to-grow flowering annual that will bloom all summer. The blossoms are cup-shaped in shades of yellow, gold, and orange. This flower will brighten up any landscape.

California poppies require full sun. Sow seed outdoors early in the spring while the ground is still cool but not frozen. The seed germinates in about 20 days. To get earlier blooms, you can sow seeds indoors about 45 days before setting plants out in the spring.

Plants sown indoors will need some exposure to outdoor life to acclimate or *harden off* prior to being transplanted in their permanent locations. Do this by taking potted plants out for a few hours each day. This will reduce the shock of outdoor life due to drying winds and wide fluctuations in temperatures (conditions that do not exist indoors). If you just transplant them without this acclimation,

This could be an "edible flower bed," but a rubber tire would probably be too small to conveniently house many edible plants.

Suggestions for an edible flower bed: Rhubarb surrounded by nonedible flowers, or edible mint plants. Strawberries can also be contained in a flower bed, as can tomatoes. Parsley is decorative on the outside circle of assorted flowers in a bed.

Edible flower bed: X = one rhubarb plant; F = perennial or annual flowers
(or)   (or) F = tomatoes.
X = 3-4 spearmint or peppermint plants; F = flowers
(or)
X = 3 tomato plants set close together for strength;
F = small flowers (such as violets, moss roses, pansies,)
and/or parsley between the flowers.

Flower bed: X = taller flowers, such as irises; F = shorter flowers, such as bright pink petunias (annual) or other flower to bloom all summer. A third row on the outside could alternate a spring bloomer (violets, tulips, etc.), with a late summer/fall bloomer (asters).

Combinations of flowers, rocks, and water pools or waterfalls are also very attractive combined to your taste, soil, and climate.

Fig. 10-1. Landscape plan #2. Courtesy of Marion Michaels.

they may all die in a short period of time.

Seeds come in packets available from your nursery or most garden stores. Instructions for how to grow these plants from seed are on the packet label. Just read the label and follow the instructions. It is that simple.

California poppies can be used in a multitude of ways. They are excellent for container growing. Their bright and colorful blooms will liven up any patio.

They are sensational when naturalized (although tall grasses and weeds will have to be controlled to prevent their hiding and shading blooms). These plants are very practical because they provide summer-long bloom that will welcome visitors to your home.

Petunias. The petunia (*Petunia hybrida*) comes in a wide range of colors. The so-called "blue" shades are almost always a disappointment. They are never a true blue, but rather off-shade hues of purple. The blooms come in both single and double forms. Petunias are popular because they bloom all summer long. Once established, petunias will provide a colorful display in your summer landscape with relatively easy care (Fig. 10-2).

The petunia flower is almost without fragrance. It is usually quite large, measuring 3 inches or more across. The plants grow from 6 to 18 inches tall, depending upon the cultivator.

Petunias can be started from seed, but in northern areas they are best started indoors. In parts of the south, they can be sowed directly into the garden. Growing petunia plants from seed is time-consuming and somewhat difficult if conditions for germination are not right. For most people, it is more practical to purchase the young plants already started and transplant them in the garden.

Plant petunias in any well-drained soil, only after all danger of severe frost is past. If your petunias are already in the ground and you hear a frost warning on your radio or TV, take precautions to protect the young transplants. Cover plants with a layer of mulch; composted leaves or straw will do nicely. Be sure to bank the mulch around the plants to help support them before covering the tops. Do not remove mulch until all danger of frost is past and temperatures have warmed up again. Then, carefully remove the mulch immediately. Keep it nearby in case you need to reapply it again in the evening when the temperatures drop. A covering of newspapers, anchored with rocks, will also serve nicely to protect tender plants from frost.

Petunias favor full sun. Plant in an area where they will receive as much sunlight as possible. They will not fare well under heavy shade. Mix plenty of peat moss and composted cow manure into the planting site. Be certain to use only well-rotted manure that will not injure tender young plants.

Control weeds so that they do not compete with the plants for nutrients, sunlight, and moisture. Also, weeds will mar the aesthetic aspects of your flower bed if left to grow. Weeds are best eradicated

Fig. 10-2. Crown Jewels, mixed colors petunia. Courtesy W. Atlee Burpee Co.

by hand-pulling. Be careful not to cultivate too deeply around plants or you may accidentally uproot them or injure roots. A summer mulch around the base of the plants will be helpful.

Petunias will bloom freely all summer long provided they receive enough moisture. Water your petunias liberally during their period of blossom. Water at the base of the plants, never directly overhead. Water droplets will stain petunia petals. The soil should be moist to the touch, but not wet.

There are many landscape uses for petunias. Because it is an annual, it should be set in those areas where it will not upset more permanent flora. Petunias are very effective in beds, borders, or rock gardens. They should not be naturalized. They are most attractive when planted in groups and set in formal arrangements. Usually one-color displays are most effective than multicolor displays. Petunias also grow well in containers. They can be set in hanging baskets, wall planters, or window boxes in sunny locations.

Petunias are a sure bet for instant floral display all summer long and, for that reason if none other, they are quite practical even though they are annuals.

Marigolds. There are two major types of marigold that are commonly planted in the annual garden: the African marigold (*Tagetes erecta*) and the French marigold (*Tagetes patula*). Marigolds are relatively easy to grow and come in varying shades of gold, yellow, and orange; there are some near-red and cream-color varieties available, too. They grow from 6 to 36 inches tall, depending upon the cultivar (Fig. 10-3).

Plant marigolds in a well-drained soil. They should be planted only after all danger of frost is past, but as early in the spring as possible. Most people start seeds indoors in pots and transplant them outdoors when they are ready.

Marigolds favor full sun so avoid planting them in shady areas. Mix plenty of well-rotted manure into the garden when setting out the plants.

Fig. 10-3. Climax, Ladies, and Nugget marigolds. Courtesy W. Atlee Burpee Co.

Marigold seed can be sown directly into the garden. A disadvantage to direct sowing is that the plants may not all come up or may come up in an uneven stand. This sometimes results in gaps where no flowers appear. Such a display is undesirable. One remedy to this situation is to dig up plants and rearrange them in a more even spacing before they become too big. Transplant when seedlings are between 4 and 6 inches tall.

Weeds are effectively controlled by a summer mulch placed around the base of the plants. Any weeds not smothered by the mulch can be removed by hand pulling.

Water plants regularly during the growing season, especially while they are in bloom. If you do not water them, or they do not receive enough moisture, the flowers can shrivel and die.

The French marigolds are naturally somewhat smaller than the African types and rarely grow over 18 inches high. They also have flowers with more bronze hues in their color spectrum. French marigolds are more tolerant of poor soil conditions than others. For best flower display, water plants during dry periods and improve soil by adding peat moss and composted manure to it at the time of planting.

African marigolds are most effective when planted in groupings. They set well in any sunny niche of your lawn. French marigolds should also be planted in groups and they are an effective flower to use for bordering walks.

Morning Glory. Morning Glory (*Ipomea purpurea*) is an easy-to-grow annual vine and works best when trained to some type of support system (Fig. 10-4). It cannot stand up on its own, but has a trailing nature. Without a support, the morning glory will spread along the ground.

Morning glories are available in several colors, but the most impressive flower is a variety called *Heavenly Blue*. This is one of the few flowers in nature that offers a true blue color. The flowers are usually an azure sky blue and open of the loveliest sights you can imagine when open.

Morning glories are an annual; some varieties reseed themselves and come back year after year once set in a location. Most do not. Morning glory plants grow best during hot weather. The hotter the weather, the faster they grow, provided that they receive enough moisture to meet their needs. Morning glories are almost always started by direct sowing in the area where they are to be grown, because they are very difficult to transplant. Sow seeds outdoors in early spring after all danger of severe frost is over. The plants favor a light, sandy soil and a sunny location. Plants that are grown under heavy shade may have some difficulty bearing flowers. When plants are 4 to 6 inches tall, thin them to 6 inches apart.

Keep weeds removed from around the base of the plants to prevent them from crowding out the morning glories. Weeds and tall grass can shade the young plants and inhibit their growth. Gently yank out weeds by hand. Cut tall grass with a grass shears or pair of scissors.

Morning glories are light feeders. They grow exceedingly well in most ordinary garden soil and do not require heavy applications of fertilizer. They are almost foolproof in that they are certain to grow and provide abundant blooms if given plenty of sunshine and ample water.

Water plants at least once a week. Water thoroughly at the base. On sandy soils, or during periods of drought, they may need additional waterings. During the most active stages of growth, and when they are in bloom, your morning glories must receive adequate water.

Train vines to a support system. Choose the type of support that best suits your landscape. This could be a trellis, a mesh fence, or simply cords tied to the top and bottom of a porch. Begin training vines when they are 1 to 2 feet tall. Tie plants to the support with soft string and gently twist the vine around the string. Once connected, the vine will tend to twist itself around the support as it climbs upward. Be careful to not tie knots too tightly and avoid use of metal ties because they may injure the vines.

Always check the vines on a regular basis to see that they have not slipped from their supports. If a heavy wind knocks your vine loose, be sure to reconnect the vine back to its supports after the wind has calmed. A vine that is left to blow in the

Fig. 10-4. Heavenly Blue morning glory. Courtesy W. Atlee Burpee Co.

wind will not be sturdy or likely to bear as many flowers as one that is properly secured.

Morning glories bloom in the late summer and continue blooming until frost. For this reason, select them as part of your late summer floral display plan. They are an unforgettable sight when trained over a porch or garden arbor. You can also train morning glories on fence posts or to trail along a split-rail or white-picket fence.

Morning glories can be planted to grow along a rural mailbox post, a rural fire-number marker, and to provide a cherry entry to your driveway. They can be effective planted upon hillsides, provided the area is one where they will not be disturbed by children playing, pets digging, or other pedestrian traffic.

Zinnias. Zinnias (*Zinnia elegans*) come in many forms, colors, and sizes, and all are equally easy to grow. In fact, one of the nicest features about growing zinnias is that they can grow without any fuss. The flowers are very showy and will provide a wealth of summer color to the landscape.

Because zinnias are easy to grow, they are usually started by direct sowing in the garden. To do this, sow seeds outdoors in the selected area after the weather has warmed. For earlier blooms, you can start zinnias indoors in containers. These pots should be set in a warm place so that the seeds germinate. This is a little extra work, but can give you a head start on the growing season.

If plants are crowded, it may interfere with their proper development later on. It may become necessary to thin out plants if they are found growing too close together. Do this thinning by selecting the plants you want to keep. The plants you remove can be repotted and given away. Rearrange the flowerbeds so that the remaining plants are spaced evenly. It is not attractive to have gaps in a flower bed. Transplant seedlings when between 3 and 6 inches tall.

Zinnias grow best in full sun. They thrive in a rich, organic loam, but seem to grow in practically any soil, provided that it is well-drained. Improve soils before planting by adding peat moss and composted manure. Do not use fresh manure, or it may burn the young seedlings.

Weed control is necessary to keep the plants from being crowded out. Weeds and tall grass can shade young plants and hinder their growth. Gently remove weeds by yanking them out. Be careful to not pull up some of the zinnia plants by accident. Hand-pulling is the safest and most efficient way to remove weeds in the flower bed. Cut tall grasses with a grass shears.

A summer mulch to conserve moisture and control weeds may be desired. Be careful not to smother plants when mulching them. Zinnias are usually grown in a group, fairly close together. Go easy on the mulching materials so that you do not injure the young plants. The mulch should be very light. If it is too thick it can hamper the plant's ability to catch natural rainfalls. Piles of leaves, straw, or other material that has not adequately decomposed may act as a "roof" to the soil near your plants, preventing the water of a light rain from reaching their roots. A weekly watering is recommended. More frequent waterings may be needed during dry weather, on sandy soils, and when flowers are in bloom.

Zinnias can serve a number of functions. They can accent the sunny southern side of a gazebo, front entrance, patio, or any number of other locations. They are very effective in container plantings, and there are varieties that can meet any need, from urns to window boxes.

Zinnias are popular bedding plants. There are tall varieties where height is desired or dwarf varieties for edging walks or bordering other flowers. A bed of zinnias in your yard cannot help but attract the attention of all who pass by.

Zinnias are excellent flowers for cut and show arrangements. Most have long, slender stems, bright colors, and showy blooms. They make attractive bouquets and lovely floral arrangements.

BIENNIALS

Biennials have a life cycle of two years. They are not popular in the northern United States owing to the extra care they require. During the first year, they grow in size and foliage. This growth is called *vegetative growth*. It is not until the second year—the last year of the plant's life—that it starts to produce flowers.

Plants die shortly after flower production or during the subsequent fall, depending upon the species. In areas of the South, some of the hardier biennials, once established will tend to reseed themselves, thus perpetuating and spreading in an area. In these regions, for all intents and purposes, they are perennials.

Biennials require the same care and high level of maintenance as most annuals. In addition, they need winter protection in the north. What they lack in practicality, however, is sometimes compensated for by their unique appearance. The exceptional beauty of some biennials in flower is so gratifying that it may make the trouble of growing them worthwhile.

Forget-Me-Not. The Forget-me-not (*Myosotis scorpioides*) is a hardy biennial. These plants are natural dwarfs, rarely exceeding 9 inches in height. They bear small, blue, starlike flowers, usually from April to June. The flowers are borne the year after planting, unless you are setting out second-year transplants. They are a true blue color, which is very rare in nature. This makes them quite impressive, even though they are so small. The flowers usually appear in small clusters of blossoms.

Forget-me-nots are best started by setting out transplants. There are some annual species that can be started by seed, but it really is not worth the effort unless you have a lot of time. In some areas, forget-me-nots may tend to reseed themselves, but this is not always the case, so do not plan on it.

Forget-me-nots favor a woodsy, organic soil. Use plenty of peat moss or leaf composts when setting them out. They like a moist soil and will tolerate almost boglike conditions. They will not tolerate drought. Regular watering during dry spells is necessary to keep these plants alive.

Semishady areas are the best location for these biennials. They do not fare well under hot, drying sun. They like a cool soil temperature, which makes them ideal for a shady spot in the backyard.

Weed control is not usually a problem with forget-me-nots, because most weeds will not grow under the boglike conditions in which forget-me-nots thrive. If weeds do appear, simply remove them by hand.

In northern states and other places where winters are severe, you should protect the plants with a mulch cover during winter. This will help prevent the plants from being heaved out of the ground due to the fluctuating freeze and thaw temperatures. The mulch keeps the ground temperature even. Remove the mulch when winter is over. (It is usually necessary to keep some mulch handy to protect the plants from spring frosts.)

The best use for forget-me-nots is in a partially shaded backyard wildflower garden. They are effective when used to border walkways and garden paths. Because of their requirements for high amounts of moisture, they are best grown separately from other species, or grown among similar cultural-demanding species, such as azaleas. Forget-me-nots should be planted in groups of at least three plants. They naturalize readily and are great for woodsy-type gardens. They are a very practical plant for people who live on boglands.

Hollyhocks. Hollyhocks (*Althaea rosea*) is a beloved biennial of yesteryear. The flowers grow on tall spires and can reach a height of 8 feet or more. There are also dwarf varieties available. Hollyhocks prefer full sun.

The flowers come in two forms: the single-blossom varieties and the double blossom types. In some areas, hollyhocks will reseed themselves so that they come up like a perennial. In the north,

however, they have a biennial growth habit.

The hollyhock is not too particular about soil, as long as it is well-drained. It is a good practice to fertilize them early in the spring, as hollyhocks are rapid growers.

The main enemy of the hollyhock is the Japanese beetle. This beetle can ruin a hollyhock planting in very short time by destroying the flowers. Organic gardeners can control Japanese beetles by use of a commercial trap that contains insect *pheromones (sex lure)*. This will greatly reduce the adult population. To control the *larval* stage (*grubs*) you can apply a bacteri called *milky spore* to the infested soil. Check with your nursery to see if they offer these items.

Hollyhocks are best started from plants purchased from the nursery. It is cheaper to grow them from seed, but faster and more time-saving to use transplants. Hollyhocks are usually not grown *en masse*, but rather only one or two groups are placed in a setting.

Although hollyhocks have stiff sturdy canes, they will need some protection from strong winds, hail, rainstorms. stake them if necessary. Control weeds around the base of the plant so that they do not compete with your flowers for nourishment and moisture.

In areas where hollyhocks reseed themselves, they multiply and usually have to be transplanted so that they can grow to their best performance. Hollyhocks should be used as specimens; they are most effective in small groupings of two or three. They are excellent background plants and can be set to frame entrances or garden paths. To protect them from strong winds, they should be planted in a sunny, but sheltered location.

Some people favor the single blossom types, others the double blossom varieties. Both are available in a wide range of colors. One of the best double blossomed hybrid cultivars is called *Powderpuff*. In those areas where hollyhocks reseed themselves, the double blossom varieties will tend to come back as single blossom types.

Hollyhocks can be a rewarding and attractive plant, but they will require a certain amount of attention. If you are willing and have the time to take care of them, this is a flower you may wish to consider. If you are however, strapped for time and prefer an easy-care plant, then this is not an appropriate flower for your landscape. Single blossomed hollyhocks in bloom will bring back a touch of yesteryear to your landscape.

Pansy. Pansies are hardy biennials and are available in a wide range of colors, markings, and sizes. *Viola tricolor hortensis* is the Latin name. (The common name "pansy" is derived from the French word, *"pensee"*, which means *thought*.) Most pansies are low-growers, which makes them ideal plants for low borders or flower beds. They are also effective when placed among other plants, especially spring-flowering bulbs like tulips. The pansies start to bloom after the earliest bulbs are through and will continue in bloom until summer flowers take over. Pansies are colorful for window boxes, containers, and hanging baskets, if they are not too far above eye level.

The ideal growing temperatures for pansies is during the spring when temperatures are about 40° F at night to 60° during the day. They grow in all areas of the United States. They produce their best flowers when the weather is mild. They fade and are usually discarded later on in the summer, when the really hot weather starts to come. In the south, and other areas where long periods of frost-free weather is common, some pansy plants have been known to bloom in the fall and during extremely mild winters.

Pansies require a good supply of sunlight. Although they will grow under partial shade, too much shade will reduce the numbers of flowers and the bloom size, causing spindly growth. Hot summer afternoon suns, however, can quickly decimate our pansy bed.

Transplanting potted plants is the best way to grow pansies. It is much faster than starting them out from seed and waiting for them to develop. Good transplants are seedlings that are stocky and display at least four or five strong leaves. When your plants first arrive, sprinkle them with water and let them stand a short while out of the sun to restore lost moisture before planting. When replanting, separate the roots and spread them in all directions to help

anchor each plant. Press the soil firmly in around the plants so that good contact is made with their roots and water them. You may have to pack a little more soil around the roots if any is washed away by watering. Gently hand sprinkle. Do not use a garden hose, or you may wash the transplants right out of their beds. Be careful not to press the soil so tightly that it will cake when dry. Space bedding plants about 3 to 4 inches apart. It is important not to plant pansies in the same location for more than three years in succession. Otherwise, *pythium*—a fungus disease—may build up in the soil.

Pansies are an easy-to-grow, practical plant that will provide beauty to your home landscape each spring.

Sweet William. Sweet William (*Dianthus barbatus*) is one of the most popular of the garden biennials. The flowers have a spicy fragrance very similar to the pinks and carnations, to which they are related. They come in many different shades, from red to white. Usually they are single-blossomed, with dark markings called *eyes*. In some areas, these markings are called *bees*. There are several varieties and many different sizes, including dwarfs.

Sweet William requires a sunny location and a fertile, well-drained soil. Sow seeds outdoors in early spring and protect from frost. If setting out young transplants, wait until after all danger of frost is past in spring before planting them in your garden.

In parts of the South, sweet William may reseed itself, thus giving it perennial characteristics. In the north, however, self-sowing is not reliable. Even in areas where this does happen, it takes a year for the plants to flower. In most of the country, a winter mulch is necessary to protect the plants.

Weeds should be kept under control; remove them by hand.

If insects appear to be a problem, apply an *organic insecticide*, such as *rotenone*. Apply it on a weekly basis, after rain, and until there are no more visible signs of the insect pest or damage. Always follow the directions on the label of the container when using any product, even an organic one.

Water plants on a regular basis, especially during dry spells and when they are in full flower.

Sweet Williams require time and labor to get them to grow successfully. They are a high-maintenance plant. Unless they are an especial favorite of yours, you may wish to grow another, more easily grown flower. They lend themselves well to a sunny niche in your lawn or garden and can be clipped for cut flowers, providing both beauty and a delightful spicy fragrance.

Chapter 11

Wildflowers and Nature Plantings

A weed is any plant growing where you (or your neighbors) don't want it. It seems to be common practice to snub our noses at any plant that we didn't buy at the nursery or set out ourselves. When we do, we are turning our back on or killing countless numbers of beautiful natural plants (Fig. 11-1).

WEEDS

Whether or not you have dandelions growing on your lawn, for example, should depend upon how well you like them. If your neighbors are not too close, or if you are a brave, independent person, there are certain advantages to letting these "coins of gold" add cheerful color to your landscaping.

Many people are ecstatic about dandelion greens and eat them every chance they get. Others, who are connoisseurs, or creators, of homemade wine, will always have dandelion wine on their shelf, along with blackberry and other varieties. And there are those who use the lovely yellow flowers as a garnish on salads. Yes, even the flower is edible. (Be sure to wash them first.)

If you are new to an area, and the former occupants of your place used herbicides on their lawn, you will probably not want to eat the dandelions—especially if they appear misshapen. Otherwise, however, they are perfectly safe and a long time favorite of many—ask your great-grandmother about dandelion greens.

If you dare defy your neighbors, this is one plant that will save you countless hours of digging time by letting it grow. (And it can ease your grocery bill when you use it!)

WILDFLOWERS

With the growing interest in getting back to nature, many people are trying their hand at creating their own "natural" landscape— a landscape composed mainly of plant materials native to the area. Such ambitions are not easily realized, and many problems may occur.

Theoretically, you will select bluebells and black-eyed susans from along the roadside and bloodroot from the swamps or marshes not too far

Fig. 11-1. Young poplar trees. Courtesy of Elizabeth Spangler.

away. Also in theory, you will go to the back of your lot and find small, perfect trees to complement your native plantings.

In actual fact, you may not have your own forest from which to find trees, it may be illegal to select plants from beside the road, and you may not even have any suitable marshes near you. For these reasons (and others), you will probably look for a good nursery for your plants.

Although wildflowers may be found growing in area woods, it is best to not disturb these plants. It may be illegal to gather any wildflowers in some states, or certain types may be illegal. In any event, it is best to purchase wildflowers from nurseries that specialize in their sale.

The natural vegetation of one region differs from that of another region. The desert, for example, provides an entirely different set of flora than does the seashore, mountain, or prairie. If you are interested in setting up a specific type of landscape, such as prairie, desert, mountain, or seashore, or whatever the natural flora in your area, you should contact your county agricultural agent. He or she can advise you on which plants to select and how to maintain them. Your county agent can also recommend nurseries that carry the type of plant materials that you want.

The nurserymen who sell these "native" plants can also provide you with advice and perhaps some ideas on their best use. Some nurseries may even be willing to help you with your landscape plan if they think they can increase their business from you. Others may charge for their services.

Neighbors

A problem you may run into when you begin your nature plantings is opposition from less "enlightened" neighbors. What you call a meadow, your neighbor may call a "weed patch."

You look forward to mouth-watering jelly and nectar from the wild grapes that you so proudly taught to climb along your fence, but your neighbor may complain that some "weed" (your wild grapes) has taken over your yard. Such problems are especially frequent in affluent neighborhoods. It is a good idea to observe the landscaping of your neighborhood. If you do anything that departs too radically from the general trend, you may face problems. Many neighborhoods, especially in the suburbs, are notorious conformists.

If you insist on your rights, you may want to hide your property from view behind tall hedges or fences. There is safety in numbers. If enough people are doing something, they can usually get away with it, but solitary individuals or couples who upset the apple cart may find themselves socially ostracized, and maybe even involved in legal battles.

Naturalizing

Most wildflowers can be *naturalized* into the home landscape. Naturalizing is simply the planting of flowers in small groups, instead of formal beds, so that they appear to have grown there naturally. When perennials are naturalized, they will come up year after year without much effort. Not all flowers can be naturalized, but those that can make an attractive landscape.

Most often, flowers are set out in formal or informal beds. The formal flower beds are usually in some geometric shape, such as square, rectangular, perfectly round, or even in a more unusual formation, such as star-shaped. Informal beds usually have more curves and less rigid lines to define them.

Usually, it is best to plant groups of similar plants together. Wildflowers are rarely planted as single specimens or accents, because most are not that spectacular. (There are exceptions, however.) In addition, some bloom for only short periods of the summer. A variety can provide color and fragrance for a much longer season.

To naturalize wildflowers, you must aim at achieving conditions that best resemble the native habitat of the species you are trying to grow. Do not forget some of the new hybrids offer superior performance—bigger blooms and longer-lived blossoms—to the native strains, so do not be afraid to use them in your garden.

WILDFLOWER SPECIES

This chapter does not attempt to provide an exhaustive list of America's wildflowers, but the flowers listed here are some of the best. There may be others that you will want to try. Check with your nursery to see what they offer. In some cases, you may have to order some of these wildflower species from special nurseries (See Chapter 31, Sources).

Most of these flowers favor the woodlands of the eastern United States and Canada. If grown west of the Mississippi, they will need special attention and care. You can recreate their natural habitats in your backyard.

Remember that flowers grow wild in the woods without any care at all, so do not smother your plants with attention. Water them and weed them, but neglect them enough so that you do not "kill them with kindness." The only exception is for people who live in the semiarid regions of the West. They will have to tend their plants more closely, because it will be harder to recreate the natural woodland habitats in some regions.

Overfeeding is probably the most common cause of failure when growing wildflowers. Raking away all their natural future soil (leaves, etc.) and not replacing it is probably the second. Go easy on the fertilizer; you are not going to get watermelon-size blooms on any of these plants. Most wildflowers are light feeders.

Wildflowers can be easy to grow as long as the site resembles, as much as possible, the natural woodland setting from where these plants come.

Astilbes. Astilbes (*Astilbe* x *arendsii)* produce attractively tall plants with towering spikes of flowers that reach 3 or more feet in height. They are available in pink, red, and white, with several hues within that range. Astilbe flowers have an airy, feathery look to them. Their leaves tend to hug the ground and are removed from their tall flower spikes.

Astilbes favor shady areas. They like a woodsy soil that is rich in organic matter. It is important to keep the soil moist around the plants; they will suffer if they are subjected to drought-stress. Plants are relatively hardy and open their flowers in early summer. They are usually through blooming by midsummer.

Weeds should be kept under control. Hand pull weeds when you see them. It will be necessary to water plants during prolonged dry spells, and it is a good idea to water them on a regular weekly basis throughout the summer anyway.

Some of the best cultivars are *Deutschland,* which has white flowers; *Europa,* which has pink flowers; and *Fanal,* which bears red flowers. There are also other cultivars available and a few other species that may be worth looking into if you are especially attracted to these flowers.

Astilbe is most effective when planted in groups. It is an excellent plant for garden borders. You can cut the flower spikes for indoor arrangements. When used as a cutflower, sprays of astilbe serve best as background material to accentuate other types of flower blossoms.

Bee Balm. Bee balm (*Monarda didyma*) is a large coarse plant with a spreading habit. It produces tall feathery flowers that are usually a lipstick-red, although cultivated varieties are available in other colors as well. The flowers bloom in summer on long stiff stems, up to 3 feet tall.

Bee balm favors a shady location. It is not too fussy about soil, provided it is well-drained. This is an easy flower to grow. Control weeds by hand removal. Add a summer mulch to help keep weeds down.

The flowers are fragrant and made excellent cut flowers. They should be set out in groups for their best display. They will attract hummingbirds to your garden, so plant them where you can see them from your window. In this way, you will be able to enjoy the sight of hummingbirds feeding upon their nectar.

This is a really nice flower that deserves greater use in the American home landscape.

Bird's Foot Violet. Bird's foot violet (*Viola pedata*) is a sun-loving species. It resembles the pansy, except for bearing smaller flowers. It has a curious face, complete with different-colored hues and the typical "cat face" that marks pansies. They are in bloom about the same time as pansies and are somewhat more difficult to transplant.

Bird's foot violet favor acid soils. They can be set out in any number of sunny areas and are most effective when planted in a large group. They provide an enchanting border for sunny walks and paths. They naturalize well. They are not as spectacular as pansies in bloom and no match for the larger flowered cultivated species of violets, but they are a charming wildflower.

Black-Eyed Susan. The black-eyed Susan (*Rudbeckia hirta*) is sometimes sold under the name *Coneflower.* This plant is originally native to the southwestern areas of the country, but has now spread throughout much of the rest of the nation. It is a biennial, but reseeds itself freely, so that once established in a location, it is not long before it spreads.

Black-eyed Susan grows up to 3 feet tall. They bear large, yellow daisylike flowers on tall, thin stems. In the center is a prominent dark brown cone.

Black-eyed Susans prefer full sun and should not be planted in shade. They should be planted on a well-drained soil. They are remarkably resistant to drought and dry weather conditions. Once planted they need almost no care. Flowers appear from mid-summer to fall.

This is an excellent flower to naturalize into the landscape and can also be used as a cut flower. There are many cultivars available, some in dwarf size and some with double blossoms.

There are other species of black-eyed Susans worth trying, and some of these "cousins" to the black-eyed Susan may be just what you are looking for.

Bloodroot. Bloodroot (*Sanquinaria canadensis*) bears very showy, large double-white blossoms in early spring. It is a low-growing plant with a horizontal or creeping growth habit that rarely exceeds 8 inches in height.

The plant produces kidney-shaped leaves that are slightly blue in color. From the center of these leaves, impressive white flowers grow.

Bloodroot favors a moist, acid soil rich in organic matter. Be certain to add plenty of peat moss to the planting site. It thrives in partial shade; if grown in full sun, be careful to not allow the soil to dry out. Keep the area around the plant moist, but not wet.

Bloodroot gets its name from the color of its red sap, roots, and stems. The sap is poisonous. For this reason, bloodroot should not be set out in areas to which small children have frequent access.

Place bloodroot among your other acid-loving plants. It is a low-grower, so be careful it is not over-shadowed by taller ornamentals.

The best use for bloodroot is in a woodland setting. It will look natural when set out in your backyard among other wildflowers. Bloodroot is an excellent plant for naturalizing, and the showy white flowers will add to your spring bouquet. It is a very hardy species and, with its trailing growth habit, it makes an unusual groundcover. It can be used alone or planted in groups.

Butterfly Flower. Butterfly flower (*Asclepias tuberosa*) is sometimes called the *butterfly weed,* because it grows like a weed! The plant bears bright orange flowers in layered clusters. Plants reach about 2 feet tall, sometimes a little taller under better growing conditions. It attracts butterflies. Blossoms practically cover the plant when in full bloom, and it stays in bloom throughout much of the summer, placing it among the everbloomers.

Butterfly flowers require full sun to perform their best. They are very tolerant and resistant to drought and hold up well even when other plants have wilted.

Butterfly flowers are fairly easy to grow, but should be grown from young seedlings, because mature plants do not transplant well.

Butterfly flowers fit well in sunny areas where a splash of color is desired. They are also useful in borders and beds. They naturalize well. For better selections of color and size, plant the new hybrids. They offer a greater choice of type than the wild, including some that look almost wild (except they have larger and longer-lasting blooms).

The butterfly flower is an informal plant and may get out of control in formal gardens. If you like to watch butterflies, this is the plant to attract them.

Candytuft. Candytuft (*Iberis sempervirens*) is a low growing perennial, usually less than a foot tall. Its branches resemble woody stems. Candytuft is a half-hardy evergreen. When it is grown in northern areas, it almost always suffers from cane tip dieback every winter, but this does not hurt the plant much. Candytuft is grown for the clusters of tufted white flowers it bears in the spring. These flowers are quite small, but because they are borne in clusters, they are very showy.

Candytuft grows best when planted in full sun. It can be set out under partial shade, but will not do so well if planted under heavy shade. It favors a rich, loam soil and plenty of moisture. Do not allow the ground around your candytuft to become too dry, or it may affect the quality of flower production.

For northern growers, it is best to prune off the dead areas of the cane each spring that show signs of tip dieback. This pruning will encourage new growth and stimulate flower production. It will also remove the dead areas,which are always a potential host for diseases. Plants should also be pruned back shortly after the blossoms have faded.

Plant candytuft in groups for best effect; it is a low-grower, so it should be set out in an area where its view will not be blocked by taller shrubs or flowers.

Candytuft can be used to form a border around flower beds. They are effective for container plantings as well.

Columbine. Columbine (*Aquilea canadensis*) grows to slightly under 3 feet tall. This plant blooms in early summer; the spurred flowers are usually bicolored with various shades of red and yellow. Columbine blossoms are very showy and consist of two parts: one part is cup-shaped, the other is long and curves away from the rest of the flower. These flowers tend to self-sow readily and multiply once established in an area.

There are many fine species and cultivars of columbines (Fig. 11-2). The *chrysantha* species is perhaps better than the *canadensis* species for home gardens.It offers a wider choice of colors, and its flowers are slightly superior. It also tends to have a bushy growth habit, so it does not need to be staked to support the plant. These plants produce an abundance of flowers.

If a dwarf is more to your liking, try *Dragon Hybrids*. This cultivar offers a dwarf columbine of many different hues. Most will grow no taller than 18 inches, so it is ideal for people with small yards or more formal gardens.

Columbine favors shade. It loves a woodsy soil rich in humus. It needs a well-drained, but moist, soil. It should be watered during dry spells. Keep the soil around them damp, but not wet, to the touch.

Tall columbines will require staking to protect them from being whipped in the wind and to help bear the burden of a heavy flower load. Tie the plants securely to stakes, but loose enough so that you do not girdle their delicate stems. A plastic-coated wire is suitable for the job. Fasten them to small, wooden stakes that are secured in the ground.

Columbine is a practical plant for naturalizing

Fig. 11-2. Columbine. Courtesy Denver Water Department, Xeriscape Conservation Garden.

in the home garden.

Dog's Tooth Violet. Dog's tooth violet (*Erythronium americanum*) is not a true violet. This plant has yellow flowers that are quite small, with nodding lilylike characteristics. It has two large leaves that come out from its base.

Dog's tooth violet is a spring bloomer. It is a bulbuous herbaceous plant related to the lily family.

The dog's tooth violet can be grown in light shade, but does not favor heavy shade. It requires a well-drained soil and is very tolerant of dry conditions. This is a fairly easy plant to grow. Set it out and forget about it—it's that easy!

Use the dog's tooth violet to line shaded paths or in a woodlands garden. It is in bloom only during the spring, so plant it among other flowers so that when the violets have stopped blooming, your landscape will not look barren.

Dutchman's Breeches. Dutchman's breeches (*Dicentra cucullaria*) is a cousin of the bleeding heart. It bears flowers early in the spring that resemble white Dutch pantaloons. It is very attractive when in bloom, but the plant will disappear during midsummer. Be sure you mark the location of this plant so that you do not accidentally dig it up while it is dormant.

Dutchman's breeches do best in shady areas and in a slightly alkaline soil. Add lime to the planting site. It prefers a moist location, but one that is well-drained. Control weeds by hand removal. A mulch may be helpful in both controlling weeds and conserving soil moisture.

Dutchman's breeches are an excellent specimen plant and are effective when planted solitaire. Visitors to your spring garden will stop and remark on these unusual flowers.

As with other spring-flowering plants, Dutchman's breeches should be set among other types of plants that will take up the floral slack when these are no longer in bloom.

Filipendula. Filipendula (*Filipendula venusta*) is a very large-growing herbaceous perennial. It falls into the category of a nature plant, rather than a wildflower, because few people expect a flower to grow 6 feet tall! Needless to say, this species is best for people with very large yards.

Filipendula is a very hardy plant and can successfully withstand the routinely tough weather of the Great Plains region and still manage to come back year after year to bloom in early summer.

The plant bears flowers that are quite delicate looking. They are pink and arranged on the stems in clusters that resemble cotton candy. These stems and flowers are sturdier than they look, however, as they hold up well to high winds and inclement weather.

The filipendula favors full sun. It is not particularly fussy about soil. It must be given ample moisture once growth starts in the spring, because it will already be in bloom at the beginning of summer.

It is most important that plenty of room be provided for its growth. Filipendulas will take up space.

Because they can be found growing wild in the prairies, filipendulas really require less care than people might imagine. If you examine prairie soils, however, you will find that they are usually quite fertile.

One of the best uses for this plant is to provide an accent in the home landscape. Its pink, cotton-candy blossoms do not appeal to everyone, but it will add a different look to your garden scene.

Goldenrod. Goldenrod grows wild along roadsides throughout the eastern half of the United States and Canada. There are many species, some types grow to 7 inches, others grow up to 8 feet tall. One of the better wild species is the Canadian goldenrod (*Solidago canadensis*). It has branches that resemble feather plumes when in flower. This flower makes an interesting display when grown en masse.

Goldenrod blossoms in the late summer and blooms until late in the fall. All goldenrods produce golden-yellow flowers of different hues, except for one species, *bicolor,* which has white flowers.

There are many new hybrids available. The hybrids are an improvement over the wild strains, and unless you have your heart set on growing strickly wild types, the hybrids are a better choice for most people. The dwarfs are best for gardens. They are easier to care for and produce an attractive display when in full bloom. One of the best cultivars is called *Golden Dwarf.* This plant grows to only about 1 foot high.

Goldenrods favor full sun. They grow well on any number of soils, provided they are well-drained. Goldenrods do not like muck soils. Plants are easy to care for and take neglect, once established. Remove weeds and cut tall grasses so that they do not interfere with goldenrod growth and bloom.

Once your goldenrods are planted, do not worry about them. Just weed them and keep them well-watered—once a week should be sufficient. In times of drought, you may wish to water them more frequently.

The new dwarf hybrids will provide late summer color to front lawns or sunny nooks in other areas. Plants naturalize well. Goldenrod is an easy to grow, carefree flower that will provide much beauty to your home landscape.

Lily-of-the-Valley. Lily-of-the-valley (*Convallaria majalis*) is a herbaceous perennial that seldom grows higher than 8 inches. It has very fragrant, bell-shaped flowers that are borne along the stem from the base to the tip in what are called *racemes.* These flowers are used to manufacture perfume in France.

Lily-of-the-valley is an easy plant to grow in shady locations. It can also be grown indoors as a house plant. It favors a moist humus soil that is well-drained. It is planted by setting out what are called *pips* or root clusters.

Lily-of-the-valley can be used in a variety of ways. They may be placed in containers that are located in shady places, and they make an excellent ground cover for shady areas where grass may not grow. It is useful to line walks and to cut for indoor bouquets. They are available with pink or white flowers. Choose the selection that best meets your needs or grow both types.

Oconee Bells. Oconee bells (*Shortia galacifolia*) is a spring bloomer, opening up in late May in most areas. The flowers come in different colors and are bell-shaped with fringed edges. The blossoms tower above the shiny, forest-green foliage.

Oconee bells require shade and a moist, woodsy soil rich in humus. They prefer acid conditions, so add peat moss or oakleaf mold to the planting site. These flowers should be kept well-watered.

Use oconee bells in shady backyards or set them out among your other woodland plantings. They are most effective when planted in groups of at least three. Solitary specimens look lonely and require too much upkeep.

Solomon's Seal. Solomon's seal. (*Polygonatum multiforum*) grows to about 2 1/2 feet in height. It bears small, white flowers in early summer, borne on pendulous (weeping) branches. This is a somewhat coarse plant with large green leaves. When it is in bloom, the white blossoms tend to hang along the stems, either in pairs or singularly.

The plant has a weedy look to it; if it is left to grow among the grass, people may assume it is a weed and wonder why you do not take better care of your yard. Use an organic mulch to help set the flowers off.

Solomon's seal favors shady locations. It may wilt if left out in the hot sun. It grows surprisingly well on ordinary soil and is not a heavy feeder. It can grow and bloom without any added fertilizer (unless your soil is absolutely starved). These plants require no special care. Like other wildflowers, their display will be more subtle than most cultivated flowers.

Their best use is in a woodland garden. They are quite attractive when set out along shady garden paths. This is a practical plant, because it is so easy to grow.

Spiderwort. Spiderwort (*Tradescantia virginiana*) has long and narrow leaves that give the plant its name. The flowers are triangular-shaped and usually a deep, almost fluorescent yellow color. Blossoms usually close during the hottest parts of the day. Spiderwort is an everblooming perennial, which flowers all summer long.

There are new hybrids that are superior in bloom and performance to the native strains. The *Tradescantia* x *andersonia* group of hybrids offers a good color selection and is recommended for people who want a more diverse and impressive floral display. These varieties will grow to about 2 feet tall.

Spiderwort favors shade and requires a rich soil, although plants seem to grow well in any good garden loam. Control weeds to prevent their interfering with the aesthetic appearance of these plants. It is usually most effective to just yank out the weeds by hand. Hold one hand over the spiderwort for close weeds, so that the flowers are not accidentally uprooted.

If you do not have a suitably shady area, plant a shade tree. Sunny areas get too hot during the summer, and the flowers will close up. In the shade, they will remain open.

Spiderwort is most effective when planted in groups and allowed to naturalize in the landscape. It readily harmonizes with other woodland flowers.

Trinity Lily. Trinity lily (*Trillium grandiflorum*) grows to about 18 inches tall. It produces large flowers, 2 inches or more across, close to the foliage. The blossoms are snowy-white. There is also a pink-flowering cultivar available.

Another popular species of Trillium is the wake-robin, (*Trillium sessile*). This attractive plant grows slightly shorter than the trinity lily, to little over 1 foot in height. This species is one of the first to bloom in spring, hence its name. It grows throughout most of the eastern half of the United States and Canada. It does not occur West of Missouri; the area is not humid enough.

Wake-robins bear chocolate colored flowers. There are two cultivars that are prettier than the ordinary variety. These are *Rubrum,* which bears read flowers; and *Album,* which has white flowers. These two plants look well when combined.

Both the trinity flower and the wake-robin favor rich, organic soils. They like partial shade and should not be planted under full sun. They do best when grown in filtered shade.

They look well when set out in a woodland garden and can be naturalized in shady areas, along backyard paths, or in other areas where wildflowers are desired. They are spring-bloomers and should not be the only flower you plant.

Virginia Bluebells. Virginia bluebells (*Mertensia virginica*) grow to about 2 feet tall, depending upon conditions. They form large clumps. In the spring, they produce sky-blue, bell-shaped flowers along pendulant stems. When the flower buds first appear, they are a rose-pink, but turn azure when fully open.

Bluebells favor shade. They like a woodsy soil that is rich in humus. Weed bluebells by hand. Add a light summer mulch around the clumps to help conserve moisture and control weeds. Add plenty of peat moss or oakleaf mold to the planting site.

Bluebells may cause an aesthetic problem later in the summer because they have the habit of *summer dieback* that causes unsightly yellowing foliage. The foliage must not be cut out, however, or it may kill the plant. Permit the foliage to die naturally.

Virginia bluebells are best used under shade in back or front yards. They naturalize quite readily. They are easy to care for and will provide a touch of springtime color to shady areas of your yard.

They look impressive along woodland paths.

Chapter 12

Iris, Daylilies, and Other Bulbous Plants

If you are looking for flowers that will dependably appear every year, with relatively little care, irises and daylilies are a good investment. These plants are ideal for an easy-care landscape. Once set into their locations, they will become a permanent addition that grows and multiplies each year.

IRISES

Irises (flags) are long-lived garden perennials that require very little care. They bloom during that period of spring when few other flowers are in bloom and continue to bloom for several weeks.

Iris varieties are easy to grow and adapted to every area of the United States. They produce bright-colored flowers in a wide range of shapes, sizes, and colors.

The principal types of iris are bearded, crested, and beardless.

Bearded Iris

The *bearded iris* is called the *German iris* (*Iris ger-*

manica). This is the most commonly grown bearded species. These plants can survive severe droughts and extreme cold. This makes them practically foolproof and especially suited to northern gardens. The plant has sword-shaped leaves that remain evergreen in warm climates and remain green until late fall in cold climates.

Most bearded irises grow from 2 to 3 feet tall. These plants are so easy to grow that they are a must for beginners. These tall, bearded irises usually bloom in May and June. There are some varieties available that bloom in both spring and fall.

There are dwarf bearded irises available, too. The two most widely planted of bearded dwarfs are *Iris pumila* and *Iris chamaeiris*. Both are well adapted to rock gardens, because they spread quickly and form dense mats of foliage. They are primarily spring bloomers.

Beardless Iris

The *beardless iris* is sometimes called *Dutch iris*. They have smooth petals and thin, grasslike leaves.

(Iris "beards" are the fuzzy growth found on the inside of lower petals. This fuzz is not present on beardless iris). Plants grow from 1 to 4 feet tall and bloom primarily during the early summer. The two most commonly grown beardless species are the Japanese iris (*Iris kaempferi*) and the Siberian iris (*Iris sibirica*). The common name Dutch iris derives from the country that exports so many of these plants.

Japanese iris have wide petals and grow from 2 to 4 feet tall. Flowers are borne on long stems. The Siberian iris has narrow petals. Stems grow to about 2 feet tall. Beardless types favor moist soil.

Crested Iris

Crested iris have a small raised area, or crest, on the middle of each of the lower petals (which are called *falls*). Often the color of the crest is in contrast with the color of the rest of the flower. One of the most popular of the crested irises is the dwarf species *Iris cristata*.

The crested iris can be used where a small unusual flower is wanted. They will add a certain charm to your spring landscape and have that same easy-to-grow quality that makes the iris such a must for any garden.

IRIS CULTURE

The first step in iris culture begins with the planting. It is a good idea to understand the significance of iris culture, because once you get them started, your irises will provide you with many years of enjoyment. First you have to get them off to a good start.

The best time to plant irises is in the late summer or early fall. They must be established in the soil before winter. Most species of iris come up from thick stems called *rhizomes*, which grow slightly below the surface of the ground or at ground level. They store the food produced by the leaves. New plants spring up from them. Many small roots penetrate the soil deeply for moisture and nutrients. These feeder roots, however, are not rhizomes.

Irises can be grown from seed, but this is not recommended. It can take up to three years for seed-grown plants to flower. Also, because most irises are hybrids, the flowers of seed-grown plants will not be of the same high quality as those reproduced from the rhizomes. To achieve uniform size and color of bloom, grow only plants from rhizomes.

You can order iris from your favorite nursery. Most mail-order nurseries will ship your plants to you at the proper time for planting in your area. Set them out as soon as you receive them.

Locations

Irises need full sun. Choose a location that has southern exposure and good air circulation. The bearded and crested varieties do best in lime soil with good drainage. Rhizomes may rot in soils where water is left standing for long periods of time in the spring. The beardless types perform better in a slightly acid soil and favor moister conditions.

Plant iris in groups of at least three for best effect. They can be naturalized or set out in formal beds, whichever you prefer. Spreading organic matter, compost, well-rotted manure, or peat moss may help to improve the drainage of heavy soils and to make light, sandy soils heavier. Add garden lime to the soil if bearded or crested irises are to be planted.

To plant, dig a shallow hole large enough to receive the rhizome. Set the rhizome just below ground level so that tops are covered by no more than 1 inch of dirt. It is very important not to plant irises too deep or they may rot and die.

Do not wad roots together. Spread them evenly throughout the shallow hole. Fill in with soil, pressing it firmly in place around the rhizome. Water immediately. Thoroughly soak the area around the roots.

Caring For Your Iris

Water plants once a week until two weeks before the ground freezes. Never water your iris plants in winter unless you live in the South or in areas of the country with warm winters.

In the spring, water plants on a regular basis, but do not overwater them. Remove weeds and grass from around plants. Hand weeding is most practical. Do not use chemical weed killers, or you may injure your irises.

While the plants are in bloom, water the area around the base. Do not use a pressure head, or you may knock down your flowers. Use common sense.

Cut faded flowers unless you want the plant to go to seed. This is not critical; it is done mostly for aesthetic reasons and to spare the plant from putting energy into seed production instead of storing up resources for next season's flowering.

Irises are not heavy feeders. An application of well-rotted manure in the spring will usually restore plants that have become small. Be sure to use only well-rotted manure. Do not cover the area to thickly. To increase bloom, add *superphosphate* or *bone meal* to your soil.

Mulch the first season after planting. Apply a light mulch of straw or evergreen boughs after the ground first freezes. A winter mulch will prevent the roots from freezing or being heaved out of the soil from the alternate freeze and thaw that often occurs during periods of winter. Irises in the far north, as in the Dakotas or Alaska, may require a mulch every winter even after they are established.

Dividing Your Irises

When plants become crowded, usually in three to five years, divide the offshoots from the irises. Divide irises in late summer or early fall, not during their bloom. Cut leaves to a third of their full height, using a pair of scissors. Dig out the entire clump of rhizomes and lift up the whole clump at once. Wash away soil with a bucket of water or a garden hose. This will enable you to see where cuts should be made.

Make small divisions if you do not want to redivide the plants for another three to five years. Make large divisions if you want to be sure to have several flowers the following spring. Large divisions may have to be separated again in two or three years. Use only rhizomes from the outer portion of the clump; rhizomes near the center are the oldest and least likely to produce healthy new plants.

Cut rhizomes with a sharp knife. Each division must contain at least one bud or fan of leaves. It should also contain a few inches of healthy rhizome and a number of well-developed roots. When separated from the original iris clump, each division is ready to plant.

IRIS DISEASES

Although diseases are not usually a problem, their prevalance may depend upon where you live and factors such as culture and growing conditions. Iris diseases reduce the number of flowers, disfigure the leaves, and can, on occasion, kill the plants.

Prevent diseases by giving the plants plenty of space, sunlight, and good drainage. Clean up dead materials quickly. Do not plant irises in crowded conditions or under heavy shade.

Bacterial Soft Spot

The most destructive disease to the iris is *bacterial soft spot*. Bacteria enters the plant through breaks in the rhizome. Leaf bases and rhizome begin to rot and the plant soon dies.

To control, dig up infected rhizomes. If the rot is extensive, destroy the iris. Cut out and discard diseased parts on less seriously affected plants. Be sure to move these diseased cuttings away from your iris bed when you are through. They should be taken away and burned, or plastic bag them with your other garbage if you have a regular pickup.

Fungus Rots

Southern blight or *sclerotic rot*, attacks irises in warm, humid areas. A fungus affects plants at or near the soil surface. The leaves turn yellow and dry prematurely or rot off at the base. Small yellowish-brown, seedlike structures appear.

Botrytis rhizome rot, another fungus, occurs in cool areas. The fungus produces small, black seedlike structures on the rhizomes and in the soil. A dry, pitchy, gray rot develops in the leaf bases and rhizomes.

Dig and burn plants that are affected with either kind of rot. Remove soil from the surrounding area; replace it with new or sterilized soil. Cut out the rotted areas of slightly damaged rhizomes to make sure all the fungus is removed before replanting.

Iris Leaf Spot

This disease will disfigure leaves and weaken plants. It causes small brown spots to appear on infected plants about flowering time, covering the leaves with these dots. Water-soaked margins around the spots turn yellow. Spots later develop a grayish center with black fruiting tufts. The leafspot overwinters in the old leaves and produces new spores in the spring.

To control, spray plants every two weeks with *Bourdeaux mixture* (a copper-sulfate fungicide available at nurseries). Also spray after a heavy rain. Continue this procedure from the time the leaves first emerge until all signs of disease has stopped.

In mild climates, cut and burn the infected leaves in the fall. If leaves are not removed, the fungus may remain active throughout the winter. In cold areas, remove and burn dead foliage in the fall.

Rust and Bacterial Leaf Spot

These two diseases weaken, but seldom kill, irises. *Rust* produces small raised, dark-red dots on iris leaves. *Bacterial leaf spot* causes dark green, watery spots and streaks. The spots later turn yellow and become translucent.

To control, remove and burn all leaves that show any sign of these diseases. Do not allow any diseased leaves to remain on the ground. Infected leaves harbor spores that spread these diseases.

Iris Mosaic

This is one of the most widespread diseases of irises. It is a virus disease that is transmitted by aphids. Infected flowers may be mottled or striped. Light green streaks appear on the leaves of some plants. Many infected plants will not show any obvious signs of the disease. Plants may show symptoms at one season of the year and appear disease-free in another season.

To control, dig up and burn irises that show mosaic damage. Reduce the spread of this disease by controlling aphids. Introduce ladybugs to the area; they will greatly reduce the aphid population.

INSECTS

Although insects are not usually a problem with irises, grasshoppers can sometimes do a great deal of damage by chewing off the flowers and leaves. They are most readily controlled over a period of time by cultural practices that keep weeds cut and lawns mowed. The introduction of a bacterial grasshopper spore is infectious to them is very effective. It is available commercially.

DAYLILIES

Daylilies belong to the *Hemeroicallis* genus, and most commercial varieties are hybrids of many species (Fig. 12-1). Daylilies are one of the easiest perennial flowers to grow and are very rewarding. They do not mind neglect. Plant them and forget about them—they are that easy! If you have a busy

Fig. 12-1. Daylilies are one of the easiest perennial flowers to grow and are very rewarding.

111

Fig. 12-2. Autumn Red daylily. Courtesy Denver Water Department, Xeriscape Conservation Garden.

schedule or want a plant that will not require too much of your time, this is a flower to consider.

Daylilies come in a wide range of colors. Some are tall-growing plants; dwarfs are also available. The flowers come in single and semidouble forms. Plants range in height from 1 1/2 to 5 feet, depending upon the variety. By choosing flowers with different blooming times, you can have daylilies in blossom throughout much of the summer. Most standard daylilies bloom in late summer.

Each blossom is only open for one day, but the daylily is so free-flowering that during its time of bloom it is constantly providing flowers (Fig. 12-2).

CULTURE

Daylilies form clumps and should be given plenty of room for expansion. They do not have to be divided, but it is the usual practice to divide clumps every five years.

Daylilies are not fussy about soil, as long as its well-drained. They can be set in either sun or shade. It will probably be to your advantage to plant them under filtered shade. By setting them out in those areas, you will be able to save the sunny spots for those ornamentals that require full sun. Do not plant daylilies under heavy shade. It may inhibit flowering.

Many people like to remove the flowers after they have faded. This is not a cultural requirement, but is done simply for aesthetic reasons.

Use daylilies lavishly; they are most effective when planted in groups. There are many kinds available, all in different color combinations and sizes. Choose the types that best fit your plans. Daylilies are excellent naturalizers and fit well into wildflower landscapes. They can be used in formal flower beds as well. They are not suitable for cutflower use, because the blooms only last one day.

OTHER BULBOUS PLANTS

There are a wealth of bulbs, tubers, rhizomes, and other bulbuous plants that will add to your spring or summer garden. These bulbuous plants are easy to grow and offer a wide selection of flower type, color, and size. Many, like daffodils, are excellent for naturalizing, and others, like tulips, are excellent for use in formal flower beds.

Crocus. The crocus is a relative of the iris family, so you know it is hardy. It is technically a *corm*, but most people call it a bulb for lack of knowledge. Some crocus plants flower in the fall; others blossom in the early spring. The autumn-flowering crocus (*Crocus sativus)* and the spring-flowering Dutch crocus, (*Crocus speciosus)* are two of the most popular species, although other species and new hybrids are available.

Crocus are among the first flowers to bloom in the spring. They are sometimes up just after the snow has melted. Once planted, they will come up yearly without any trouble and increase in number.

Plant corms anytime during the fall before the ground freezes. Plant about 3 inches deep. They grow well in most types of soil, provided that it is well-drained. Crocus favors sun, but will grow under partial shade.

They are best planted in groups of ten to a dozen corms in one setting. Crocus naturalizes very well. The autumn types, however, perform better when they are planted in a formal bed. The regular spring-flowering types are best for naturalizing.

After bloom, allow the foliage to turn brown and wither before removing it. This is very important, because it is the foliage that stores up nourishment for next spring's bloom. Be careful not to mow the crocus foliage when mowing your lawn.

Crocus is a practical flower for people who like maintenance-free landscapes. These are one of the easiest plants to grow and will make a beautiful floral display each spring and for many springs to come.

Daffodils, Narcissus, and Jonquils. The daffodil (*Narcissus pseudonarcissus*) is a large-flowered member of the *Narcissus* genus. In com-

mon usage, the term "daffodil" refers to any member of this genus that has a large trumpeted flower on a tall sturdy stem (Fig. 12-3).

The word "jonquil" (*Narcissus jonquilla*) refers to any member of this genus with clustered flowers. Plants that resemble small-flowered daffodils are called narcissus (*Narcissus poeticus*). If it all sounds confusing, it is. This is partly because botanists classify plants according to certain features, and horticulturists sometimes classify these same plants according to different features than those used by botanists. Whatever name you call them, they are all related and enjoy the same culture.

Daffodils need a well-drained soil. Soil that has a high water-holding capacity is not acceptable, because standing water can encourage rot organisms that attack the bulbs. The bulb part of the plant is where the flower stores up it reserves of food necessary for bloom.

The time to plant daffodils is in the month of September, although they can be set out anytime in early fall. This gives the roots a chance to row and establish themselves before the ground freezes. Plants that are set out too late in the season may have difficulty coming up the following spring.

Some varieties are bred for indoor *forcing*. These varieties can be forced to flower indoors during the winter after they have undergone a sufficient chill period of from six to eight weeks. Forced daffodils are usually only good for one flowering, because the process drains a lot of energy from the bulb.

Most daffodils today are hybrids, the result of crossing superior selections. Wild daffodils are more on the order of the small-flowered narcissus.

Weeds must be controlled. Plants should be kept watered, especially just prior to and during periods of bloom. Be careful when watering not to aim pressure hoses at flower stems. Such pressure can destroy a bed of flowers. Water around the base area of the plants and water thoroughly.

Do not cut back foliage after the flowers are gone. Rather, foliage must be allowed to die back naturally. The plant's foliage needs to be protected, because it will provide the nourishment for next spring's bloom. Be careful that it does not get cut

Fig. 12-3. Daffodils need a well-drained soil.

when mowing lawns, or you will be mowing away next year's flowers. Cut foliage after it has browned and has a dead appearance, but not before then.

Daffodils are ideal for naturalizing in a landscape. Remember to fertilize them each spring to keep them blooming their best. Composted manure, superphosphate, or bone meal will be helpful. If you do not fertilize them, they will start to decline in vigor.

Certain varieties of daffodil, narcissus, and jonquils are good for indoor forcing and can be grown in containers for winter bloom.

Daffodils look lovely strewn along woodland paths and add a touch of sunshine to any spring garden. Flowers can be cut for indoor arrangements or given to friends and relatives in bouquets.

Dutch Hyacinth. The Dutch hyacinth (*Hyacinthus orientalis*) bears little resemblance to its ancient progenitors. Almost all cultivated hyacinths are fragrant. They come in many different colors. Some are single flowered; The double blossomed types are the most popular.

Hyacinths have attractive, swordlike leaves that offer an interesting feature even when not in bloom. They bear clusters of flowers on erect spikes.

Plant hyacinths in September or early fall. They favor a rich, humus soil that is well-drained. It is usually best to plant hyacinths to about 6 inches deep. The round side of the bulb should face the bottom.

Control weeds by hand removal. Be careful not to injure plants or pull up any hyacinths by mistake. Hyacinths favor full sun, but will grow under partial shade.

After blooming, allow the foliage to turn brown and wither. Do not remove the foliage until after it has withered, or you will damage next spring's crop of flowers.

Hyacinths look exceedingly well when set in formal beds. They are excellent for growing in containers and window boxes as well. Some types can be forced indoors for winter bloom. When planted outdoors, they are most effective when set in groups of the same color.

Garden Tulip: The garden tulip (*Tulipa* x *hybrida*) is a spring-flowering bulb related to the li-

ly. Although there are many species of tulips, the hybrids are the most sought after. One of the best known of the hybrids is the *Darwin*. These are usually May-flowering, although they bloom earlier in more southernly climes. These tulips are distinguished by their sturdy long stems and large, cup-shaped blossoms. There are many other excellent hybrids on the market today, and some are even bred for their fragrance.

Tulips have an interesting history. They first came to Holland from the Middle East in the early 1600s. They became very popular and there was wild speculation in the tulip trade. Enormous prices were paid for single bulbs. Many people lost a fortune in the tulip trade until the government stepped in to regulate it. Tulips are still a major Dutch industry and export.

Modern tulips are the result of hybrid crosses. They are far superior to their ancient relatives. Some varieties are even multicolored. They get their strange coloration from a virus that is transmitted by aphids. The virus does not damage the plant, it only affects the blossoms. These flowers should be set out in separate beds from your other tulips or they may affect them.

Tulips favor a well-drained soil. A sandy loam is best. They flourish most favorably when grown in full sun. Areas where water is likely to stand for long periods of time in the spring are a poor place to plant tulips (or any other bulbs for that matter). Tulips store up reserves in their bulbs. If rot organisms attack these bulbs, the plants literally starve to death.

Plant tulips in September or early fall—the same time you are planting your daffodils. Do not attempt to plant them after the ground has frozen. They will not develop roots under those conditions and may rot when warm weather returns.

Tulips are one of the first flowers to bloom in the spring. By planting several varieties, you can extend the tulip season for several weeks. Certain varieties are good for indoor forcing as winter blooms. Many people grow them, they are very practical, easy to row, and quite carefree. You will never regret planting tulips. They are most effective in groups of the same color and type.

Chapter 13

Peonies

The peony is one of the loveliest of the herbaceous garden perennials. Their flowers are among the largest and showiest blossoms of any of the hardy temperate-zone ornamentals. Peonies are available in many colors and types, depending upon your personal preference.

Peonies are also among the easiest of flowers to grow and, once established, are among the most rewarding of flowering shrubs (Fig. 13-1).

For people who live in areas where winters are severe, the *garden peony* is preferred to the *tree-type*. Tree peonies may not be sufficiently hardy in the far north, but garden peonies can be grown as far north as Alaska. Because they are such a hardy plant, they should be used in abundance.

Even when not in bloom, the green, shiny foliage of your peony will provide an attractive asset to your landscape. During the winter, the colder areas, your peony plants will disappear totally from view, to reappear the following spring.

Peonies are handy herbaceous perennials. They require little care and live through severe winters.

In most areas, the tops die back each winter (in parts of the South, this is not so).

Once peonies become established in a garden, they will bloom each spring for many years. They are excellent for cut flowers and as a bedding plant. They are also quite effective as single specimens. Most modern peonies are hybrids belonging to the genus *Paeonia*.

Plant peonies in clumps of three, in larger groups, or among other plants. They are most impressive flowers, whether planted singly or in groups. Peony leaves have a waxy appearance and are excellent background plantings for smaller ornamentals. Grow them with garden phlox for a contrast of foliage and time of bloom.

Peonies do not grow well in the deep south. Some varieties can grow there, but they seldom bloom because winter temperatures are not low enough for the flowers buds to develop properly.

TYPES OF PEONIES

Garden or herbaceous peonies have full bushy stems

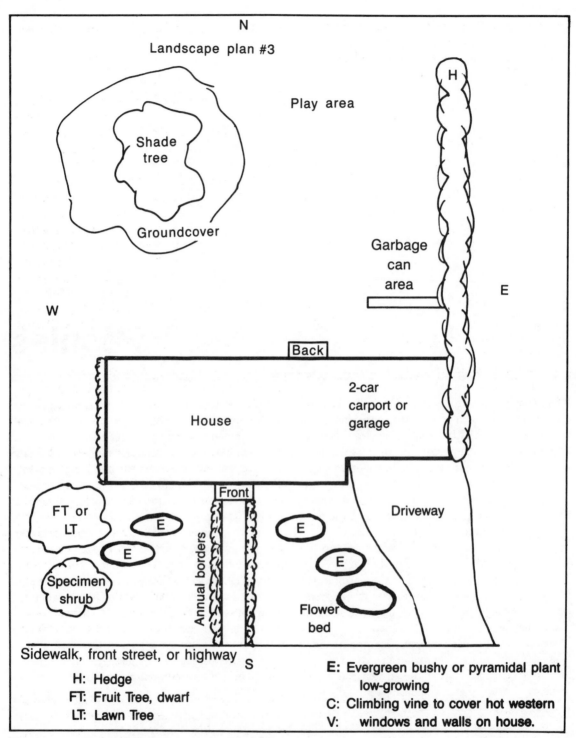

N

Landscape plan #3

Play area

H

Shade
tree

Groundcover

Garbage
can
area

E

W

Back

House

2-car
carport or
garage

FT or
LT

E

E

E

E

Front

Annual borders

Driveway

Specimen
shrub

Flower
bed

Sidewalk, front street, or highway

S

H: Hedge
FT: Fruit Tree, dwarf
LT: Lawn Tree

E: Evergreen bushy or pyramidal plant
     low-growing
C: Climbing vine to cover hot western
V: windows and walls on house.

Fig. 13-1. Landscape plan #3. Courtesy of Marion Michaels.

that grow from 2 to 4 feet tall. Tree peonies can reach eye level on woody stems with few branches. Tree peonies do not die back to the ground each winter. Their woody stems remain visible throughout the winter and develop new leaves as soon as spring arrives.

Garden Peonies

Garden peonies are grouped into five types according to the shape of the flower petals. These types are single, semidouble, double, Japanese, and anemone. Each type includes many varieties.

Single or *Chinese* peonies have a single row of broad petals that enclose a cluster of yellow, pollen-bering stamens. Other flower types have central petals in place of stamens. *Semidouble* types have broad central petals. *Double* peonies have central petals that are as wide as the outer ones. *Japanese* peonies have long, thin central petals. *Anemone* peonies have broad central petals.

Garden peonies bloom most often in May and June, depending upon where you live. They come in a wide array of colors. Some very popular selections are *Festiva Maxima,* which is white and blooms early; *Sarah Bernhardt,* which is rose-pink and blooms fairly late in the peony season; and *Mikado,* which bears red blossoms and blooms midseason.

Tree Peonies

Tree peonies are not as hardy as garden peonies. They do not form large trees, but rather miniature trees, rarely over 7 feet in height. They produce many flowers and come in a wide variety of colors. The centers of the flowers are usually yellow, pink, or red. Petals are mottled at the base.

The stems of tree peonies stay alive all winter. They do not die back to the ground each year as garden peonies do. They are less common than garden types and also much more expensive. Many, perhaps most, tree peonies are grown from grafts, where two plants are spliced together to become one plant. The top part of the graft is called a *scion,* and the bottom part is called a *rootstock,* or sometimes just *stock* for short.

There are several varieties of tree peonies available. A couple of the popular ones are *Flambeau* and *Argosy.*

CULTURE

Peonies grow from *tubers*—underground stems that store food produced by the leaves. New growth develops from buds, called *eyes.* These eyes appear on the tuber. A single tuber may have many eyes, but it must have at least three to thrive.

Plants grown from tubers with less than three eyes may take several years—five or more—to produce more than a few small flowers. Peonies that are grown from tubers with three to five eyes may very well flower the second year after planting.

Young shoots are bright red, succulent, and easily injured. The mature leaves are dark green with a shiny surface.

Peonies do not like to be disturbed once planted. This is because they have a *tap root system.* The tap root is a straight, thick, central root that extends further into the soil than all other roots. Once peonies are planted in an area, they should not be moved. Every time a plant is transplanted, it suffers from a certain amount of setback. Tap root plants suffer from greater setback because they do not have as many little feeder roots.

Hybrid tree peonies will produce larger flowers than regular tree peonies. Both hybrid and regular tree peonies have a serious fault, however, in that the stems are weak at the top.

Tree peonies can be grown from either seed or from grafts. When grown from seed, they usually take six or more years to reach blooming age. Plants grown from grafted tubers bloom years earlier and usually produce larger flowers with a greater variety of choice. Because grafting is a difficult process, most people will find it easier to purchase plants from nurseries, rather than attempt to graft their own.

Planting

Plant both garden and tree peonies in the early fall so that they will have time to become established in the soil before winter. Although fully grown peonies can be planted in the spring, it is not advisable to do so. They will be much harder to keep alive than plants set out in the fall, because they are already in a state of active growth when you plant them. Serious setback may occur, and the plant may die.

Peonies require well-drained soil. They do best in slightly raised beds that provide good drainage. Roots may rot in soils that hold water around them. Peonies favor a rich, fertile clay loam, although they will perform well in most good garden soils.

Peonies need full sunlight. They will grow under partial shade but should not be grown under heavy shade, because they may have difficulty flowering, or not flower at all. Peonies should be set out in areas where they will have some protection from strong winds. They need good air circulation to help control fungus diseases, but must be kept out of places where gusts of wind are likely to knock blossoms off the bush.

It is worthwhile to carefully prepare the area where you are going to set out your peony plants. Once planted, they will remain in place for many years. They will not grow well in poorly prepared beds. Spade organic matter, compost, peat moss, and well-rotted manure into the soil.

When setting out your peony, dig a hole to break up clumps of dirt. Plant garden peonies so that the eyes are not deeper than 2 inches below the soil surface. It is better to plant them too shallow than too deep. If they are planted too deep, they will never flower. Put a little soil around each tuber and water them in thoroughly. Press the soil down and add a little more dirt if tubers become uncovered during the first watering. Tamp the soil firmly. Water again to settle the tuber.

Plant a tree peony tuber with 4 or 5 inches of soil covering the graft. You will recognize the graft by the ridging on the stem and the different texture of the bark. Deep planting allows the grafted section to establish its own roots in the soil, which should make for a sturdier plant. Add soil and water to the planting hole the same as you do when planting a regular garden peony.

Mulch peonies in both summer and winter. A winter mulch will keep plants from being heaved out of the soil by the alternating freeze and thaw that occurs during so many winters. A summer mulch conserves moisture and will help to keep weeds down.

About two weeks before the ground freezes, cover the clumps with a mulch for winter. Three to 4 inches to straw or some other organic material is usually sufficient. Do not use plastic. It is not as effective as other mulches and, if applied too early, can prevent the normal root development that occurs during the fall. (Roots are still actively growing even after tops have gone dormant. Plastic mulches prevent water from reaching roots.)

In the spring, after all danger of frost is past, remove the winter mulch and place it into your compost pile. Spread a summer mulch of straw or peat moss 1 to 2 inches thick around the base of the peony. Do not touch the plant with the summer mulch and be sure that it is no thicker than 1 or 2 inches. In the fall, remove the summer mulch and place it in your compost pile before applying a new mulch for winter. Changing mulches helps to control insects and disease pests.

Control weeds by hand removal. Hand weeding is preferable to using tools. You can weed with a hoe, but be careful to not injure plant roots. An accidental whack at the tap root can destroy your peony.

Water peonies frequently after the tubers are set out in the fall until about two weeks before the ground freezes. Water on a regular weekly basis during the growing season.

Peonies are heavy feeders and respond well to spring applications of well-rotted manure. If you are using fresh manure, keep it at a distance so that it does not come in direct contact with the plant (about a foot away in a circle is a safe distance). Be extremely careful to not get manure or any other fertilizer on the stems, roots, or leaves of your peonies. The exception is that you can apply a liquid foliar fertilizer without danger of burning plant tissue.

Plants that are taken care of can be left in place for 10 to 15 years before they become too crowded. Never fertilize after August first. To do so would promote succulent growth and could result in winter injury.

Staking

Tall plants should be staked to keep them from being blown over in the wind. Special stakes are available at garden and hardware stores, but you can usually improvise with materials around your yard. Select stakes that will be 6 to 12 inches shorter than the grown plant.

Place plant stakes where they will be out of sight, behind the peonies. Never place them in the center of the clump. Loosely tie the plants to the stakes using wire covered with plastic or green paper. Do not use string or uncovered metal wire. String is unsightly, and bare metal wire breaks the stems.

Tie the plant, making a double loop of the wire with one loop around the plant, the other loop around the stake. Never loop the wire around both stake and plant. Otherwise, the peony may hang to one side and the wire may girdle the plant.

Flowers

Remove side buds on each stem as soon as they are visible. If you remove them later, it will adversely affect the appearance of the stump. Roll the buds out with your fingers to keep from scarring the stems. Leave the *terminal (end) bud* on each tip. This will develop into a large showy bloom.

A few flowers may appear two to three years after planting. When peonies are well cared for, blooms increase in number and quality with each season for several years.

Peonies will bloom earlier in the season if you plant them where they will have southern exposure, and place a protective screen around the beds. Covering the beds with snow will cause a later bloom.

If you want flowers for indoor arrangements, cut the stems when buds begin to unfold. Often, they can be kept in the refrigerator for one to three weeks. When cut flowers are handled, the stems may crack and fall over. Attach each stem to a florist's wire to support the flower.

Dividing Peonies

If peonies are planted in a favorable site, with good spacing and adequate care, they should grow well for several years without dividing.

Divide and replant peonies only when they become crowded, usually in 10 to 15 years. Because transplanting upsets the plants and retards flowering for several years, never divide a plant less than three years old.

Divide peonies in early fall. Carefully dig around and under clumps. Be extremely cautious so that you do not accidentally break off any roots, especially tap roots.

Wash off any soil that clings to the clumps and strip off the plant's leaves. Cut tubers apart with a sharp knife that you have sterilized with alcohol to avoid infecting the plant with any bacterial disease. Rubbing alcohol works well for this operation. Sterilize the knife after each cut.

Each section should have three to five eyes. Be sure to leave a tap root attached to each tuber that has eyes on it. As you cut, look for signs of disease. Cut out and burn any diseased portions. Replant tubers as soon as possible in a new area that has been prepared for them.

Failure to Bloom

Often peonies fail to bloom even though roots and tops may appear healthy. If your plants do not bloom, look for signs of disease and examine the growing site. Too much shade, dry soil, or poor drainage may prevent blooming.

Peonies will not bloom if they are planted too deep in the soil, or if plants are cut back in the fall before the foliage turns brown. Other causes of failure to bloom are lack of growing space because of tree or shrub roots and late spring frosts that kill flower buds.

DISEASES

Peony diseases disfigure foliage, reduce flowering, and rot roots. Buy disease-free plants from a reputable nursery, and plant resistant varieties if they are available. To prevent foliage diseases, water plants early in the day so that they have time to dry out before night falls.

Most fungus diseases can be controlled by use of a fungicide, like Bourdeaux mixture. There are other fungicides on the market, but Bourdeaux mixture is still one of the best and safest to handle. Apply Bourdeaux mixture when the disease is first noticed, with repeated applications every seven to ten days, and after rains. More frequent applications may be needed during damp weather.

Botrytis Blight. Botrytis blight is caused by a fungus that winters over in dead peony leaves, stems, and roots. The disease usually appears in midsummer and is most damaging in cool, rainy weather.

Early in spring, infected shoots turn gray-brown. Mature stems rot at ground level. A mass of gray-brown, feltlike spores appear on stems and leaves. Young buds dry up, and shoots and mature buds and flowers soften and rot. Infected petals drop onto healthy leaves and spread the disease.

To control, remove diseased parts as soon as you notice them. Pull out and burn badly infected plants. Cut plants to the ground after the foliage turns brown in the fall. Remove and burn dead material. Do not throw diseased plants or plant parts onto your compost pile. Spray with a solution of Bourdeaux mixture at weekly intervals during the growing season until the disease is gone.

Phytophthora Blight. Phytophthora blight is less common than botrytis blight, but it causes more damage to individual plants. Infection spreads down the stem from the buds. Stems dry up, turning dark brown and leathery. Plants rot at the ground line (crown of the plant).

To control, remove diseased plant parts as soon as you notice them. Pull out and burn badly infected plants. Cut plants to the ground in the fall. Remove and burn dead material. Spray with Bourdeaux mixture at weekly intervals during the growing season until all signs of the disease are gone.

Wilt. Wilt is caused by a fungus that lives in the water conducting tubes of the stems. Infected plants wither and die quickly.

To control, dig infected plants out immediately. Do not replant peonies in the same location for at least three years.

Leaf Blotch. Leaf blotch is a disease that usually does not occur until after plants bloom. The leaf blotch fungus winters over in dead plants. Infected plants have small red or reddish-brown spots on stems, leaves, and flowers. The spots on the leaves later change to purplish-brown blotches on the upper surfaces. Dull brown blotches appear on the lower surfaces.

To control, cut plants to the ground in fall. Remove diseased leaves as they appear in spring and summer. Spray plants with Bourdeaux mixture at weekly intervals during the growing season, until the disease is no longer evident.

Crown and Stem Rots. Crown rot is caused by an unidentified fungus that rots the area where roots join stems. Sometimes small circular spots appear on roots of infected plants.

Two *stem rot* diseases, each caused by a fungus, attack peonies. The diseases rot shoots and full-grown stems. They cause white molds on the surfaces of stems and leaves. Both fungi produce *sclerotia* (small brown granules about the size of a mustard seed). Sclerotia winter over in stems or on roots. They reinfect new shoots in the spring.

To control, dig in infected plants. Cut away decayed areas. Burn badly damaged plants. Replant peonies in a different spot in your garden. If you want to put plants in the same place, remove the soil and replace it with new soil before so doing.

If you use manure in your peony bed, mix it in thoroughly with the soil. Do not use it on top of crowns. Used this way, manure helps to foster crown rot organisms.

Lemoine Disease. Lemoine disease is a root ailment. Its cause is not known. Infected plants do not produce flowers, shoots are weak, small knobby swellings appear on the small roots, and soft yellow areas appear on the large roots.

To control, dig up and burn infected plants.

Root Knot. Root knot, which is sometimes called *root gall,* is caused by *nematodes.* These tiny worms feed on the roots and damage them. They are most injurious where winters are mild, and where the growing season is warm and the soil light.

Nematode-infected plants lack vigor, producing only a few small flowers. Stems are short and thin, leaves are light green, large roots become swollen and stubby, and small roots develop knobby outgrowths.

To control, dig out and burn heavily infected plants. If possible, plant lawn grass on infected soil and let it grown for two years before you replant peonies there.

Virus Diseases. *Mosaic* is the most common virus disease of peonies, but it does not cause much injury to the plants. Yellowish blotches and rings appear on the leaves.

Crown elongation, another virus disease, causes many long-branched crowns to develop from the tubers. Plants develop many slender, weak shoots. These dwarf shoots produce no flower buds.

Leaf curl virus has a dwarfing effect upon plants. Leaves grow close together on the stem and curl up. Leaf surfaces crinkle, and no flower buds form. To control all virus disease, dig up and burn infected plants. Purchase only virus-free plants from the nursery.

INSECTS

Insects seldom attack peonies. Peonies are one of the few flowers that have only a very limited insect pest problem. This, in itself, is a good reason to grow this flower. Those most likely to cause damage are the rose chafer, the Japanese beetle, and flower thrips.

Rose Chafer. This small tan or gray beetle feeds upon the flowers. Control by picking these bugs off by hand (wearing gloves is advised for the fastidious) and dropping them into a bucket of kerosene.

Japanese Beetle. Japanese beetles, if you have them, will devastate your peony flowers and quickly destroy their aesthetic value. Control by biological means. The adult beetles can be controlled with commercially available traps. These Japanese beetle traps use an insect pheromone (sex lure) and floral lure to entice the beetles into the trap, where they are held. The larvae of young Japanese beetles can be controlled by spreading milky-spore bacteria over the areas where the beetles are concentrated.

Flower Thrips. Flower thrips are an easy-to-control nuisance. Mostly, they disfigure the flower blossoms by feeding upon the petals. They can be controlled by spraying plants with a solution of water and shavings from a bar of mild soap, such as Ivory.

Chapter 14

Garden Perennials

Wouldn't it be fabulous if a riot of beautiful flowers would just magically spring up in your yard every year? By planting perennials, you can make that magic happen! Although most perennials are easy to grow, most are not maintenance-free, however, and some species are hardier than others. Every few years, a perennial flower bed may have to be renewed and clumps broken up to eliminate overcrowded conditions. This work is minimal when compared to all the labor that goes into growing annuals.

Certain perennials have an *everblooming habit;* an example is the butter daisy *(coreopsis)*, which blooms all summer. Other perennials, such as mums, are fall bloomers. They flower during the late summer and fall, when few other plants are in bloom.

Other perennials bloom for only a few short weeks during the summer. When growing perennials with a limited season of bloom, you may wish to arrange your flower plantings to schedule the sequence of blossom times. That way, when one flower is through blooming for the year, another one starts,

and you will always have something in blossom in your yard.

Many people like to naturalize perennials. They simply scatter them about the yard, usually in small groups. When they come up, they look as though they were placed there by nature. Of course, you can always grow them in formal beds as well.

There is labor involved in growing perennials. Some species require more work than others to get them to grow successfully. Other species will be almost carefree, while still others may require a little pampering. By learning a few simple rules for their culture, you will be able to master the art of growing perennials.

Baby's Breath. Baby's breath *(Gypsophila paniculata)* is an easy-to-grow perennial. It should be planted in a sunny location, because it will not tolerate heavy shade. It is a large plan that will take up quite a bit of space in your garden. There are dwarf varieties available.

The flowers on the baby's breath plant come in single- and double-blossomed varieties. There is good reason why the double-flowered are favored; the flower size is very small and individual flowers are relatively insignificant. When clustered with other flowers, however, the plant has an airy, cloudlike look when in full bloom. It is for this gracious quality that it is cultivated. Flower sprays are also cut for indoor arrangements.

Baby's breaths are somewhat fussy plants. They prefer an alkaline soil. It is usually best to add garden lime to your planting site. Plants will not tolerate acid soil conditions. An application of lime each spring helps to keep the soil "sweet," the way that baby's breaths like it.

These plants should be set out in a permanent location where they will not be disturbed. They need a well-drained soil. Do not plant baby's breath too close to other plants, because as all but the dwarfs grow quite large and will crowd out your other shrubs. Give them plenty of room in which to grow.

A winter mulch is desirable for protecting the plants in northern climates. Do not apply the mulch until about two weeks before the ground freezes. Some pruning of the plants may be desired to keep them within limits and to control size.

Baby's breath should be used for specimen planting only. They grow too large to plant more than one, unless you are planting only dwarf, in which case, you could plant more. There are trailing types available that are suitable for rock gardens and container plantings.

The cut flowers are collected in sprays (small branches covered with flowers). They are useful for flower arrangements.

Some of the best cultivars of the *paniculata* species are *Snowflake*, which has white, double blossoms and grows to 4 feet in height and about the same in width; *Pink Star*, which bears pink blossoms; and *Bristol Fairy*, the most widely planted cultivar: it is large with double, white blossoms.

Bleeding Heart. The bleeding heart (*Dicentra spectabilis*) has pink, heart-shaped flowers in early summer that form panicles along the branches. The branches have a tendency to arch under the heavy flower load. It favors semishady areas of the yard.

Bleeding hearts form clumps about 2 1/2 feet tall and 3 feet wide. The plants require fertile soil. It is best to add organic matter, such as peak moss, to the soil when planting.

There is one landscape problem that occurs with this plant. It dies down to the ground during the summer. For this reason, bleeding hearts must not be planted *en masse,* or there will be an empty spot in your landscape until next year when they come back up again.

Select a choice location for your bleeding heart. A partially shaded area is best. Avoid either full sun or heavy shade. Be sure that your plants receive plenty of moisture, especially when they are in bloom. Bleeding hearts are not especially heavy feeders, but, like all plants, they respond favorably to fertilizer. A dose of composted cow manure in the spring is usually sufficient. If you use fresh manure, be careful to not place it too close to your plant.

Plant bleeding hearts in the spring. They should be set out in a permanent location where they will not be disturbed. Once they are located in an area, they should not be dug up and moved to another location.

The bleeding heart is ideal as a single specimen. It should not be planted in groups, or during the hot summer months, your landscape will look empty when they die down. Bleeding hearts are not suitable for container plantings for the same summer-dieback reason.

Coreopsis. If you are an extremely busy person and have very little time to care for your home landscape, then you may wish to consider planting this beautiful perennial. Coreopsis are easy to care for and will withstand neglect that would result in the failure of other flowers. Coreopsis thrive and flourish, even when totally ignored! It is a hardy perennial with almost no insect or disease problems, and, best of all, they bloom all summer long!

The coreopsis genus contains both annual and perennial species. Several species grow wild throughout the United States. The annual species is called, *Calliopsis* (Fig. 14-1).

English Violets. English violets (*Viola odorata*) are low-growing plants that add color and interest to those shady areas ion your lawn or

Fig. 14-1. Sunray coreopsis. Courtesy W. Atlee Burpee Co.

backyard. Violets come in many colors besides violet. They are quite hardy and fairly easy to grow.

Violets prefer filtered shade and rich, moist soil. Add plenty of peat moss to the soil when planting. Avoid areas where the shade is too dense, or your violets may not flower freely or at all.

English violets are very easy to maintain. It is important that they be planted on well-drained soil. It should not be allowed to dry out, however. The soil should be moist, not wet, to the touch.

Plants grow to less than a foot under most circumstances, yet have large blooms of an inch or more across. Best of all, violets tend to be everblooming. The English violets are among the best, as they are sweetly scented and quite hardy.

Violets are most impressive planted *en masse*. They are low growers and make ideal border plants when set along garden paths. They can be used in formal beds as well. Violets naturalize quite readily. They can also be planted in window boxes and other containers. These are an easy-care perennial for the home landscape.

Some of the best cultivars are; *Royal Robe*, which

has the traditional violet-purple flowers; *Red Charm*, with flowers of rose-red; and *White Czar*, which has white flowers for those dark areas where white blossoms will brighten up the place.

Garden Phlox: The garden phlox (*Phlox decussata)* requires a fertile, well-drained soil. It is a high-maintenance plant and will require much time and labor. Garden phloxes grow as high as 4 feet, but the most desirable cultivars are those in the 2 foot range. Each shoot produced has its own cluster of flowers. Although the individual flower is very small and almost insignificant, when grouped in this manner, they produce a spectacular effect.

Garden phlox can be planted in light shade or full sun. If set out in full sun, be sure to keep the plant well-watered. During dry periods, the plant will need to be watered even when in partial shade. Phlox are very sensitive to drought and require a plentiful supply of moisture, especially when they are in full bloom.

Watering and weeding will be among the main chores when growing phlox. They also have other problems: phlox are frequently attacked by mildew.

This can be controlled with applications of bourdeaux mixture (a copper-sulfate fungicide). Red spiders may also become a nuisance. Bordeaux mixture will help to reduce their population as well as that of mildew.

Phlox are a formal plant and belong exclusively in formal settings. They are excellent for beds, borders, and to line walks. They are best when grown in groups. A single specimen planted alone is not especially attractive by itself and requires more effort than it's worth.

Phlox come in many colors. Usually they are most effective when planted in groups of the same color.

Geraniums. There is some confusion about geraniums because there are two genuses of plants that are called "geraniums." One is the true geranium. The other uses the common name of geranium because their flowers resemble the real geranium flowers. They actually belong to the genus *Pelrgonium,* which is not relation to real geraniums. (Pelargonium are the house plant "geraniums" so often grown on windowsills.)

True geraniums are a carefree perennial. Most are drought-resistant, and some species produce flowers all summer long. Plants grow up to 1 1/2 feet tall and form a mound. There are dwarfs available. Best of all, just a few short weeks after setting out the plants, you will have flowers.

Geraniums prefer full sun, but will flower in partial shade. They should not be planted under heavy shade. The size and color of the flowers depend upon the species. One of the best is *Geranium endressii* var. *wargrave pink*. This cultivar is an everbloomer and will bear vivid, pink flowers all summer long.

Geraniums do not require much care. They are not especially finicky about soil, as long as it is well-drained. This is truly a "worry-free" perennial that will survive much neglect, some abuse, and still bear flowers!

Formal flower beds, borders, or sunny garden paths are all suitable areas for geraniums. Because they are fairly low-growing, they should not be hidden behind other plans if set out in mixed flower beds.

Geum. Geum (*Geum reptans)* has vivid flowers in shades of scarlet and orange. It favors full sun and should not be planted in shady area. Geum produces its biggest display of flowers in early summer, but it continues to bloom until fall frosts.

Geums like a rich, humus soil. Add plenty of peat moss to the planting site. Because it is an everbloomer, it should be fertilized for best flower production.

Plant only on well-drained soil. It does not tolerate dry soil very well. Keep the ground moist to the touch. A hardy perennial that requires little care, geums need to be watered regularly and especially during periods of dry weather.

These plants are excellent for naturalizing. They produce a bright show of color that will set sunny areas of the yard ablaze when in flower. They are best planted in groups, although it will not be ignored if used as a single specimen.

Geums can be used as a cut flower. Species that have a trailing growth habit can be useful on problem areas, provided they receive full sun. Check with your nursery to see what types they offer.

Helenium. A good border plant, Helenium (*Helenium autumnale*) can grow up to 6 feet tall. It comes in a variety of colors; the red and bronze hues are the most popular. There are dwarfs available; these tend to grow just under 3 feet and are best for most people, unless you happen to want a 6-foot flower.

Heleniums are fall bloomers with daisylike flowers that begin to open up in late summer. Heleniums require staking to support their tall stems. They must be protected from heavy winds, rain, hail, and pets. They are an easy-care perennial that requires little maintenance.

Plant in full sun, and avoid shady areas. Heleniums need a well-drained soil. They are not heavy feeders, but, as with all plants, they respond well to fertilizer. Apply composted manure in the spring. Be sure to use only well-rotted manure; if you use fresh manure, do not touch the plants with it.

Heleniums are most useful in borders. The tall varieties are good background plants. Small varieties can be set in front of them.

The tall varieties are not practical for naturalizing, as they need to be staked. The dwarfs can be naturalized, provided they are placed in a sunny area. Grow them in groups for best effect; single specimens are not practical.

Missouri Primrose. Although not related to the many other plants that are called primroses, the Missouri primrose (*Oenothera missouriensis*) is among the easiest plants to grow. This species is in bloom during the late afternoon and evening. They are low-growing plants with a trailing habit, rarely exceeding a foot in height. This is an excellent flower for easy-maintenance landscapes.

If a shrub form is desired, plant another species called the *Sundrop (Oenothera tetragona)*. These are somewhat similar to the Missouri primrose, except for growth habit. Sundrops form a small mound about 2 feet in height. Both species produce huge saucer-shaped flowers of buttercup yellow. (There are also varieties available that have deeper golden tones.) They are everbloomers, in blossom from early summer to fall. Some species are more free-flowering than others.

Plant in full sun. Do not plant in shady areas. It grows well on light, sandy soil. It will not tolerate poorly drained soils.

These plants can take a great deal of neglect and still bear beautiful flowers. They are very hardy. If you do not have too much time to put into your landscape, this is a very practical flower for you. You can plant it and forget about it.

The Missouri primrose is best suited for those areas where a trailing plant is required. It can cover up soil banks and problem areas of a lawn, and it can also be grown in containers for a "hanging garden" effect.

Sundrops are best suited as border plants. They may be used as single specimens or as entry plantings. These plants naturalize very well into the landscape. Both species really deserve to be planted much more often than they are. They have no major insect or disease problems.

Oriental Poppies. The oriental poppy is a perennial species of poppy that comes up year after year. It produces the largest blooms of all the poppy plants and is quite hardy. *Papaver orientalis* is a tall flower, sometimes reaching 3 feet or higher. It depends upon the cultivar; dwarfs that grow only 2 feet tall are available. Oriental poppies come in many colors, all bright and vibrant.

Plants usually go dormant by midsummer and disappear into the garden until the next year. Oriental poppies spread from root clumps.

Oriental poppies favor a sandy loam soil. They need full sunlight and should never be planted in the shade. The time to transplant poppies is during the late summer or early fall, while the plants are dormant. Be sure to cover transplants with mulch the first winter. It is actually a good practice to cover plants with mulch every winter to protect them from fluctuating temperatures that can heave them out of the soil.

Control weeds and tall grasses so they do not shade young plants. A yearly application of manure in the spring will be beneficial. Do not place fresh manure too close to the plants or it may burn them.

Although they can be grown from seed, poppies are best purchased as transplants.

Oriental poppies are most effective when planted in groups of the same color and size. They can be naturalized into your landscape or grown in formal planting beds. The plants will go dormant during the middle of summer and can leave a flower bed looking quite empty, so you may wish to avoid planting them in formal flower beds. You should at least mix in some plants that will take up the slack when your poppies are dormant.

Pyrethrum. The *painted daisy*, or *pyrethrum*, has the unique ability among plants to produce its own very powerful insecticide. For this reason, if none other, they are a must for your perennial garden. They will help to keep insects away from your other prize flowers as well (Figs. 14-2 and 14-3).

Painted daisies (*Chrysanthemum coccineum*) are among the easiest flowers to grow. They bear daisylike flowers that are in bloom throughout much of the summer. They grow to about 2 feet tall. Painted daisies come in many shades, provided exciting colors to your yard. Some flowers have semidouble blossoms.

These plants require full sunlight to perform their best. Painted daisies should not be planted in

Fig. 14-2. Gloriosa daisy. Courtesy W. Atlee Burpee Co.

Painted daisies are not as popular as they deserve to be considering their easy culture and attractiveness. If you want to spend more time in your hammock, or pursuing your other interests, then these flowers are ideal. This is an excellent flower for beginners, because it is almost foolproof.

Like most perennials, painted daisies are available as potted transplants. This is quicker and easier than growing them from seed.

This flower is a perennial plant that stays in bloom for a long time. It holds up well as a cut flower. In addition, the extract from this amazing flower is used for organic insecticides, which have an almost instant effect upon harmful insects. A combination like this can hardly be beaten!

Shasta Daisies. Most people grow shasta daisies because of their beauty as cut flowers. *Chrysanthe maximum* is a member of the Chrysan-

Fig. 14-3. Painted daisies. Courtesy Denver Water Department, Xeriscape Conservation Garden.

heavily shaded areas. They like a good loam soil. Add organic matter, such as peat moss, to the planting site.

Painted daisies multiply rapidly and should be divided every three years. This is not as much work as it may sound. It also will enable you to spread these plants around your yard or give a few away to envious friends and neighbors.

Painted daisies require practically no care. They should, of course, be watered during droughts. Plants respond well to fertilizer.

Painted daisies are ideal for naturalizing. They also make excellent cut flowers for indoor arrangements. Plant them in groups for their best effect, although they are very colorful and will be noticed even when they stand alone. They are useful in borders and for formal flower beds. This is a very practical flower that you will want to use lavishly in your landscape plan.

themum family. They produce excellent cut flowers and are available with single or semidouble blossoms. The flowers are true daisy form and usually appear in varying hues of white. The exception is the cultivar *Cobham's Gold*, which is a rich, creamy yellow (Fig. 14-4).

The shasta daisy is a tender perennial with the same cultural requirements as chrysanthemums. Unlike mums, shasta daisies prefer partial shade and should not be planted in full sun. They like a moist, humus soil, and they must be watered during dry spells. They are not an easy-to-grow flower and require a certain amount of attention for best results. This is not a flower you will be able to neglect.

Shasta daisies are suited to several purposes in the home garden. Because they make such an excellent cut flower for indoor arrangements, many people grow them solely for that purpose, but they are also quite decorative in the garden. They should be grown in groups in their own bed for easier maintenance and best effect.

Shastas can be set in semishady spots where other flowers may not perform. Being white, or near-white, they will not provide sufficient contrast against a white house.

Swamp Rose. The swamp rose (mallow hibiscus) thrives in areas that may be too wet for other flowering shrubs. *Hibiscus moscheutos* has large, showy flowers, sometimes up to 12 inches across when open. They come in many shades. They are single-blossomed with a vague resemblance to the wild rose, except that the size of their blooms surpasses any others. Plants grow up to 8 feet tall and bloom in midsummer. Dwarfs are available.

Hybrid swamp roses that are a mixture of species are available. They are one of the largest-flowered of all perennials.

This is an ideal plant for people who have a high water table or drainage problems. Swamp roses love such damp sites.

They prefer rich, moist loam soil. Add plenty of peat moss when planting. They like to have sun for most of the day and, for best flowering, should not be planted under heavy shade. Once planted, do not disturb them.

Swamp roses have only one major problem: they are subject to attack by Japanese beetles. These beetles can destroy the beauty of the blossoms in short order. You will need to control these pests, if they are a problem in your area.

Swamp roses are easy to grow and just need to be kept well-watered so that the soil underneath them does not dry out. Swamp roses are best planted in wet spots. Trim trees to allow sunlight to filter through, where necessary. The 3 foot dwarfs are probably the most impressive. Even though the plant is dwarf size, the flowers are not. They add a real splash of color to the landscape.

Sweet Pea. Perennial sweet pea flowers come in shades of red, pink, or white and are very fragrant. They bloom early in the summer. The vines of *Lathyrus latifolus* grow to 6 feet in length. The plants need to be staked to grow upright, otherwise they will tend to sprawl over an area. Perennial sweet peas come up year after year in a location and are very hardy (Figs. 14-5 and 14-6).

Sweet peas can be grown from transplants or started from seed. If started from seed early, they will bloom the very first year. To get blooms in a hurry, start seeds indoors in pots about 45 days before setting them outside in their permanent location. Sweet peas take about 20 days to germinate.

Sweet peas can also be sown directly in the garden in late spring. For best results, follow the planting instructions that are written on the seed packet.

Sweet peas require full sun. They should not be planted in shady locations, because it may hinder flowering, and they may not even flower at all. They are very vigorous growers and will soon take over an area. Unsightly weeds and tall grasses should be controlled around sweet peas. Cut the weeds with grass shears.

Water plants on a weekly basis; more often during dry weather and when the plant is in full bloom. Water around the base of the plant so you do not destroy flowers.

There are many uses for sweet peas. They are an excellent cut flower, adding beauty and fragrance to any room in your house. They can be trained as a vine on a trellis or porch and are useful for screen-

Fig. 14-4. Alaska Shasta daisy. Courtesy W. Atlee Burpee Co.

Fig. 14-5. Perennial sweetpea. Courtesy W. Atlee Burpee Co.

Fig. 14-6. Perennial sweetpea. Courtesy W. Atlee Burpee Co.

ing out unpleasant views when trained to a chain-link or other fence.

Violas. Violas, or Johnny jump-ups, as they are sometimes called, are quite hardy and come up without much care. They are easy to maintain. *Viola cornuta* is a perennial cousin to the pansy. They are also related to the English violet. Although they have a slightly different growth habit, they are not as fragrant.

Violas grow in clumps, usually under 1 foot tall and about a 1 1/2 foot wide. These plants grow best under filtered shade. They should not be planted in full sun. Violas are everbloomers and will blossom all summer long. This makes them an excellent choice to add color to the drab, slightly shady areas of your backyard. And color they have! They come in a wide range of hues from purple to apricot.

Plant in a well-drained soil. Violas prefer a woodsy soil, rich in humus. Add peat moss to the planting site. The soil underneath the plants should not be allowed to dry out. It must not be wet, but should feel moist to the touch.

Violas can be used in the same manner as English violets. They are most effective when planted in groups of the same color.

Some of the best cultivars are *Chantreyland*, which has apricot blossoms—a rare and exciting color; *Jersey Gem*, which produces blooms of the traditional violet color; and *Lutea Splendens*, which are a bright, golden-yellow. There are other colors available. Check with your nursery to find the ones that best fit into your landscape plan.

Chapter 15

Cut-Flower Perennials

Most of your landscaping will concern itself with how plants look in your yard, but some plants present both a pleasing appearance outside and offer sufficient blooms of a type suitable for cut flowers for your dining room table, for a sick friend, for a wedding or anniversary party, and perhaps even to sell. (June is traditionally a popular month for weddings because of the availability of cut flowers.)

Naturally, you would like to think there will always be abundant water for all your landscaping needs. In the world of reality, however, this is not always the case. If you see that your beautiful rosebush is dry, and you do not have water for it, this is a splendid time to make use of cut flowers for the home and to take to your friends. Rather than dismally watching your flowers wither on the vine, cut them and use them for indoor arrangements. The flowers will come to life and produce a beautiful display that can be enjoyed by all who see them. Or, if you or your children have a roadside stand, you can sell the beauties to passersby.

As for your yard, do not let your plants die from drought. Even when there's a ban on lawn sprinkling, as occurs in summer in many cities, there's likely to be no law against your emptying your shampoo water near your favorite plants. Nor letting toddlers splash around in a rubber pool that you later empty on your flower bed. Even these "little dabs" of water will help plants to survive.

By removing blossoms for cut flowers use for yourself and friends, you are also helping the plant to survive drought. Less energy is going into flower production and more water can be conserved to help maintain the plant's vital functions. Of course, water conservation is not the only reason for cutting flowers, but it is a very practical one.

Some flowers are grown specifically for the purpose of using them as cut flowers. It is best, when growing these flowers, to plant several and not take all of them for cut flowers, unless very dry weather demands it. By leaving some flowers, you will not disrupt the beauty that they can add to your landscape.

CHRYSANTHEMUMS

For cut flowers galore during the late summer and

early fall, plant the chrysanthemum—usually called "mums" for short. Few plants are as showy or as hardy.

Mums come in a variety of colors, both bold and pastel. Flowers may be shades of red, yellow, orange, bronze, pink, or white. They vary in size, from clusters of small, round pompons to individual decorative blossoms 4 inches across or more. Because of their long-lasting flowers, mums are popular in indoor arrangements as well as in gardens.

Although most North Americans consider the mum a joyous flower, often wearing them in wedding corsages, some cultures do not. In Mexico, the mum is a flower of mourning and is used extensively in funerals. It is probably not a good idea to give any Mexican friends a bouquet of mums. Unless they are familiar with customs in these United States, they may think something terrible has happened.

CULTURE

Chrysanthemums bloom during that period of late summer and early fall when few other flowers are in blossom. Because they have so little competition, and because they are so versatile and decorative, they are almost a "must" for the home landscape. Usually, mums are planted in groups. They can also be planted as single specimens, and almost every garden setting is suitable for mums.

The plants are relatively easy to grow throughout most of the United States. Even when neglected, they often produce flowers, but such mums are likely to have weak branches, yellowish leaves, and only a few small flowers. When they are properly tended, they will be the glory of your late summer and fall garden. You will not regret a generous use of mums in your landscape plans. This is especially true for people who do not live in the south or in California, where they have other plants always in bloom.

Hardy varieties of mums produce underground shoots called *stolons*. These stolons enable the mums to persist year after year without replanting. Usually, hardy varieties thrive in the home garden.

Commercial florists grow nonhardy mums in greenhouses. Garden mums can be just as attractive as those offered by commercial florists.

Nonhardy mums produce very few stolons or none. They will not persist from year to year. They are usually winter-killed by the alternate freezing and thawing of the soil, or they bloom so late in the season that their blossoms are killed by frosts. You can grow some of the nonhardy types in your garden if you give them winter protection, but it is best to grow the hardy types.

Planting

Chrysanthemums should be planted in fertile, well-drained soil. They prefer full sun and should not be set out under heavy shade. If you buy packaged mums in the fall, plant them early enough for the roots to become established before winter (about six weeks). If planting in the spring, wait until after killing frosts have ended before you set them out.

Prepare your planting site a couple of weeks before setting the plants out. Dig and loosen the soil to a depth of about 6 inches, breaking up all clumps. Spade organic matter—peat moss, compost, or well-rotted manure—into the soil. Be sure to use only well-rotted manure, because fresh manure can injure the young transplants. Just before planting mums, respade the soil bed to kill any weeds that may have germinated.

Dig a hole that is big enough to accommodate the mum plant or cutting. After it is set in, firm soil around roots to prevent air pockets from forming between the roots and soil. Water thoroughly to settle the plant. If necessary, add more soil where the water washed any away so that no roots are exposed.

Plant low-growing bushy varieties 2 to 2 1/2 feet apart; plant other mums 1 to 1 1/2 feet apart.

Place a coarse mulch (1 or 2 inches of straw) on soil around the plants. If straw is not available, you may use evergreen boughs as a substitute. Use at lease an extra inch of mulch if you are planting in the fall.

Care

In most areas, at least in the eastern half of the

United States, rainfall will provide mums with enough water. In times of drought, or if their leaves start to yellow, they should be watered. Do not let mums wilt.

Mums respond well to fertilizer; apply composted cow manure in spring and then again later in the summer. Do not fertilize plants after August first, or it may make them more susceptible to winter injury.

If you use chemical fertilizers, a balanced water-soluble formula is best. Such fertilizers feed the foliage as well as the roots and are absorbed almost immediately. They can quickly correct any nutritional deficiencies that exist.

Stake tall or weak plants to support them. Each branch of large-flowered varieties needs support. If heavy, pounding rains are common, protect your large-flowered mums with a frame covered with cheesecloth.

Pinching and Disbudding

When small-flowered varieties (cushion mums) are 6 to 8 inches high, pinch off the light green growing tips to encourage branching. Unless the growing tips are pinched, the plants may develop tall, weak stems that produce only a few flowers. Pinching encourages new branches to develop along the stems. Pinch all shoots every two weeks until June 10 for early varieties, and July first, for late varieties. Flowers may not form if you continue to pinch later than these dates.

Your nursery should give you instructions for the care of your variety of chrysanthemums with your order. If they do not provide this information, and you are uncertain whether your mums are early or late bloomers, call the nursery and ask.

To encourage the size of bloom on large-flowered mums, a practice known as *disbudding* is used. The purpose is to concentrate growth in a few select flowers by taking off side buds. To do this, pinch off the growing tips when plants are 5 to 6 inches high. New shoots will develop along the stem. Break off all but two or three of these new shoots. Let the remaining shoots grow into branches. Every two weeks, remove all side shoots that grow from these branches. When flowerbuds show, remove all except those on the top 3 inches of the branch.

As these top buds develop, notice the first or *crown* bud. When you are assured it is healthy and well-developed, pinch off all other buds. Do this by carefully bending the stem of the branch downward and sideward with your thumb. The stem should pop off without much effort at the point where the stem joins the branch.

If the crown bud is injured or gives the appearance that it may not develop or may develop deformed, pinch it off. Select the second flower bud from the tip. Take care to not damage or break off the flower bud that is left. No new flower buds will develop after you have taken the others off.

Continue to remove side branches until flowering time. *Note*: this practice is for use only with large-flowered varieties. Disbudding small-flowered varieties will not make them have larger flowers.

When plant tops die after blooming, cut them to the ground. Clean up fallen leaves. Put down a mulch to protect new stolons from the winter months ahead.

Selecting Plants

Mums are sold in the spring as *cuttings*; in spring and fall as *packaged plants*; and year-round as *potted plants*.

Well-rooted cuttings establish themselves quickly. They bloom the same year they are planted.

Packaged plants are larger than cuttings. They bloom at the normal time for the individual variety. If you do not want to spend time to grow the cutting, purchase packaged plants with well-developed buds.

It is best to buy only the hardy garden varieties for landscape purposes. Many of the potted chrysanthemums that florists sell are not sufficiently winter hardy and may die during the first winter outdoors.

Chrysanthemums are among the most versatile of the herbaceous flowering perennials. There is a type of every preference, garden design, and purpose. Mums are categorized according to their size, shape, and flower-type.

Cushion mums are dwarfs that form a mound

or "cushion." They are low bushy plants that rarely exceed 3 feet in height; some are smaller. Most cushion mums are early flowering. Nearly all varieties are hardy. Check with your nursery to select the ones you will be using in your landscape.

Pompon mums have small stiff stems and almost globular flowers. They are usually not as hardy as the cushion mums, but some varieties are quite hardy.

Anemone mums resemble the anemone or Grecian windflower, as it is commonly called. Nearly all varieties are hardy. The petals of the crest are usually deeper colored than the other mums.

Single mums are characterized by their daisylike flowers. They have one to five rows of long petals radiating from a central eye; nearly all varieties are hardy.

Decorative mums have *incurved* flowers (close, regular petals curving toward the flower center); incurving (loose, irregular petals curving toward the flower center); or reflexed (all petals curving away from the flower center). There are many hardy varieties.

Spoon mums offer flowers with spoon-shaped petals. Some varieties are hardy. Check with your nursery to see if the varieties they offer will be hardy in your area.

Spider mums have long tubular petals with hooked ends. They give the appearance of a spider's legs. There are very few hardy varieties among this species. You will probably not find them as attractive as other mums.

Quill mums have long straight petals that are somewhat tubular. There are few hardy varieties.

Single, pompon, cushion, and anemone mums are normally considered *small flowered*. Usually they are varieties selected to bloom before killing frosts in the fall. Mums that have blossoms over 3 inches in diameter are *large flowered*. Most large-flowered types are grown under greenhouse conditions.

GARDEN MUMS

Chrysanthemum morifolium, or garden mums require more attention than many of the other flowering perennials. They are heavy feeders and should be supplied with plenty of fertilizer, especially during the early part of the growing season. Most will require some winter protection. (Even hardy varieties should be mulched each winter.) They should be protected from both extremely dry weather and heavy rains—especially the large-flowered varieties.

DISEASES

Chrysanthemums are subject to attack by many diseases. Although these diseases rarely kill, they damage and often disfigure plants. There are several practical ways to prevent disease problems:

☐ Do not plant in wet, shady places.

☐ Do not crowd plants. Give them plenty of room for good air circulation.

☐ Water early in the day so that leaves can dry out before nightfall. Fungi thrive on wet leaves.

☐ Stake tall plants to keep their branches off the ground.

☐ Remove and burn dead or diseased leaves, stems, and flowers.

☐ If mildews are a problem in your area, treat the plants to a solution of a copper-sulfate fungicide (such as Bourdeaux mixture) on a weekly basis and after heavy rains. Be sure to spray the undersides of leaves, too. Stop treatment when flower buds show color.

If your mums do not look right, they may have a disease. Disfigured leaves, wilting, or stunting are all indicative of mum sickness and/or insect-pest problems. Insects usually serve as *vectors*—transmitters of disease.

Mildew causes a grayish-white powdery patches to appear on leaves. Later, leaves turn yellow and wither. Control this disorder by weekly applications of Bourdeaux mixture. Also apply this fungicide after heavy rains. Stop treatment when the flower buds show color.

Rust causes small brown blisters to appear on the undersides of leaves. Areas around the blisters turn light green, and leaves curl and die. Control with Bourdeaux mixture.

Bud rot causes growing tips and buds to soften and turn brown. Affected buds do not open. Control with Bourdeaux mixture.

Septoria leaf spot causes leaves to turn brown, yellow, or reddish. Then black spots develop. Infection starts at the bottom of the plant and spreads upward. Control by spraying with Bourdeaux mixture.

Verticillium wilt is caused by a soil fungus. Diseased plants usually wilt, turn brown, become stunted, and produce poor flowers. In extreme cases, they die. If the plants do not wilt, the areas between the leaf veins turn yellow. To control this disease, do not plant chrysanthemums in areas where *solanaceous* crops have been growing—that is tomatoes, potatoes, eggplant, etc. Also, do not plant mums too close to strawberries, or where strawberries grew previously. If you are planting in containers, you can avoid this problem by use of a sterile planting medium. You may run into this problem in garden soil. Control by removing and burning infected plants.

Chrysanthemum stunt is cause by a virus. Diseased plants are stunted; they often bloom earlier than healthy plants. Leaves fade to light green or turn a reddish color. Control by planting only virus-free chrysanthemums.

Aster yellows is caused by a virus transmitted by leafhoppers. Diseased plants develop many distorted flowers and several small, weak shoots. To control, plant only virus-free stock, and do not plant near asters.

INSECTS

Many species of insects attack chrysanthemums, and they can do a great deal of damage. Perhaps the worst damage is done when flowers are spoiled. A few eaten leaves can go unnoticed, but devasted blossoms destroy the aesthetic quality of the plant itself. Some species to watch out for are aphids, leaf nematodes, leaf miners, thrips, and plant bugs.

Aphids spread viruses from one plant to another during their feeding. They also suck plant juices, thus weakening the plants. To control the spread of viruses by aphids, use ladybugs.

Leaf nematodes are microscopic, parasitic worms that feed upon many garden plants. If your mums are infested with leaf nematodes, they may develop dark spots on the undersides of their leaves. They can also form brown areas between the leaf veins. Leaves wither and dry, but tend to remain on the plants after they die. Plants are stunted, and buds do not develop.

Leaf nematodes can live three or more years in dead chrysanthemum leaves. They can also live in the soil. Do not plant healthy mums in the soil where infested mums have grown.

Leaf miners, when adult, are small golden-brown moths with silver markings. The larvae are small worms found inside leaves in thread-shaped, irregular tunnels. The worms deform the leaves and create dead areas. To control, pick damaged leaves (likewise, any fallen leaves should be gathered), and burn them.

Thrips, when adult, are a small black insect with feathery wings. It injures mums by its habit of laying eggs in the blossoms. Control with an organic insecticide such as *rotenone.*

Plant bugs overwinter as adults in sheltered places such as fence rows, roadsides, ditch banks, and other locations where weeds are abundant. The best way to control plant bugs is to reduce the weeds where these bugs hibernate in the winter and late spring by hacking them down. To control pests on the mums, use an all-purpose organic insecticide such as rotenone.

Note: some people consider chrysanthemums a difficult flower to grow. Their clumps often need to be divided annually in fertile soils and under ideal growing conditions. The large-flowered varieties require staking, as well as protection from rainstorms and hail. If you are willing to go through the little extra effort and care that mums require, there are not many flowers that will reward you with as much satisfaction as your mums in bloom.

OTHER CUT FLOWERS

Chrysanthemums are not the only flower that is suitable for cutting. There are many other species. The important things to look for in any cut flower is a long stem, showiness of bloom, and fragrance. Three other species that you may wish to try are carnations, pinks, and delphiniums.

Carnations. The garden carnation (*Dianthus caryophyllus*) is the most loved of flowers. It has been in cultivation for over 2,000 years in parts of southern Europe. There are many species in the carnation family including annuals, biennials, and perennials. The hardiest of the perennial carnations are the *grenadines*.

Carnations are a tender perennial in most areas of the United States and are best suited to greenhouse production in the north. The garden carnations offered by nurseries can be grown successfully in the home landscape if given proper winter protection.

Carnations have spicy, fragrant blossoms. They grow up to 3 1/2 feet tall, depending upon the variety grown, and there are dwarfs available. They are usually available in shades of red, white, pink, and sometimes yellow.

Plant carnations in groups for their best effect. They are ideal in formal flower beds and can also be used for naturalizing. Carnations favor a slightly alkaline soil. Check your soil's pH (acidity or alkalinity) before planting carnations. it is usually a good practice to add garden lime to carnation soils.

Carnations are everbloomers. They require a sunny location and a rich, fertile soil. Never plant carnations under heavy shade, or they may have difficulty flowering, or may not blossom at all.

These are an excellent cut flower for table, corsage, and indoor arrangements. Plant several so that you will have plenty for cut flower use.

Delphiniums. When in full bloom, delphiniums are impressive to behold (Fig. 15-1). The common delphinium (*Delphinium elatum)* is usually available in its hybrid forms. The most

Fig. 15-1. Giant mixed colors, Pacific delphinium. Courtesy W. Atlee Burpee Co.

popular of the hybrids are *Pacific Giants* and a more compact cultivar called *Connecticut Yankee*. The blue shades are the most loved, although there are other colors: red, white, pink, etc.

Delphiniums are a great deal of work to grow and require an enormous amount of time, effort, and patience. They are tender perennials that are apt to be quite bothersome in their maintenance requirements. This is not a flower that can be neglected.

They are available in a wide range of colors and some grow as a flower-laden column, as high as 6 feet. There are dwarfs, such as *Connecticut Yankee*, that grow only about 3 feet tall, so even the so-called dwarfs are tall plants. Delphiniums often have a darker center color in their blossoms called a *bee*.

Plant in full sun. Delphiniums prefer a somewhat alkaline soil that is well-drained and fertile. Flowers grow on tall spikes. Stake each individual spike to keep them from collapsing under their own weight when in full bloom. To do this, tie the young plants to sticks or bamboo in the ground. Tie them with string, never bare metal wire. Bare wire can cut through plants. Use a soft string and do not tie them too tightly, just securely.

Because they are so tall, delphiniums will need to be protected from hail, wind, and heavy rains. They must not be planted in any area where they may be accidentally injured by young children or pets. There is too much work involved in growing them to fail to protect them.

Sometimes delphiniums have problems with insects and a fungal disease called *mildew*. To protect plants from mildew, set them in an area where they will receive full sun. Be sure to give them plenty of room for air circulation. Crowded plants have more mildew problems than those that are located where the air can flow freely.

Spray plants with Bourdeaux mixture. If you live in a humid climate, weekly treatments may be necessary.

To protect plants from insects, use an organic insecticide such as rotenone. If mites are a problem, they can be treated with a solution or soapy water. Always use only a gentle bar soap, such as Ivory. Never use detergents or deodorant soaps. An insecticidal soap is commercially available.

Mulch delphiniums heavily for winter, especially in the north. Often they do not live long.

Delphiniums are best used as a background flower for formal beds. They are not suited for naturalizing. If you truly love this flower and have the time and patience to grow it, its beauty is worth your efforts. For most people, however, delphiniums are probably not too practical, but they are popular!

Pinks. A cousin to the carnation, pinks are hardier, but smaller flowered. There are many species, all belonging to the *Dianthus* genus. Available as dwarfs or standards, they come in a wide range of colors. One species, the *sweet William* is biennial. They usually have single or semidouble blooms. Darker markings called *eyes* or *bees* appear on the flowers. Pinks are a tender perennial with the same cultural requirements as carnations. They are excellent cut flowers; they also look good in borders or flower beds. They are best planted in groups.

There are many excellent cultivars available including *Helen*, which is salmon color; *Doris*, a pale pink with a deep pink bee; *Sweet Memory*, which is white with a red bee; *Tiny Rubies*, which is a dwarf, deep pink in color; and, *Her Majesty*, another dwarf with white flowers. There are many other fine cultivars and species. Check with your nursery to find the ones that you want for your garden.

Chapter 16

Lawn Grasses

A good lawn is one of the most important features of any successful landscape. A finely manicured lawn catches the eye and provides a background to trees, shrubs, and flowers. Lawns have utility value as well. They hold soil in place to prevent erosion, cool surrounding air, keep dust down, provide oxygen and serve as functional outdoor "carpets" for recreational activities.

The most commonly used plants for lawns are the lawn grasses. Other grass-type plants are sometimes grown and, in problem areas, substitutes for grass are often more practical (Fig. 16-1).

The selection of the grass you grow in your lawn will be based on several factors: your climate (amount of rainfall and winter temperatures), your life style (whether you have the time to care for the grass, or need something that will grow almost maintenance-free), and what purpose the grass will serve (is it for beauty, or are the kids going to play on it regularly?). Not all grass species have the same qualities. Some are best suited for specific uses. Certain grasses can tolerate a lot of "roughhousing" and

are well adapted to recreational activities. Others need extra care and are very sensitive to abuse. Examine your nursery catalog to locate the type of grass or grasses that might be best for your lawn. Do not hesitate to call on your county agricultural agent or area nurseryman for advice. Starting a lawn is an important step in your landscape plan.

SOIL

Have your soil tested before you plant your lawn. A test can be made by your county agriculture extension service for a small fee. You can test for pH, as well as soil fertility. Most grasses prefer a neutral or slightly alkaline soil. Plan on adding limestone. Dolomitic ground limestone is best. It contains both calcium and magnesium, which grasses need. Any kind of barnyard lime will be sufficient.

Sandy soils should be improved by the addition of peat moss, composted organic matter, and well-rotted manures, in addition to lime. Heavy, clay soils should be improved by the addition of peat moss,

139

Fig. 16-1. One of the most important features of any landscape is the lawn.

composted organic matter, well-rotted manure, and sand, if need be, to lighten them.

You can also add organic matter to the soil by use of a green manure crop the season before planting to lawn. This is one of the cheapest and simplest methods to enrich soil in a hurry. You grow a crop to improve the soil and till it under. In the north, soybeans, clover, and sudan grass are good green manure crops. In the south, vetches, rye grasses, and clovers work well. When the crop is tilled under in the fall, it rapidly decomposes into rich humus, ready to plant in lawn the following spring. This greatly improves the soil, whatever type of soil you have, and will give you a head start to an attractive lawn.

Before planting, till the soil to get rid of any weeds or vegetation that might compete with the grass seed or sod for moisture and nutrients.

SOD VERSUS SEED

When most people think of starting their lawn, they usually look over the various grass seeds that are available. Seeding can be the most economical way

to start a lawn, but it is often neither practical nor efficient. Too often, people have problems starting a lawn by seed. Problems include:

☐ Planting seed too early, so it does not germinate.

☐ Not sufficently preparing the seedbed.

☐ Failing to keep the soil moist (but not drenched) while the seed tries to germinate.

☐ Failing to keep the kids off the seedbed.

☐ The most trying of all—waiting for the seed to germinate.

It may take a couple of years or more to finally get a good stand of grass—one that makes for an attractive, yet durable lawn.

A better route, especially for people who have light, sandy soils, is the use of sod. Grass sod is available from many sources (Fig. 16-2). Plant only those types appropriate for your area. Many garden catalogs offer *zoysia grass*, which they usually sell in sod plugs. What they often fail to mention is that this type of grass is not sufficently winter hardy north of central Illinois. Many smart homeowners have lost their investment by purchasing this product. Do not plant grass that will not survive the climatic conditions of where you live. This is the first rule, whether you are using seed or sod.

There are two routes to go with the sod method. The simplest and most expensive is to buy *carpet grass* and cover the entire lawn at one time. This is very time-consuming and heavy work. It usually takes more than one person to lay the grass into place properly. Most people find it easier to hire a landscape firm to lay out their carpet grass, which adds even more to the expense. Grass sold in carpet form can range in price anywhere from one dollar a square foot to ten dollars per square foot, before adding in the costs of hired labor, which makes the figures soar even higher. If you can and want to spend the money, this will provide an "instant lawn."

Once planted, you will have to maintain the grass through regular waterings, usually once or twice a week. During dry weather, you may need to water more often.

The cheapest and most practical way to sod a lawn is to use *plugs*. This can be a one-man or one-woman operation. It is exactly the same method used to establish zoysia grass, except that you can use any grass species that you desire. (Providing that it is hardy in your area.) You do not need any special equipment, other than a shovel, to put plugs into place, and you can incorporate plugs into the existing lawn.

Grass sod is usually cheaper to buy locally than through the mails. For quality lawns, buy only from a reputable dealer. If you are not fussy and want to do it the cheapest way possible, a friend or neighbor may be willing to provide you with some grass plugs for free. If they like you well enough, you may even be able to talk them into helping you plant the plugs.

It is important that the plugs of grass make contact with the soil. Once the hole is dug and the grass plug put in, it should be tamped into place, firmly, but gently. If there are spaces around the sides of

Fig. 16-2. Grass sod is available from many sources.

the plug, they should be filled in with soil. There must be no air pockets left, or they can kill off the new plug of grass.

Another cheap way to get grass plugs is to dig them from parts of your own woodland, being careful to not take too much from any one spot, thus potentially damaging trees. If you do not have your own forest, however, you may wish to buy carpet grass and cut it into squares of at least 3 × 3 inches. Or, if you want faster results, plant larger 1-foot squares of carpet grass in a checkerboard pattern throughout the lawn.

Once the grass has been planted and is securely in place, water it thoroughly on a weekly basis. During dry periods, it should be watered more frequently. It usually takes about one season to get the grass firmly entrenched and spreading into a lawn. Occasional applications of fertilizer of high nitrogen content will be helpful. Do not fertilize your lawn after July first. Your lawn, in the north, will need to prepare for the frigid winter months ahead.

It is important to water lawns well into the fall until a week before the ground freezes—usually a couple of weeks before Thanksgiving, or the last week in October in the far north.

Fall is the ideal time to plant grass. The warm autumn days help the grass to grow and spread. If you lay out sod in the fall, you will want to mulch your lawn the first winter to help protect the young plugs. This is not as necessary if the sod was laid in the spring, because the plants will have had a better chance to become entrenched.

Some grasses turn brown after the first frost, but their roots will still be growing even while the top (green blades) is dormant. This is why watering should be kept up until a week before the ground freezes. Never water frozen ground, or it may cause severe damage to your lawn.

SEEDING A LAWN

Seed is usually the most economical way of planting a lawn (unless you can obtain free grass plugs). Seeding lawns is not as simple as it looks and can run into expense if it is not done properly. The best time for seeding a lawn is in the fall. The warm autumn days helps to insure the rapid germination of seeds. Spring is the second best time to seed a lawn, but is not nearly as good as fall. The ground may still be cold, and other problems can occur in the spring to hinder results. Summer is never a good time to sow lawn seed, because hot temperatures will keep seeds dormant or interfere with the other complicated biological processes involved in germination. Needless-to-say, no one in the north plants seeds in winter, and although it may be possible to do this in many areas of the south and California, it is not an option for northern gardeners.

Most old soils will usually benefit from the addition of barnyard lime. The lime must be spread evenly over the entire lawn area. If you are seeding by hand, mix some sand in with your seed. Stir it so that it is a fairly even mix. This will help to give a more uniform stand when you start sprinkling the seed. Sow half the seed in one direction and the other half at right angles. Lightly rake the seed into the soil surface, covering the seed by not more than 1/4-inch of dirt. Grass seed needs light to germinate. The seed must be in contact with the soil, however. If the seed is just sitting above the ground caught up by the blades of the old grass, it will not be able to germinate and you will have wasted your money and time.

PREPARATION

Before you start your lawn, there are a few steps that you will want to take. These are the same whether you are seeding or preparing for sod culture.

The land must gently slope away from the house. It may already do so, but in some cases it will have to *graded*. The land *grade* is the degree of slope in the land. It is important that the land be graded so that it slopes away from the house; otherwise, you can have flooded basements and drainage problems in certain areas where water collects. The grade should not produce a sharp drop, (unless you are planning on a moat around your home). A gentle, barely detectable grade of 2 inches every 10 feet is sufficient to provide for good drainage.

It may be necessary to protect existing trees if the new lawn is to be raised above the existing level.

Some trees are killed by root suffocation when too deeply buried by soil. Protect trees by building a *stone well* around them up to the new level. Naturally, any low branches should be removed so that the tree looks in place. If the new lawn is raised quite a bit higher, you may want to consider moving the tree altogether. It is doubtful this would be necessary with deep-rooted trees such as oaks.

The subsoil must be properly drained. Most grasses will not thrive on poorly drained soil. If you think water drainage is a problem on your land, contact your county agricultural agent for advice. He or she can put you in contact with a company that can install landscape drainage tiles, if necessary, for proper drainage.

NORTHERN GRASSES

Grasses selected for growing in the north have to meet certain criteria: they have to be hardy, to survive extremely cold winters; they must produce a good stand without gaps or barren areas; and they have to look nice. In general, the finer textured grasses are better looking than the more coarse types. Because a mix of different kinds of grasses is perhaps the best way to meet the utility needs of most homeowners who want an all-purpose lawn, you must try to balance the mix so that coarse and fine-textured types are in harmony.

Buffalo Grass. Buffalo grass *(Buchloe dactyloides)* is a valuable pasturage grass of the western plains region of the United States. It is also suited for and used as a home lawn grass in these same regions.

Buffalo grass is a drought-resistant perennial. If forms a dense sod and can take abuse well, which makes it an excellent grass for play areas. It has a dwarf growth habit, rarely exceeding 6 inches in height and rarely requiring mowing (once or twice all summer long)! Although it is most common in states like Nebraska, Kansas, and the Dakotas, buffalo grass is an excellent grass for any dry climate. It deserves to be planted more widely than it is. If water conservation is a problem in your area, buffalo grass may be the answer for your lawn.

Buffalo grass prefers a fertile, "prairie-type" soil. It spreads by underground runners (stolons).

It forms a dense mat and should not be planted under trees right up to their trunks. It is established by seed or sod. Both are very expensive. (Sod culture is recommended.)

Colonial Bentgrass. Colonial bentgrass *(Agrotis tennis)* is one of the highest quality lawn grasses. It is fine-textured and forms a dense turf. It is more expensive to keep up than other grasses, because it has high maintenance requirements.

Colonial bentgrass requires a rich, fertile soil and frequent applications of fertilizer (it is a heavy feeder). It must be watered during drought and mowed closely. If it is cut much above an inch, its appearance is destroyed.

There are several strains available: *Highland* is the hardiest cultivar; *Astoria* is another popular variety, but not as drought-tolerant as the *Highland* strian.

Creeping Bentgrass. Creeping bentgrass *(Agrotis palustris)* forms a dense sod with a creeping growth habit. It must be mowed closely, under an inch, and raked to prevent the formation of thatch.

It requires a rich, moist soil, slightly alkaline and well-drained. It is a high-maintenance grass and must be cared for, or its appearance will suffer. There are many selections available, all established by sod. Some of the best are *Seaside, Toronto,* and *Arlington.* There are many others.

Kentucky Bluegrass. Kentucky bluegrass (Poa pratensis) is the standard lawn grass by which all other grasses are judged. It is the most popular lawn grass in the United States and is usually propagated by seed.

There are numerous strains of Kentucky bluegrass. Common Kentucky bluegrass will not tolerate acid soil; it favors a rich, lime soil. It is highly drought resistant and tends to go dormant during hot summer months. There are many excellent cultivars. Some of the best are *Monopoly,* which is the fastest germinating—in less than a week; *Baron; Adelphi; Park; Glade; Merion,* and many more. Check with your nursery to see what varieties they offer and which best suits your needs.

Perennial Ryegrass. Perennial ryegrass is best for the humid, cool climates of the eastern half of the country. Although it can be grown west of the Mississippi, it will require watering in the drier areas of the Great Plains. *Lolium perenne* is not sufficiently winter hardy in the far north. New cultivars are being developed each year, however, so it is a good idea to check hardiness with your nursery.

There are many reasons for planting ryegrass. It is one of the quickest of the lawn grass seeds to germinate—often within a week! Perennial ryegrass can succeed in many areas where Kentucky bluegrass will not. It grows under less fertile conditions and some of the newer fine textured cultivars resemble the bluegrasses in their neat appearance.

With perennial ryegrass you can have an almost "instant" lawn, but because it grows so fast, you will have to mow it more often as well. If you do not like mowing your lawn, you may not want to plant this species.

Ordinary perennial ryegrass is fairly wide-bladed and presents a somewhat coarser lawn when compared to Kentucky bluegrass. Some of the better strains, however, rival bluegrass in beauty. Two excellent fine-bladed varieties are *Pennfine* and *Manhattan*.

Red Fescue. Red fescue (*Festuca rubra*), sometimes called *creeping red fescue*, is second only to Kentucky bluegrass in commercial importance. Red fuscue thrives on sandy soil and in shady areas where regular bluegrass does not grow. For these reasons, it is popularly used in seed mixtures.

Red fescue has fine texture and forms a dense turf when seeded heavily. It resists wear quite well. It will not take close mowing (below 1 1/2 inches). If you mow too low, you can cause serious damage to the turf. It grows slowly and when injured, repair takes time.

Redtop. Redtop (*Agrotis alba*) is a short-lived perennial. It rarely survives for more than two seasons. It is useful in providing a quick cover in the north, while more permanent grasses are developing. In the south, it is used for winter overseeding of Bermuda grass.

Redtop grows in highly acid, poorly drained soils. It is drought-tolerant and survives areas of low fertility. It is usually established by seed.

Velvet Bentgrass. Velvet bentgrass (*Agrotis canina*) is the finest textured among the bentgrasses. It makes a dense turf of the highest quality, spreading by creeping stems. It is established by seed or sod.

Velvet bentgrass grows best on well-drained alkaline soils. It does not take abuse well and is slow to recover from injury. It is a high-maintenance grass, requiring much work to keep it up.

SOUTHERN GRASSES

Southern grasses are not hardy enough to survive most northern winters. Most of the finer lawn grasses are capable of standing up to the hot summers and mild winters so common to Dixie.

Although some northern grasses can be grown in the south, it is not recommended. Most northern grasses are not suitable for any permanent lawn when grown in the southern climate (especially the deep South).

Bahaia Grass. Common Bahia is rarely used for lawns: it has a coarse texture and is mostly used as a forage crop for animals. *Paspalum notatum* is a perennial with a low growth habit. It spreads by thick, short runners. It grows best along the Southern coastal plains. It is usually established from seed.

Bahia grass is most important for covering large fields, where grass quality is not necessary. One of the best strains is *Pennsacola*, which has a finer texture. It produces a dense, somewhat uneven, coarse turf.

Bermuda Grass. Common Bermuda is the only strain that is grown by seed, all cultivars are established by sod culture. *Cynodon dactylon*, is a popular southern grass. It grows by underground roots and above ground runners. It is a vigorous plant and can invade flower beds. Once it is established, it is difficult to get rid of.

Bermuda grass favors lots of fertilizer, an alkaline soil, and plenty of sunshine. It will not thrive in shade, acid soil, or on infertile or poorly drained soils. It must be mowed closely to form a dense turf.

Some of the best cultivars include: *Tiflawn*, which has a finer texture than common Bermuda grass. It grows vigorously and forms a dense mat. *Everglades No. 1* has a finer texture and is a dark green. It is one of the easiest-to-maintain of all the bermuda grasses. If low maintenance is a feature you are looking for in a southern lawn grass, this is a species worth trying. *Tiffine* has a fine texture, but is lighter in color than some of the other varieties. It requires high maintenance and is used for golf courses.

Centipede Grass. Centipede grass (*Eremochloa ephiruroides)* is one of the best low-maintenance grasses for the south. It forms a thick turf that stands up well to wear. It will require less care than other grasses. That translates into more free time for you and less time doing lawn work.

Centipede grass should not be planted near the ocean, because it is highly sensitive to the saltwater spray that occurs in such locations. It differs from most other grasses in another important respect: centipede grass favors a slightly acid soil.

On ordinary soil, centipede grass may suffer from *iron chlorosis*. This disease will cause it to yellow and brown out. It can be corrected by acidifying the soil so that the grass can take up the necessary amount of iron from the soil that it needs to survive and thrive.

Centipede grass is drought-tolerant, but does better if watered during periods of dry weather. This grass spreads rapidly. You can plant seed or sod to develop a lawn from this species.

Japanese Grass. Japanese grass (*Zoysia japonica*) is a perennial with a low growth habit. It spreads by runners and roots, forming a dense turf. This grass turns the color of straw after the first killing frost in the fall and will not green-up until the following spring.

Common zoysia grass has a coarse texture, but it is all right for recreational areas. *Zoysia japonica* var. *meyer* is the strain most often used for home lawns. It has vigorous growth and retains its color later in the fall. It greens-up earlier in the spring as well. It is sold by sod only. There is no seed.

Zoysia grass is drought-resistent and stands up to wear and close clippings, once established. It is not hardy north of central Illinois.

Manilla Grass. Manilla grass (*Zoysia matrella*) is a cousin of Japanese grass. If forms a dense carpet of turf that is highly resistant to wear and insect damage. It spreads by stolons (underground runners).

Manilla grass requires an alkaline soil and fertilizer. It is a heavy feeder and very sensitive to acid soils. It turns brown after the first killing frost in the fall and stays that way until spring. It is established by sod.

St. Augustine Grass. St. Augustine grass (*Stenotaphrum secundatum*) is the most important shade grass in the south. It is a perennial that spreads by creeping runners. It is established *vegetatively* by sod culture or grass plugs. There is no seed.

St. Augustine grass is highly salt-tolerant; it will withstand the saltwater sprays near the coast. It favors rich, moist soil.

LAWN PROBLEMS

Some of the problems that lawns face are acidic soils, surface compaction, neglect, and too much shade. Insects are not a problem on a healthy lawn. Contact your county agricultural agent for advice, should insects become a nuisance. Your agent can identify the insect pest and prescribe treatment to eradicate it. If you are an organic gardener, ask for organic solutions to insect pest problems. Do not let anybody try to tell you there are none. Go to your library if need be. There are many books on how to deal with insect pests.

By controlling insects, you will also control the pocket gophers, moles, and field mice that feed upon grubs in the soil.

Acidic Soil. Moss never grows on a healthy lawn. Its presence usually indicates poor drainage, acidic soil, too much shade, or a combination of all these factors. Moss can be controlled by spraying the grass with Bourdeaux mixture, but to eliminate it permanently, add lime to your soil to change its acidity. this will also help your grass grow better, because few grasses can thrive in acidic soils.

Herbicides. Proper maintenance is the best method of weed control. Herbicides are not necessary. A well-kept lawn does not have weed problems. Hand removal of weeds is the safest route to follow. Herbicides can injure other foliage if handled carelessly.

Lawn fertilizes with mixed-in herbicides are also not practical. For one thing, weeds have growth cycles. At certain points in their growth cycle, they are more vulnerable than during any other time. Most people apply these chemical mixtures rather carelessly, without knowledge of the life cycle of the weeds they wish to destroy. Often, they end up killing a lot of vegetation, but not the weeds! For the best lawn, do not bother with dangerous chemical herbicides.

Diseases. Lawn diseases are mostly fungal in nature. Different grass species have varying levels of resistence to these diseases. A copper-sulfate fungicide, such as Bourdeaux mixture, is one of the safest fungicides to use. It will take care of most lawn disease problems.

Sometimes other forms of injury are mistaken for disease symptoms. (Incidentally, an injured lawn is more susceptible to attack by disease and insect pests.)

Fertilizer Burn. Caused by too heavily applied doses of chemical fertilizer or too fresh manure, dog damage, or herbicides are often the real culprits. And, of course, a yellowed lawn may be the result of drought.

Soil Compaction. Soil compaction can become a problem on lawns that are used for recreation, and especially on heavy clay soils. To prevent this problem *aerate* the lawn from time to time. You can do this by one of many ways. You can rent a machine especially built for this purpose from a local garden center, hire a professional, or simply take a pitch fork and poke holes in the grass as you walk along. The pitchfork method is the cheapest.

What you are trying to do is to open up your lawn so that oxygen can get to the roots of the grass.

Shade. Most grasses do not grow well (if at all) under shade, especially heavy shade. Lawn planted near shallow rooted trees and under heavy shade can easily become unsightly barren ground. To remedy this situation, try growing shade-tolerant grasses. In the north, try red or chewings fescue for shady areas. In the south, try St. Augustine grass.

If grass absolutely does not grow in an area, you may want to try a different groundcover. If nothing wants to grow, try using decorative bark or stones to help hold the soil in place and improve the area's appearance.

You can allow more light to filter through to grass by pruning branches on trees.

If you find yourself faced with any long-term or serious lawn problems, seek help. Contact your county agricultural agent for assistance.

Chapter 17

Groundcovers

If your land has steep banks, rocky terrain, badly eroded soil, heavily shaded areas, drainage ditches, or terraces, you will probably need to utilize a groundcover. The alternative may be dusty, barren soil, no matter how much time and expense you put into trying to seed and maintain a lawn.

Groundcovers are also desirable in places where shallow-rooted trees compete too vigorously for moisture and nutrients. To leave these problem areas barren would be unacceptable, and, in some cases, it would worsen their condition. A groundcover is needed not only for beautification, but to protect the landscape by controlling erosion and dust. Low-growing plants and vines are often used as groundcovers.

There are many excellent groundcovers on the market. Some are better suited to shade than sun; others do better in sunny locations. Each groundcover has its own unique qualities which either makes it a candidate for selection or removes it from your list of likely choices.

There are many features about a good groundcover that you will want to consider before you decide upon yours. The groundcover must be hardy in your area. It should also meet your need. That is, if you want a groundcover that will stand a lot of trampling, you do not want to plant anything too tender. A groundcover should be examined for its aesthetic qualities as well. Is the texture fine or coarse? What does it look like in the winter? In the fall? In the spring? In the summer? What is the color?

To select a groundcover for your landscape, you will need to know where it is going to be used—rocky hillsides, under shade, in full sun, etc. Should you select an evergreen or decide upon a deciduous species that offers a change with each season? Finally, how much care do you want to invest?

The decision is yours, but it is important to weigh all considerations carefully. What may have looked good in a park or at a neighbor's house, may not really fit into your landscape or your tastes. Before you decide upon a groundcover, make a checklist of your needs.

Bird's Foot Trefoil. For people with problem terrain, the bird's foot trefoil is very practical.

Although not terribly attractive as an ornamental, *Lotus corniculatus* is a rapidly growing groundcover, widely used for soil conservation. It forms a dense mat that helps prevent soil erosion and improves the soil at the same time. Bird's foot trefoil bears yellow flowers with a tinge of orange color in late spring and early summer. The blossoms often attract bees and various butterflies.

Plant in a sunny location. This plant is tolerant of wet, acid soils. It will thrive in poorly drained soils where other plants would drown. Bird's foot trefoil is very winter hardy and can be grown throughout the far north. They are sensitive to drought stress, and light, sandy soils are not ideal for growing them. Water the plants frequently during dry weather.

Once established, bird's foot trefoil is a relatively carefree plant. It grows densely, choking out most weeds. It tends to be invasive, so do not plant too close to flower beds.

It gets its name from the plant's three-lobe leaves, which are said to resemble bird feet. It is a coarse and aggressive plant and should not be set out in refined areas. An excellent bank cover, it is most effective for controlling soil erosion problems.

Bird's foot trefoil is never grown for its beauty, but for its utility. It is much more appealing, however, then a barren spot or eroded gully in your garden.

Creeping Oregon Grape. The creeping Oregon grape (*Mahonia repens*) is a better groundcover than the Oregon grape holly: it hugs the ground closer than the regular Oregon grape (Fig. 17-1).

The creeping Oregon grape bears yellow flowers in the spring and fruits later on in the summer. It is a broadleaf evergreen, with glossy leaves that reflect the light and make it a very attractive plant.

Creeping Oregon grape grows well in the shade, but a filtered shade that permits some sunlight to

Fig. 17-1. Oregon creeping grape. Courtesy Denver Water Department, Xeriscape Conservation Garden.

Fig. 17-2. Dwarf arctic willow. Courtesy Denver Water Department, Xeriscape Conservation Garden.

pass through is preferable to heavy shade. These plants like a rich, moist soil. They are vigorous growers and spread from underground suckers.

In northern areas, where this plant is only half-hardy, it must be protected from severe winter temperatures. Mulch plants heavily before winter begins, take off the mulch each spring, and reapply it when frost is imminent.

The plants should also be protected from windy sites and watered during periods of drought. Add plenty of peat moss to the planting site. Composted manure will have a beneficial effect upon plant growth. It can be set out anywhere in your yard where an attractive groundcover is desired.

Dwarf Arctic Willow. The foliage is the most interesting feature about the dwarf arctic willow (*Salix purpurea* var. *nana*). The long slender leaves sway in the slightest breeze, and the silvery foliage reflects the sunlight for a fascinating display (Fig. 17-2).

Dwarf arctic willow is a low-growing shrub,

reaching about 2 1/2 feet. It has weeping foliage and an open growth habit.

This plant favors moist, but sunny locations. Add plenty of peat moss to the planting site. It is better able to tolerate poor soil drainage than most ornamentals.

Water on a weekly basis throughout the growing season and in fall until a week before the ground freezes. Water more often during dry weather. When watering, do not merely sprinkle the plant. Rather, let the water soak into the area around the base. The ground surrounding the willow should be moist, not wet, to the touch.

Avoid planting in shade. Plants set out under shade are more subject to fungal attacks. If these diseases do appear, spray plants with Bourdeaux mixture on a weekly basis, until the disease is no longer apparent. It is also a good practice to spray plants after heavy rains.

Dwarfbush Honeysuckle. The dwarfbush honeysuckle (*Diervilla lonicera*) will grow under

149

somewhat adverse conditions, on poor, dry, and a sandy soils. Actually, this plant is an imposter: it is a low-growing plant that looks suspiciously like a honeysuckle, even though it is not related. Although a dwarf bush, its low-mounded form makes it better suited for a groundcover than for any other use.

It is a mound of green throughout the summer. Set plants 1 1/2 to 2 feet apart for a dense groundcover. Plant 3 feet apart in a row where a separation to distinguish individual plants is desired.

Dwarfbush honeysuckle loves shade. It can be placed in those barren, shady spots of your yard where few other plants will grow. Do not waste it in a sunny location. Save those areas for something more colorful that requires heavy sunlight.

Dwarfbush honeysuckle can grow on rugged terrain. For best results, be sure to follow the planting instructions that your nursery will provide with your order. It makes a good bank cover, helping to control soil erosion. These plants are usually set out in groups. They are also quite effective in rock gardens.

Indian Currant. A shrub that helps in the fight against soil erosion is an asset to any yard. The Indian currant (*Symphoricarpos orbiculatus*), also sometimes called the *coralberry*, is such a plant. Although called a currant, this is a misnomer, because this species is not any relation to the fruit bush currants. The coralberry is a low-growing plant with a crawling or creeping growth habit. Once established in an area, it spreads rapidly by underground shoots called *suckers*. This plant bears pink fruits that resemble currants, except they are slightly larger (Fig. 17-3).

Indian currants are very hardy plants. They grow well on any good, drained soil. They are very tolerant of shade and thrive in shady areas where other ornamentals may have difficulty in staying alive. They produce their best fruit display, however, when they receive sufficient sun.

These plants are vigorous growers and are very tolerant of dry weather. They even manage to retain their ornamental beauty under summer heat. They should be watered during dry spells, however.

Fig. 17-3. Indian currant. Courtesy Denver Water Department, Xeriscape Conservation Garden.

Fig. 17-4. Manhattan euonymus. Courtesy Denver Water Department, Xeriscape Conservation Garden.

Indian currants are excellent for bank covers. They help to prevent soil erosion and are a good substitute for grass under shade trees.

Japanese Fleeceflower. The Japanese fleeceflower has a remarkable ability to withstand much environmental stress, such as drought and neglect, and still be a vigorous grower. *Polygonum cuspidatum compactum* has compact dense growth. It bears pink flowers on spikes that rise above the foliage. This is a summer-flowering species and will be in bloom after many spring-flowering ornamentals have given their last hurrah for the season. The Japanese fleeceflower has a coarse texture and aggressive nature. It has red foliage in the fall.

This plant is also known as *knotweed*, which suggests that the plant is easy to grow, and it is. It grows like a weed once established. It thrives in ordinary garden soil. It grows well in sun or under partial shade, producing its best flowering and fall color display when grown under full sun.

The Japanese fleeceflower can survive even though neglected, but you will want to give it good care for best results—at least until it becomes well established. Neglected plants have a scrawny and

unloved appearance. No one wants a landscape that looks like a still life of death and dying.

Do not use in formal areas. The coarse texture of the plant and its aggressive nature suit it to problem, rather than showcase areas. It is an excellent choice for a bank cover and is quite effective in controlling soil erosion. The Japanese fleeceflower is a plant for problem areas that you can hide and improve at the same time.

Manhattan Euonymus. If you have sufficient space and a little extra time, you may want to consider the Manhattan euonymus (Fig. 17-4). *Euonymus kiautschovicus* var. *manhattan* is very attractive, with its showy red berries contrasting against the glossy, green foliage. Manhattan euonymus grows in a horizontal fashion, spreading its branches up to 9 feet in length. It has fine textured, broadleaf evergreen foliage. In northern areas of the United States, it tends to have only a semievergreen habit.It will need protection when grown in the north.

Euonymus favors shade, although it will grow in sunny areas. It needs a rich, moist soil, and plenty of room for its branches to spread. Because of its

Fig. 17-5. Moneywort. Courtesy Denver Water Department, Xeriscape Conservation Garden.

horizontal growth, it should not be cramped for space in the location in which it is set out. If your yard is very small, you may want to consider carefully whether or not to plant this specimen.

Prune branches to control their size and keep an even balance, when necessary. Control weeds and provide a summer mulch to conserve soil moisture. The mulch should be very light and blend in with the plant. It must not cover the foliage. This is a fancy plant, and it will take some work to maintain it, especially if you live in the north.

Moneywort. Moneywort (*Lysimachia nummularia*) is also sometimes called *creeping Jenny*. The plant grows in a horizontal fashion, rarely getting over 3 inches high. Its long, trailing stems stretch several feet in length. The plant bears yellow cuplike flowers that are quite small but abundant when the plant is in full bloom (Fig. 17-5).

Moneywort bears a whorl of round leaves on very short stalks. The leaves are usually silvery-green and said to resemble small coins, from whence the plant gets its name.

Grow in sun or partial shade. It should not be planted under heavy shade. It favors a fertile, moist soil. Moneywort is a vigorous grower, tends to be invasive in a landscape, and should not be planted in areas where it is not expected to take over, such as near flower beds.

Control weeds by hand removal. Keep plants well-watered for best growth. They will not tolerate drought. A good rule of thumb to test whether they need to be watered or not is to touch the soil with your finger. If it is dry, water the plants. The soil should be kept damp, not wet, to the touch.

Moneywort is a practical plant for the home landscape and sure to impress your friends, who will look twice just to be sure there really are no coins out there.

Myrtle. Myrtle (*Vinca minor*), with its little blue blossoms and glossy leaves, looks sensational under trees where grass cannot grow, and its springtime bloom is a welcome addition to any landscape. It is sometimes called *periwinkle* in certain parts of the country. This plant is a broadleaf evergreen. It is a natural groundcover with its horizontal, creeping growth (Fig. 17-6).

It is hardier than many evergreens because it hugs the ground. Although an evergreen, its leaves

152

This red-brick, walled-in English garden has Chippendale panels in the wall. Photo by Gale Nurseries.

Arbors are used here for shade and to create an intimate space for a terrace next to a pool. Photo by Gale Nurseries.

A geometric Knott garden containing Ilex helleri with herbs. Photo by Gale Nurseries.

Lentenboden bulb garden. Photo copyright Derek Fell.

Landscaped house and lawn. Photo copyright Derek Fell.

Ashland Hollow patio garden. Photo copyright Derek Fell.

Allee at Meadowbrook Farm. Photo copyright Derek Fell.

Seven Pines garden. Photo copyright Derek Fell.

may turn off-color in northern regions. They will revert back to green after the temperatures warm up again in the spring.

Myrtle likes a rich, garden loam, but will grow in poor soils. It is a vigorous grower. Control weeds and water plants on a regular weekly basis. Weeds are best removed by hand. Water during dry spells. A winter mulch may be necessary for those who live in areas with severe winters. Usually, the natural snowfall will insulate plants, but it is a good idea to use a mulch anyway because some winters do not have much snow. If there is not adequate snow in the early part of the winter, the ground may freeze, thus harming or killing the plants.

Myrtle is well-suited for shady areas: in fact, it favors shade. It produces a fine-textured foliage that always looks neat.

In addition to regular myrtle, there are two cultivars you may wish to try: *Alba*, which produces large white flowers, and Bowles, which is an improved version of regular myrtle producing larger flowers and blooming more profusely.

Oregon Grape Holly. Oregon grape holly (*Mahonia aquifolium*) is not a true grape. It is so-called because its hollylike foliage resembles grape leaves and because it bears a cluster of blue fruits that look something like grapes. (They are not edible.) It is an ideal urban plant, because it is extremely well-adapted to the stresses of the city environment (Fig. 17-7).

Oregon grape holly bears clusters of yellow flowers in the spring on racemes about 3 1/2 inches long. It is a broadleaf evergreen with shiny, attractive leaves. It may not be sufficiently winter hardy in some northern areas.

These plants are quite tolerant of shade, although they produce a better flower and fruit display when grown under maximum sunlight. They favor a rich, moist soil.

In the north, plant in a protected location, in an area that will not be open to the drying winds of summer or the bitter, cold winds of winter. Mulch plants heavily each winter. Uncover plants in the spring when temperatures have warmed to a safe level. They will be off-color, but will regain their color as the season progresses. Protect plants from

Fig. 17-6. Myrtle. Courtesy Denver Water Department, Xeriscape Conservation Garden.

Fig. 17-7. Oregon grape holly. Courtesy Denver Water Department, Xeriscape Conservation Garden.

frosts and late spring freezes by covering with mulch any time the temperature threatens to dip below 35° F. Plants may not survive in the extreme north.

The plant tends to spread rapidly from underground shoots. Although they are vigorous growers, they are also interesting when used as specimens.

Phlox. Phlox is a good choice for those cold areas where many groundcovers winter kill. *Phlox douglasii* grows to 6 inches in height. This low-growing species tends to form a mat over the ground's surface. It bears flowers in the late spring and early summer. The colors of bloom vary according to variety. Some of the best cultivars of the Douglas phlox are *Snow Queen*, which has white flowers; and *Supreme*, which bears lavender-blue blossoms.

Another species of phlox that is useful as a groundcover is the *moss phlox, Phlox subulata*. Its needlelike leaves are evergreen in the south, semievergreen in the North. Moss phlox bears small, clustered pink or white flowers.

Plant phlox in sunny areas. It tends to produce an unkempt effect if grown in the shade. These fine-textured plants grow well on dry, poor, and infertile soils. They have vigorous growth and multiply rapidly. These phlox species are easy to care for and are best for groundcover use. Do not confuse them with the showy garden phlox, which takes a great deal of care and is not suited to groundcover use. The moss phlox is an excellent bank cover for problem areas.

Plumbago. If you live in the far north, you may not want to consider plumbago as a groundcover. For rock gardens, or for those with less severe winters, however, its tiny blue "stars" are really eye-catching.

Plumbago (*Ceratostigma plumbaginoides*) is a tender groundcover. The plant grows in clumps that reach 1 1/2 feet across and can get to be 6 to 8 inches tall.

Plumbago flowers in late summer. Though small, the star-shaped blossoms are borne in abundance and are of the true blue color that is so rare in the plant world. Plumbago is easy to grow. Plant in full sun or partial shade. It is best to avoid heavy shade.

A winter mulch is advisable. Layer straw, 3 to 4 inches deep, spread evenly over the entire area. Do not lay mulch too early; wait until about one week before the ground freezes. Do not wait until after the ground freezes, or the plants may die.

Plumbago is most effective when lining pathways and walks. It looks nice in rock gardens, or when planted under trees that permit filtered sunlight.

Purpleleaf Wintercreeper. The purpleleaf wintercreeper (*Euonymus fortunei* var. *colorata*) grows in a sprawling fashion along the ground. It has a fine texture to its small glossy, dark-green leaves. The purpleleaf wintercreeper is a broadleaf evergreen, but has only a semievergreen habit when grown in the north. Its leaves turn purple after the first frosts and stay that way throughout the entire winter (Fig. 17-8).

Purpleleaf wintercreeper is not fully hardy in the north. When grown in such areas, it needs to have a sheltered location. It also should be mulched heavily in the winter to help it survive severe cold.

Fig. 17-8. Wintercreeper. Courtesy Stark Bro's Nurseries & Orchards Co.

It grows best under filtered shade. It likes a fertile, moist soil,and it needs room for its branches to sprawl. It should not be cramped into a small space.

You may wish to prune off dead areas or other unkempt parts that can come about by winter kill (especially in northern areas) to maintain the orderly appearance of the plants.

Water plants each week with a thorough soaking. Water more often during periods of dry weather.

The purpleleaf wintercreeper is an excellent grass substitute for those shady areas where grass may have difficulty growing. It is also a welcome relief from the monopoly of grass in a lawn. It requires more maintenance than some groundcovers, but produces an attractive display, combining beauty and utility.

Spurge. Spurge (*Pachysandra terminalis*) grows to only about 6 inches in height. This sprawling groundcover blankets an area with its dense cover. It has an apple-green foliage (sometimes darker) with fairly large leaves. It is somewhat coarse, but a very useful groundcover (Fig. 17-9).

Spurge is a vigorous grower. It is not fussy about soil and seems to perform well in dry, infertile soil. It does require good drainage. Spurge grows better in areas where organic matter, such as peat moss, has been added to the soil.

Spurge grows best under shade. These plants seem to flourish in those areas where grass cannot grow because of insufficient sunlight. They will crowd out most weeds,and any remaining weeds can be pulled by hand.

Use to cover barren spots in shady areas of your yard. Spurge can be substituted for grass or ground ivy, where a coarse groundcover is not offensive. It will provide a very attractive woodland floor.

Stonecrop Sedum. Stonecrop sedum, true to its name, does well on dry, stony soils. And it even grows in Alaska! A summer-flowering species, it bears small, yellow clusters of flowers. *Sedum acre,* rarely exceeds 5 inches in height. It has a mostly horizontal growth and multiples vigorously. Sedum forms a dense mat on the ground's surface (Fig. 17-10).

There are many other species and cultivars of sedum that have different colors and flowering times. The *spectabile* species offers several varieties

Fig. 17-9. Spurge. Courtesy Denver Water Department, Xeriscape Conservation Garden.

Fig. 17-10. Stonecrop sedum. Courtesy Denver Water Department, Xeriscape Conservation Garden.

that produce a larger plant than stonecrop. Some of its cultivars are: *Autumn Joy*, which has salmon-color flowers; *Meteor*, which bears carmine-red flowers; and *Atropurpureum*, which has pink blossoms. This species flowers from late summer into the fall. Check with your garden nursery to see

Fig. 17-11. Thimbleberry. Courtesy Denver Water Department, Xeriscape Conservation Garden.

what species and types of sedum they offer.

Sedum is a sun-loving plant. It grows best in areas where it receives plenty of sunshine. Never plant sedum under heavy shade. It is very easy to grow and grows on any well-drained soil. It thrives on poor, infertile, sandy, dry, stony soils.

Although a succulent (like cactus), stonecrop sedum is one of the hardiest of plants. (Some of the other sedum species may not be as hardy, be sure to check hardiness with your nursery before buying any plants.)

It is mostly used in rock gardens, but in the semiarid regions of the west, it is often used in place of grass. It is a very practical plant anywhere that water may be scarce.

Thimbleberry. The thimbleberry (*Rubus deliciosus*) is notable for its somewhat weeping (pendulant) growth habit (Fig. 17-11). Its long branches tend to arch, rather than grow erect. It is a deciduous plant that can grow from 8 to 10 feet tall under ideal conditions. It rarely gets that tall.

Although this species is one of the so-called "flowering raspberries," it is not grown for its fruit, which is small and flavorless. It produces large flowers in late spring. The blossoms are white, single, and 2 or more inches across. The flowers always occur on 1-year-old wood. This is the wood from the previous season's growth.

Thimbleberries favor full sun. They will grow in partial shade, but may have trouble flowering when grown under heavy shade. Plant in a semiacid sandy loam. Plants like a soil that is rich in organic matter. Add peat moss or oakleaf mold to the planting site.

Prune to control size and encourage flowering wood. Cut back plants immediately after flowering. This will stimulate the production of next year's flowering wood.

The thimbleberry will add charm to any landscape. It should be given plenty of room to grow and a sunny location. It is thornless and, even though it can grow quite tall, is a practical groundcover for trouble spots in your landscape, such as sunken gullies or ditches.

Chapter 18

Vines

Vines can be grown in areas where there is not enough room for a shrub, but some form of plant life is desired (Fig. 18-1). As screens, they give needed privacy. As groundcovers, they help to prevent soil erosion and hide ugly areas where grass refuses to grow. Vines can be used to soften and lessen the intrusion of aluminum, steel, and concrete into the natural surroundings of your home. They can provide flowers and fragrance as well as plenty of summer color. Some vines bear brightly colored inedible fruits that provide a pleasing contrast, especially in the fall when leaves are gone. The careful selection of vines to fit your needs is a wise step.

SELECTING VINES

All landscapes could use at least one or two vines. They can enhance the character of walls, or provide filtered sunlight or shade into a room with western exposure. They can hide unsightly walls and fences, garbage cans, sheds, or clotheslines. They can screen off children's play areas, parked cars, patios, or porches, and they can be used as groundcovers.

Vines offer a solution to many landscape problems.

Because they do not take up much space, vines are very versatile and useful. Most vines provide a lush of green growth throughout the summer, yet take up very little ground space. Some vines have flowers in the early part of the summer and late spring. Other vines, such as climbing roses, can be everblooming and are grown chiefly for the beauty of their flowers.

(Caution: masonry walls are good for vines; wooden walls are not. Wooden walls are easily damaged by the weight of the vine and the moisture held in the foliage. Do not train vines against wood frame houses.)

Do not allow your vines to row above the rain gutters of your house. If they become established on rooftops they may be very difficult to remove, and if they are not removed, they will cause a great deal of damage to shingles.

TYPES OF VINES

Clinging vines, such as Boston ivy, should be planted

Fig. 18-1. Vines have numerous uses in the home landscape.

close to the supporting wall. The shoots of clinging vines may need to be held in place until they can establish their own contacts. If you plant Boston ivy (or similar clinging vines) too far from its support wall, it will be difficult to grow and will lose some of its aesthetic appeal.

Waterproof tape can be used to help plants establish contact with the wall. Be careful when removing this tape later on: the vines are very delicate, and if you yank off the tape, you could pull down half the vine as well.

Some vines are hardier than others. Be sure that the vine you select for your landscape is sufficiently hardy in your area. A mulch around the base of vines can help protect them from winter injury, but if the vine is not hardy to begin with, it may die.

Some vines have a herbaceous nature; that is, they die back to the ground each winter but will come back up when the spring arrives. Some vines are woody perennials. They do not die back to the ground each winter, but form a permanent woody frame with their branches. An example of this is the Boston ivy. Annual vines are not practical, except as accents. Annual vines may sometimes reseed themselves in warmer climates, but usually are more labor-demanding than are perennials.

Not all vines have spectacular flowers. Some vines have flowers that are inconspicuous and insignificant from a landscape viewpoint. The vines that are not grown for their flowers are usually grown for their foliage or fruit display. As a rule, the large-flowered vines require more attention and time to take care of them properly.

Bittersweets

Bittersweet vines are characterized best by their clusters of fiery orange-red berries, which appear in profuse, pendulant clumps in late autumn.

Bittersweet vines are among the few members of the plant kingdom that carry the sexes on two separate plants. Only female plants produce berries.

American Bittersweet. American bittersweet *(Celastrus scandens)* is much like the oriental bittersweet (see below), except it is much hardier. This species can be grown in those northern areas where oriental bittersweet would die out because of winter cold injury.

American bittersweet has a twining growth habit. For support, it twines around an object. Its yellow and red fruits grow in terminal (end) clusters. Like the oriental, it is *dioecious* (single-sex; male or female). In order to obtain fruit, you must plant both sexes. The female plants bear the colorful fruits, and the male plants provide the necessary pollen.

American bittersweet favors filtered shade and is very tolerant of dry soil and drought. It is especially attractive in the fall landscape.

Oriental Bittersweet. Its bright orange fruits are the most noteworthy feature of the oriental bittersweet. *Celastrus orbiculatus* is an excellent selection for planting on soil banks, and it also climbs walls and other garden supports. It often reaches a height of 35 feet. Bittersweet has small yellow flowers in the spring. Its inedible autumn fruits add to the character and attractiveness of the landscape.

Bittersweet has male and female flowers that are borne on separate plants. You must have the female plant to bear fruit and the male plant for pollination. If favors a sunny location and well-drained soil.

Clematis

The Clematis genus is noted for its large, showy blossoms that appear on tall, woody-stemmed vines. Clematis are all very tough (in their suitable climates) and long-lived. They make an excellent choice for a low-maintenance screening vine.

Anemone Flowered Clematis. The anemone flowered clematis is a southern shrub, not suited to the north. *Clematis montana* is a hybrid, with medium-size flowers that appear in midsummer, usually during June and July. The flowers are shaped like anemones. They come in colors of white, pink, or red.

Like other clematis species, the anemone flowered clematis requires a support system, such as a trellis or fence. It does not make a good groundcover. The flowers bear on 1-year-old wood. Do not prune the vine until after it has flowered. Pruning before that time will likely eliminate the flowers.

Jackman Clematis. Jackman clematis will make a spectacular display of summer color to brighten up your landscape. *Clematis jackmanii*, with its purple flowers, is very popular.

When Jackman clematis blooms in midsummer, the flowers are often 5 to 7 inches across. This plant prefers a slightly alkaline soil and a partially shady location. Mulch roots to keep the soil and prevent drying out of the soil.

You can use a string as a support system for this vine. Jackman clematis grows by twisting its leaf stalks around the support. Jackman clematis is a hardy vine that will add summer beauty to your porch, trellis, or garden arbor.

Scarlet Clematis. The scarlet clematis (*Clematis texensis*) is native to Texas, although it is hardy enough to grow in most parts of the county. It can be grown as far north as Minnesota if given some winter protection.

The scarlet flowers are unique in their distinctly urn shape. It blooms mostly in July, but often flowers sporadically until frost. Plants reach a height of 6 feet. The species may die back to the ground in the winter, but it will usually sprout back up again the following spring. It blooms on the current season's growth.

Scarlet clematis is especially appealing when trained to climb the entry to a white-painted gazebo, or to frame a porch or patio.

Sweet Autumn Clematis. Would you like the luxury of perfumed breezes in late summer and early fall? Sweet autumn clematis (*Clematis paniculata)* bears a profusion of clusters of small, richly scented white flowers. Although the individual blossoms are quite tiny, the effect of the clusters is tremendous. When in bloom, they produce clouds of blossoms.

This is an easy plant to grow. It is especially suited for use as a screen. It usually grows 10 to 15 feet, but can reach heights of 30 feet when set in a warm location with plenty of fertilizer and water. This hardy vine requires a support system to stand up; it completely covers chain-link fences in rapid order.

Clematis flowers are borne on the current season's growth. Prune heavily in the spring to encourage rapid growth and to stimulate flower production. This is one of the most common and most vigorous species of clematis.

Train sweet autumn clematis along fences or garden trellises. It also can be used on a porch. It is not suitable for groundcover use, because the flowers would get all muddy after a rainstorm and become unsightly. It should not be placed too close to driveways or in places where it may block desired views. It is a vine with utility value, especially to screen out unpleasant sights. It can hide garbage cans and make the area smell sweet.

Honeysuckles

All members of the Lonicera genus are famous for their fragrant, nectar laden blossoms. These vines are a prime source of food for bees, hummingbirds, butterflies, and other nectar-seeking insects.

Everblooming Honeysuckle. Everblooming honeysuckle (*Lonicera heckrotii)* is a twining vine equally at home in sun or shade. It produces fragrant pink and yellow flowers and blossoms throughout most of the summer.

The everblooming honeysuckle is a good vine for screening off an unsightly view and areas with a foul odor, such as garbage cans. The perfume from the flowers will camouflage unpleasant scents. It needs a support system on which to climb.

Hall's Honeysuckle. Hall's honeysuckle (*Lonicera japonica* var. *halliana*) is a tall-growing vine, often reaching 20 feet. It is best as a screen, but can also be used for a groundcover. It grows wild in parts of the south.

The very fragrant flowers of Hall's honeysuckle appear in midsummer and continue to bloom into the fall. They come in shades of white and cream. It is a delightful plant to use on border fences that divide neighbors, or to line garden paths or driveways.

Sweet Honeysuckle. The most fragrant of the honeysuckle species is sweet honeysuckle (*Lonicera caprifolium)*. Its trumpetlike flowers appear in early June and are a creamy ivory in color. They are about 2 inches in length and give off the most delightful scent, like a heavy perfume.

Sweet honeysuckle can be used anywhere there is a desire for a fragrant ornamental. It also makes an excellent background plant for backyards and patios. The growth can be used to screen out undesirable views, such as gas tanks, bottle gas, oil barrels, or garbage cans. Sweet honeysuckle provides warmth and charm for any sunny area.

Trumpet Honeysuckle. The trumpet honeysuckle (*Lonicera sempervirens)* is a somewhat fanciful vine because of the trumpet-shaped flowers it bears. It climbs by twining around an object and grows equally well in sun or shade.

Trumpet honeysuckle produces yellow, orange, and red flowers in the spring. It later bears red fruits for late summer color.

Ivies

Both American ivies (genus *Parthenocissus*) and European ivies (genus *Hedera*) are excellent green covers for masonry walls. It is wise, however, to periodically check the condition of such walls to determine if the ivy is deteriorating the wall's mortar. If this is the case, the vines will have to be removed and the wall repaired.

Boston Ivy. Boston Ivy (*Parthenocissus tricuspidata*) is one of the best vines for masonry walls (Fig. 18-2). This is the ivy of Harvard and other celebrated Ivy League universities. It has inconspicuous flowers and is best noted for its lush, yet orderly and extremely dignified dark-green summer leaves, which turn a blaze of color in the fall. The leaves do not mingle, as with most plants, but line up neatly into rows so that each individual leaf can capture some sunlight.

Boston ivy sends out rootlike *holdfasts*, which cling to any masonry or stone wall. They have the strength to support the vine when it is planted tight to the masonry building.

Although a very hardy plant, it may need some protection in areas with severe winters. The plants grow fast and are heavy feeders. Be sure that they receive plenty of fertilizer, especially nitrogen, each spring. If you use commercial fertilizer, a time-release pellet can be added to each plant. These pellets will usually last for two seasons of growth. Otherwise, apply manure each spring. Fresh manure should not touch the plant. Spread it evenly around the base of the vine and cover it with a few shovelfuls of dirt. Never fertilize after July first. Too much fertilizer late in the season will promote succulent growth and leave the vine susceptible to winter-injury problems.

Prune vines to keep them out of rain gutters and off rooftops. Do not use this plant on trellises. Boston ivy has great weight and needs the support of solid masonry walls (brick, block, stone, or stucco).

Boston ivy is a beautiful vine with multiseasonal appeal. It usually provides brilliant fall color, unless planted under too heavily shaded conditions. This plant will lend a formal and elegant, if not "educated," look to your home.

Thorndale English Ivy. The thorndale English ivy (*Hedera helix* var. *thorndale)* is among

Fig. 18-2. Boston ivy. Courtesy Stark Bro's Nurseries & Orchards Co.

the hardiest of English ivies, but it still may not be sufficiently winter hardy for many northern areas. Plant in a sheltered, but sunny location. This broadleaf evergreen is very fine-textured and favors shady conditions.

The thorndale English ivy supports itself by *aerial rootlets*. It is often used as a groundcover under trees where grass refuses to grow. If it is hardy in your area, this is a very fine species and makes an attractive display in your garden.

Veitch Boston Ivy. Veitch Boston ivy (*Parthenocissus tricuspidata* var. *veitchii)* is a fine-textured cultivar of regular Boston ivy. It is less aggressive than the regular species, and its leaves have a finer texture. The young leaves are purple and turn green as they mature.

An elegant vine with all the same fine traits as Boston ivy, this plant requires a masonry wall for its support. Plant in full sun for its best fall color display.

Virginia Creeper. Virginia creeper (*Parthenocissus quinquefolia)* is one of the hardiest ivy vines, an excellent choice for northern areas where Boston ivy may be only marginally hardy. Virginia creeper hangs on to masonry walls by holdfasts and tendrils. It has blue, inedible fruits, and its leaves turn red in the fall.

Virginia creeper grows in sun or shade. It grows rapidly and does not take long to establish itself. If a finer-textured type is desired, try the cultivar *Engelmanii.*

A cousin to the Boston ivy, this species is hardier and can be grown in areas where other vines will not survive because of winter kill. Like all vines, it should be pruned to keep it within bounds. Unbounded vines can do great damage to rooftops.

Other Vines

There are literally hundreds of vines that could be

162

chosen as landscape plants, depending on your local climate and your requirements. The few listed here have showy floral displays and are most hardy in temperate climates. If you live in the deep south, your choices are immensely increased by the profusion of fine tropical vines, or lianas, available.

Dutchman's Pipe. Dutchman's pipe (*Aristolochia durior*) is a twining vine for the shade. Its curious purple flowers and huge leaves form a privacy screen, and it is an excellent vine to screen off unpleasant views, such as garbage cans, oil barrels, or a busy highway.

Because of its twining growth habit, you will have to use some support base on which this vine can climb. A chain-link fence works nicely. The large leaves will quickly cover up the area and provide an excellent screen.

Silver Lace Vine. The silver lace vine, sometimes called *silver fleece vine*, has a fleecy, feathery look to it when in full bloom. *Polygonum aubertii*, its Latin name, bears flowers late in the summer, usually around August. When small thick clusters of flowers appear, most are white in color; sometimes they appear light green or pastel pink.

The silver lace vine will reach great heights. It should be trained to a trellis or screen for best effect. The vines do not show up as impressively against a white porch as when trained to a chain-link fence, where they can cover the whole fence with clouds of blossoms. An excellent background plant, it will add a delicate texture to formal gardens.

Trumpet Vine. The trumpet vine (*Campsis radicans)* will attract hummingbirds to your landscape. The birds like to hover over the trumpet-shaped blossoms and sip nectar with their long bills.

There are two colors available; one has golden flowers, the other, red. The trumpet vine clings to masonry by means of small rootlike holdfasts.

Trumpet vines favor moist soil, but they prefer full sunlight. They also need plenty of space to spread. They tend to multiply by suckers and will come up all over if they are not kept in bounds by pruning out suckers.

Wisteria. Spectacular is the only way to describe wisteria when it blossoms in the springtime. *Wisteria floribunda* is a leguminous plant that prefers a slightly alkaline soil. It should have a sunny location and plenty of moisture.

Although a fairly hardy plant, wisteria may need protection from severe winters in parts of the country. It should be planted on the wind-sheltered side of property. Never plant wisteria on the north side of a building or in an area where it will receive too much shade. If grown under heavy shade, it may have difficulty flowering or not flower at all.

The vines are a woody ornamental and their trunks grow in circumference each year, but they will need a support system. This plant can be trained to grow as a dwarf tree. (Check with your nursery to see if they offer the *tree* wisteria.) The vines should be trained and will need strong supports, because they can become quite heavy when in full bloom.

Wisteria vines can grow to great lengths (25 feet or more), but they produce the most flowers when they are pruned to contain their size. The plant's green leaves make it an attractive summer vine, even when not in bloom. When in blossom, wisteria is one of the most beautiful sights to behold. The vines produce clusters of highly scented flowers that hang like grapes, 12 inches or more in length. They are available in colors of lilac, pink, or white.

To achieve the best flower display, prune the plant to a main stem. All side branches should be pruned to encourage the production of short spurs. It is these short spurs that will produce the flowers. For largest flowers, purchased grafted plants. They will bear in a shorter time than those grown from seed and will usually have superior flowers.

The importance of providing a strong support system for wisteria vines and to train the vines to that support system cannot be stressed too often. A collapsed vine (or roof) will not be any joy to deal with.

Chapter 19

Roses

Roses are America's favorite flower. Although renown for their flowers, they are actually a woody ornamental shrub. Grown in all parts of the country, roses are used for many landscape purposes. Different varieties of roses are available for planting in borders, on lawns, for climbing arbors and trellises, for use as bedding plants, as hedges, as miniature trees, and as a source of cut flowers.

If you choose to have a completely natural landscape and use only wild roses, care can improve their performance. Watering, pruning, fertilizing, and protection from insect and disease pests, will result in larger and more plentiful blooms on the wild plants.

Neglected wild roses can grow quite large and may not bear any flowers. In such a case, you have a thornbush, which is not especially attractive. A little loving care, and a lot of pruning, watering, and fertilizing can turn your thornbush into a lovely specimen with blooming, fragrant roses.

Though some types of wild roses are desirable in a natural landscape, they are gradually being replaced by new hybrid varieties. There are many advantages to the new hybrids:

☐ They flower for longer periods of time, sometimes blooming from midsummer into fall.

☐ Hybrids usually have larger blooms.

☐ There are hybrid varieties that resemble the wild, but are superior in performance (larger blooms, and longer flowering period).

Every year new varieties are introduced by plant breeders. These new cultivars are available in a wide range of colors, shapes, sizes, and some have a stronger fragrance than others.

CLASSES OF ROSES

Roses are separated into two main classes by the habits of their growth: bush roses and climbing roses. Full-grown bush roses can be reached anywhere from 1 to 7 feet in height. They are erect and require no support. Climbing roses produce long canes and must be provided with some kind of support.

Bush Roses

Bush roses are grouped into types depending upon their flowering habit, winter hardiness, and other traits. *Hybrid tea, floribunda, grandiflora, polyantha, hybrid perpetual, shrub, old-fashioned, tree or standard,* and *miniature* are all types of bush roses.

Hybrid tea is the so-called "everblooming" rose. It is the most popular of all the rose family and more widely grown throughout the United States than all other types of roses combined. When the word rose is mentioned, it generally suggests a hybrid tea variety.

Mature hybrid tea roses are 2 to 6 feet in height. The height depends upon the variety and frequency of pruning. The flowers vary from singles, which have but one row of petals, to doubles with many rows. Usually, the buds are long and pointed, and the flowers are borne one to a stem or in clusters of three to five. They offer a wide color selection, and all varieties are good for cut flowers.

Most hybrid teas have some fragrance, but this will vary with the cultivar. When fragrance is present, it is usually most intense in the early morning, before the scented oil (a complex of at least 30 essential oils) has evaporated from the base of the petals.

Hybrid teas vary in cold hardiness. Most are winter hardy in areas where temperatures do not drop below 0° F. The hardiest class of hybrid teas were developed by Dr. Walter Brownell, a rose breeder. He made crosses from selections of roses known for their hardiness in the north. These types are called *sub-zero roses,* or *Brownell roses,* after the man who bred the original stock. They are usually hardy to −10° F. When given winter protection, they can withstand temperatures to −30° F.

Floribundas bear their flowers in clusters, with the individual blooms having a close resemblance to the hybrid teas, but not as large. They are gaining in popularity, especially for bed plantings where a large display of color is desired. Floribundas will tolerate neglect more than any other type of rose, with the exception of some of the shrub roses.

Grandifloras resemble the hybrid teas in bloom type (single flower on a long stem) and in hardiness. Though the flowers are somewhat smaller than hybrid teas, grandifloras bloom more abundantly. The flowers are good for cutting.

Polyanthas are smaller than those of the grandifloras and are borne in rather large clusters. The clusters are similar in form and in size of the individual flower to many of the climbing roses, to which they are related. Polyanthas are very hardy and can be grown in many areas where hybrid teas (with the exception of the Brownells) are too tender. Their chief use is in bed plantings or in borders with other perennials. They are effective in groups, but tend to flower only once a year, during early summer.

Hybrid perpetuals are the so-called *June roses* of yesteryear's garden. They have large flowers, generally lacking the form of the hybrid teas. An exception is the white-flowered variety, *Frau Karl Druschki,* which many consider to be the finest white rose in existence.

Before hybrid teas were developed, hybrid perpetuals were very popular. They are an everblooming type, though most do not bear continuously throughout the growing season, as do hybrid teas. They develop into large, vigorous bushes.

Shrub roses are actually a miscellaneous group of wild species, hybrids, and varieties that develop a large, dense growth useful in a landscape setting. They are hardy in all sections of the country. Although their flowers do not equal in size or form those of other roses, they are useful for hedges or screening. These roses produce fruits called *rose hips* that have a high content of vitamin C. Rose hips are edible (though not tasty raw) and can be used to make jelly, tea, tonics, etc.

Old-fashioned roses include the varieties that were popular in colonial gardens. Though the flowers of old-fashioned roses are not as attractive as those of newer varieties, they are usually more fragrant. These roses are hardy, require little care, and furnish an abundance of flowers in June.

Tree or standard roses are distinctive because of the form of growth, rather than the type of flower. Most modern tree roses are made by grafting any of the bush-type roses on upright trunks. Many of the better-known varieties of bush roses are also available as tree roses. Tree roses form miniature trees rarely exceeding 6 feet. They are useful in formal plantings or as accents in a garden. In areas where winters are severe, the plants will require special protection. They are not recommended for the north.

Miniature roses are very small. Not just the flowers and leaves, but the plant, itself, is small. The tallest some varieties get is about 6 inches. They are available with all the colors, form, and fragrance of the large-flowered plants. Miniatures are especially becoming in rock gardens, to edge flower beds, or border sunny garden walks. They can also be grown indoors in containers during the winter.

Climbing Roses

Climbing roses include all varieties that produce long canes and require some method of support to hold plants off the ground. Usually trained on trellises and porches, they can also be staked to fences and cover garden arbors as well. Certain varieties can be used as groundcovers, but most varieties cannot. Climbing roses are gaining in popularity.

Like bush-type roses, the climbers are also grouped into several types. There is some overlapping in categories and certain varieties could fit into more than one class. These classes are *ramblers, large-flowered climbers, everblooming climbers, climbing hybrid teas, climbing polyanthas, climbing floribundas,* and *trailing roses.*

Ramblers are very rapid growers. They sometimes develop canes as long as 20 feet in one season. They have small flowers, usually less than 2 inches across, which are borne in dense clusters. The flowers appear only once during the season and on 1-year-old wood (canes that were produced the previous year). The foliage is glossy, however, it is extremely sensitive to mildew. Although still available, most ramblers are being replaced by other climbers that bear larger flowers over a longer period of time and are less susceptible to mildew.

Large-flowered climbers grow slowly when compared with ramblers. They are often trained on posts. These roses are good for small gardens,

where they can be trained against a wall, fence, or trellis. The blossoms are large and can be used as cut flowers.

Everblooming climbers usually bear their heaviest bloom in early summer. After that, they produce a few scattered flowers until fall. Then, if conditions are favorable, the plants may bear heavily again. New varieties of this type of climber appear on the market each year. Some everblooming climbers are available that bloom as continuously as the hybrid teas and are more winter hardy.

Climbing hybrid teas originated as seedlings and as chance *sports* (mutations) of hybrid tea bush varieties. When a bush variety produces a cane that has climbing characteristics, the new plant is usually given the same name as the plant that originated it.

The climbing forms of hybrid teas do not bloom as continuously as their bush parents. The flowers, foliage, and other characteristics, however, are usually identical. The climbing hybrid teas bear the same level of hardiness as their bush parents.

Climbing polyanthas and *climbing floribundas* originated as sports (mutations) and seedlings from regular polyantha and floribunda roses. The flowers of these climbers are genetically identical to those of the bush form of the species. They also seem to bloom as continuously as their parents do, but they are less hardy than bush-types and will require extra attention and protection from severe winters.

Trailing roses are suitable for groundcovers. They are adapted to planting on banks or against walls. Their flowers are not as pretty as some of the other types, but plants are hardy. If used as a groundcover, set them in a sunny location where there is not traffic.

BUYING PLANTS

Buy your roses from reputable dealers. Mail-order nursery houses are often the best source of quality plants. Garden centers and local nurseries are acceptable, but be wary of plants already growing vigorously on the store shelf or, worst yet, in a sunny parking lot. These plants may suffer serious setback when they are finally transplanted. *Dormant* plants are the best for transplanting. Plants that are growing have already broken dormancy and may give you problems or die.

Mail-order nurseries usually offer a wider selection of roses, and they almost always offer a guarantee. Do not buy from any source that refuses to guarantee that their plants will grow and bloom if given normal care.

Look through your garden catalogs to see which roses capture your eye. Try to visualize the rose or roses as a part of your landscape. Keep in mind the additions and limitations of your yard (that is climate, size, etc.). That way, you will be able to make the best judgment.

CULTURE

Roses grow and bloom best if set out in sunny areas. They will grow satisfactorily under partial shade, if given a minimum of six hours of sunshine each day. They may not bloom if located under heavy shade.

If you must plant your roses in an area where they will be shaded for part of the day, let it be a place where they can receive the morning sun. If plants are shaded in the morning, their leaves remain wet with dew a few hours longer than if they receive the morning sun. Moisture on the leaves is favorable to the development of leaf diseases.

Rose roots grow close to the surface, so do not cultivate around them. You can control weeds by hand-pulling or cutting by them down to the soil surface, being careful to not injure the plant.

A summer mulch is recommended to control weeds and conserve moisture. Organic mulches are best, because they can also leach fertility into the soil as they decompose. Peat moss, straw, well-rotted manure, and many other composted items make effective mulches.

Roses need a liberal amount of water. Even in areas where rainfall is plentiful, occassional waterings are beneficial. Roses should receive the equivalent of an inch of water every seven days throughout the growing season. Soak the soil thoroughly. Direct a steady, slow-moving stream of water around the base of the plant. A heavy blast aimed at the plant is wasteful, because most of the water runs off and fails to penetrate the soil more than a few inches. Also, if you are not careful, you can erode soil around the plant and expose roots to drying winds and sun.

Time to Plant

The proper planting time for roses depends upon the severity of the winters in the region where they are to be planted. In the north, plant in the spring only; in the south, you can plant in either spring or fall. *Container-grown* roses can be set out at any time in the spring or fall, but they are very expensive.

Dormant *bare-root plants* are cheapest and best to plant. After they are set out and break dormancy, they will grow vigorously and bloom the same year they are planted, unless there is some other problem preventing this. (Late spring frosts can weaken and even kill newly set rosebushes.)

Planting

If you are planting only a few roses, dig individual holes for each rose. Make the hold at least 1 foot deep and 1 1/2 feet wide. Be sure the hold is large enough to accommodate the plant's roots without crowding. If you are planting a large number of roses in a bed, you can dig trenches in which to lay your roses.

Any good garden soil will produce good roses. The condition of peat moss and well-rotted cow manure will be beneficial to most soils. Roses are heavy feeders; they will appreciate a spring application of manure.

Roses do best when they are planted shortly after their arrival. If you cannot plant them the same day, moisten the packing material around the roots and repack the plants. Keep them in a cool room (but not freezing), away from any heat source. They will keep for three or more days. If they must be held longer than that time, *heel-in* plants in a protected spot in your garden until you are ready to plant them in their permanent locations.

To heel-in roses, simply place them in a shallow trench and cover their roots with moist soil. Be sure to select a shady location. Keep the soil moist, but not drenched. When you are ready, you can set the plants out.

Pruning

Annual pruning of roses is necessary and serves many purposes: it improves the plant's appearance, removes dead wood, and controls the quality and quantity of flowers produced. If roses are pruned, they soon grow into a bramble patch producing flowers that are small and of inferior quality. Shoots sometimes come up from understock. Usually these shoots can be identified by their many, small dark-green leaves. Ordinarily, these should be removed as soon as they appear, or they may dominate the plant.

It is not difficult to prune roses. It is advisable to wear a pair of leather gloves. These will protect your hands from the cuts and scratches of the thorns. Also wear a long-sleeved shirt or blouse to protect your arms.

To prune, always use sharp tools. Prune bush roses early in the spring, just before growth starts. First remove the dead wood. Be careful to cut an inch or so below the dark areas. If no live buds are left, remove the entire branch or cane. Next, cut out all weak growth and any canes growing toward the center of the bush. Anywhere two branches cross, remove the weaker. Shape the bush by cutting the strong canes to uniform length.

In some areas, the winters are so severe that much of the top plant is killed, and it may not be possible to do much toward shaping the plants. Just cut out all the dead wood, saving all the live wood that you can.

To prune tree roses, trim back the tops heavily in the spring. You may have to prune later in the growing season to prevent the tops from becoming too large for the stem. After cutting out the dead wood, shape the rest of the canopy so that it is fairly well balanced.

Prune shrub roses after they have bloomed and the blossoms faded. These plants are usually quite hardy, so pruning is needed to thin out and remove old canes. They will not require shaping. Shrub roses are most attractive when they are allowed to develop their natural shape.

Prune hardy climbers shortly after they have finished their flowering. This stimulates new cane growth and the development of new *laterals* (branches), on which next year's flowers will be borne.

Where ramblers are trained to a support that is so high that one season's growth will not cover it, cut off some of the older shoots. Shorten strong, vigorous canes. This pruning will stimulate laterals to develop and continue to elongate and cover the trellis. In spring, remove all dead canes and weak branches. Be careful not to remove too much wood. If you prune too heavily at this time, it will reduce flower production.

Most of the large-flowered everblooming climbers do not produce as much growth each year as the hardier climbers. For this reason, prune lightly.

Winter Protection

All roses benefit from some winter protection, except in parts of Florida and California where there are no true winters. Plants must be protected not only against low temperatures, but also from fluctuating temperatures. Sometimes rose varieties are hardy in the north where winter temperatures are constantly low, and are injured in areas further south where the winter temperatures fluctuate considerably.

To avoid winter injury, keep you rose plant healthy during the growing season. Healthy roses are better able to withstand winters than plants that have lost their leaves during the summer because of disease, insect pests, or nutrient deficiencies.

To protect bush roses, immediately after the first killing frost, while the ground can still be easily worked, pile soil 8 to 10 inches high around the canes. It usually works best to bring in soil from another part of your garden for this. Do not dig it from the rose bed, or you may injure the other rose plants. After mounding the soil around the canes, tie the canes together to keep them from whipping in the wind and loosening the root system.

Look at plants frequently to see that the soil is not washed away by rains before the ground freezes. Protection by mounding alone is effective in southern areas where the temperatures rarely dip below 0° F. In the north, however, further protective measures are necessary. A winter mulch of organic matter, such as straw, shredded leaves, or hay is advisable. Hold the mulch in place by tossing a few shovelfuls of sand over it. Cover the entire plant with mulch.

Remove the mulch and soil mound in spring when severe frost is past. Be gentle when removing the mulch so that you do not injure the plant. Keep some mulch nearby so that you can reapply it if there is danger of a late spring frost some evening.

To protect tree roses in areas where the temperature does not often drop below 0° F, wrap the plants with straw and cover with burlap. In areas where the winter temperatures frequently dip below freezing, you must also cover the base of the plants with soil. Tree roses are not recommended for the severe north.

EXHIBITION ROSES

For exhibition roses, disbud the plants while the buds are very small. Remove all but the terminal bud on each stem. This will cause the terminal bud to develop into a much larger flower than would otherwise be the case.

Polyanthas and other roses bearing many flowers per stem will also be improved by disbudding. Remove some of the buds from each stem. The more buds you remove, the larger the remaining flowers will develop.

Cutting Roses

Cutting roses is an important operation and must be done properly to prevent injury to the plant. Use sharp tools to cut flowers. Breaking or twisting off roses will injure the remaining wood.

During the first season, cut flowers with short stems only. Removal of foliage with long-stemmed flowers robs the bush of its food-manufacturing capacity and will reduce subsequent flower yield and plant growth. It also makes the plant more susceptible to winter injury.

Even with well established plants, it is not recommended that stems be cut any longer than is actually needed. At least two leaves should remain between the cut and the main stem.

Hybrid tea roses have three leaflets at the top of the rose stem and below that, a spray of five leaflets. On weak stems, make the cut above the spray of five leaflets. If the stem is strong, pencil thick in size, the cut may be made slightly higher.

Roses cut just before the petals start to unfold will continue to open normally and remain in good condition longer than if they are cut when fully open. If you do not cut the roses, remove them when their petals fall. Withered flowers in a cluster should be removed to give the blossoming flowers room to develop. After all flowers in a cluster have withered, cut off the entire stem just above the top leaf. This insures that new side shoots will begin to develop.

Preparing Cut Rose For Show

You begin preparation of show roses at the time the first buds appear. Allow the center flower bud to develop and pinch out all others along the stem as you see them. This allows the center bud to develop faster and into a much larger flower than if the other buds were allowed to remain.

Just before the show, cut the bloom with a long stem. It should be in tight bud at the time of cutting. Immediately immerse the stem of the rose into cold water. Wash the leaves of the plant to rinse off dusts, fungicides, or organic insecticides. Then store the bloom in a refrigerator at 32° F to 40° F to delay its opening. Remove it from the refrigerator to allow it to open between one-half and three-fourths at the time of the show.

Transport the rose carefully to the show. Take extra care not to damage the flower or the leaves. At the show, set the stem straight in a vase of proper size to hold the flower upright. Attach to the vase a label identifying the rose by name (and with your name on it).

DISEASES AND INSECTS

Many different insects and diseases attack roses. These pests vary in severity and type from area to area. Most of them can be effectively controlled no matter where you live by following the following recommendations:

☐ Buy plants that are free of insects and diseases.

☐ Keep your rose garden clean. Remove weeds, fallen rose leaves, and diseased or insect-infested canes and burn them.

☐ Control insects and diseases by biological means where possible. Use ladybugs to reduce the aphid population. Bourdeaux mixture is an excellent fungicide and will also help to rid plants of mites (Ivory soap will help rid mites, too). Organic insecticides, such as rotenone and pyrethrum, are available and will be very helpful in combating tough pest insects. (To control the Japanese beetle, see Chapter 13, Peonies).

The rose is a plant with many uses and it is also a practical plant that can enhance the beauty of your home and garden.

Chapter 20

Lilacs

April in Paris! To some the scent of lilacs in the air brings to mind April in Paris! Lilacs can add enchantment to your yard with color and fragrance. Lilacs come in many sizes, shapes, and colors. To the snow-weary residents of the north lavender, pink, red, or purple lilacs are usually favored over the white-flowering varieties (Figs. 20-1 and 20-2).

Although most enchanting during the spring, when in full bloom, they remain an attractive shrub during the summer after blossomtime has ended and the old withered flowers are removed. Lilacs are without any special interest during the fall and winter, but they make up for it in the spring. Their spring bouquet alone makes them worth planting.

Lilacs are quite versatile plants and have a wide range of uses in the home landscape. Depending upon which varieties you choose, you can have lilacs in flower from April to June. Naturally, they bloom earlier in places where temperatures are warmer.

Lilacs can be grown as single specimens or in a row as a flowering hedge. They are excellent for bordering walks and driveways. Taller varieties can be used effectively as windscreens. They can hide your garbage cans or offer privacy to your backyard. The dwarf varieties are useful for foundation plan-

tings and in areas where you want a shrub that will not get too tall or become too large. Dwarfs are often an excellent choice for a small yard.

Although their flowers are quite delicate, lilacs are among the hardiest of the woody ornamentals. Some varieties can survive winter temperatures down to −60° F and still bloom the next spring.

Lilacs perform well in all but the deep south. In the south, winters are too mild to provide lilacs with the seasonal rest period that they need. Lilacs do not require much care. They often grow and flower for many years, even when totally neglected. With proper care (water, pruning, and fertilizer) lilacs will produce better displays of flowers.

Most lilacs grow to less than 10 feet in height. This, however, depends upon the type and/or age of the plant. There are dwarfs that seldom get beyond 3 feet tall, and there are tree lilacs, such as the *Japanese tree lilac*, which can reach a height of 30 feet or more.

LILAC SPECIES

There are many species and cultivars of lilacs. The hybrids are the most popular today. Extensive cross

Fig. 20-1. Purple lilacs. Courtesy of Charles Webb & Mary Borofka-Webb.

Fig. 20-2. White lilacs. Courtesy of Charles Webb & Mary Borofka-Webb.

breeding has caused many of these species to closely resemble each other. Sometimes even botanists find the different lilac species difficult to classify.

Cheyenne Cultivar. If you live where winters are severe, you may wish to try *Cheyenne*, a free-flowering cultivar. It will withstand extra-cold temperatures. This lilac grows to a height of 8 feet and has dense symmetrical growth. The flowers are highly fragrant and a distinctive shade of light blue, quite different in color from most lilacs.

Common Lilac. The common lilac (*Syringa vulgaris*) is one of the best known species in the United States. This shrub can grow up to 20 feet. It has fragrant flowers that are usually lilac-color, although they can be white or other hues as well. Leaves are heart-shaped and smooth. Common lilacs tend to send out shoots of new growth each year from the base of the plants. These shoots are called *suckers*, and this habit is called *suckering*. If suckers are not removed by pruning, the lilac will quickly get out of bounds and form a thicket. This is one of the disadvantages of the common lilac and why the new hybrids, which do not sucker, are rapidly replacing it in popularity.

One of the advantages of the common lilac is that these suckers can be transplanted each spring and a new lilac plant will form. In a short while, a person can have an abundance of lilacs and some plants to give away each spring.

Dwarf Korean Lilac. The dwarf Korean lilac (*Syringa palebinina*) produces a smaller bush than the little-leaf lilac, rarely getting over 4 feet tall. It, however, has large flowers that are a typical lilac color. The blossoms are delicately scented with familiar lilac perfume.

Fragrant Lilac. The fragrant lilac (*Syringa pubescens)* has pale flowers that are among the most highly perfumed of all the lilacs. The leaves are hairy or pubescent. The fragrant lilac grows up to 12 feet tall.

Himalayan Lilac. The Himalayan lilac (*Syringa villosa*) is one of the latest to bloom within the lilac family. This is an excellent plant to extend the lilac season. It grows to about 10 feet but, like the others, can be pruned to a lower height if desired. The leaves are pointed and have hairy veins. The flowers are fragrant and borne in clusters; they have a rose-color hue.

Hungarian Lilac. The Hungarian lilac (*Syringa josikaea*) resembles the Himilayan lilac in many features, but it has darker flowers and smooth leaf veins, void of the hairlike pubcscence of the Himilayan species.

Japanese Tree Lilac. The Japanese tree lilac (*Syringa amurensis japonica*) is the most popular of the tree lilacs. They can reach a height of 30 feet and bear huge clusters of ivory or cream-color blossoms relatively late in the season. One drawback to the Japanese tree lilac is that it tends to have alternate bearing cycles. That is, it will bear flowers one year and skip the next year. One way to deal with this problem is to prevent it from bearing too heavily in one season. That way you can attempt to equalize the *C/N ratio* (carbon/nitrogen balance responsible for flowering) in the plant so that it will bear flowers annually. This is done by pruning.

Large-Leaf Lilac. The large-leaf lilac (*Syringa oblata*) is one of the first lilacs to open up the spring. It has scented blossoms and can grow to 12 feet tall. It is noticeable again in the fall when its big, broad leaves turn red. Most lilacs do not display fall foliage color, so if you are interested in a lilac for an autumnal landscape, this is an excellent variety.

Little-Leaf Lilac. The little-leaf lilac (*Syringa microphylla)* is a naturally dwarf plant. Both leaves and flowers of this species are small. It has a round, bushlike growth and rarely exceeds 5 feet when mature. It flowers late into the season, and has the famous lilac scent, but the blossoms are decidedly smaller than most other types.

Nodding Lilac. The nodding lilac (*Syringa reflexa)* has pink flowers that hang limply on the 10 to 12 foot bush. It "nods" in the wind, hence its name.

Peking Lilac. The Peking lilac (*Syringa pekinensis)* is an attractive shrub with yellow-white flowers. The flowers are not fragrant, although they are very ornamental.

Persian Lilac. The Persian lilac (*Syringa persica)* will grow to around 10 feet in height and is a truly grand sight when in full bloom. They have a pale lilac color, and its fragrant flowers fill the air with their heavenly perfume. This lilac is excellent for hedge use.

Preston Hybrids. The Preston hybrid lilac (*Syringa* x *prestoniae)* is a cross between the nodding lilac and the Himilayan lilac. It is a very hardy species with pale lilac-color blossoms that bloom late in the season. Its scent, although not as strong as some, is nevertheless lovely. These varieties can grow a tall shrub or be trained to tree form. They will reach a height of 15 feet.

Rouen or Chinese Lilac. The Rouen lilac (*Syringa* x *chinensis)* is actually a hybrid cross between the common lilac and the Persian lilac. It grows somewhat taller than the Persian. The highly scented, lilac-purple flowers are very similar to those of the common lilac, but they appear in greater profusion. The leaves are smaller than those of the common lilac, and the foliage looks more like the Persian lilac. Many nurseries confuse the two, calling this plant the Persian lilac, and vice versa. If you order it by the scientific (Latin) name, however, you will know what plant you have. The Rouen lilac does not sucker like common lilacs.

CULTURE

Lilacs do not require much care. They seldom need to be watered once established, except under conditions of drought, or if you live in an area where natural rainfall is inadequate. If weeds become a problem, pull them out by hand and then apply mulch. Do not cultivate around the base of the plant.

Lilacs grow best in an open area with good drainage. They favor a slightly alkaline loam. They will grow well in all types of soils excepting those that are too acidic.

Use

Lilacs are indeed versatile. Their use will depend on type or variety you have chosen, as well as on your individual tastes.

The Persian lilac makes such a beautiful hedge that it seems almost wasteful to not plant more than one in a row. Beautify your sidewalk or border your property with this variety, or use them to hide your garbage cans, unsightly gas or oil tanks/bottles, or a backyard work area (provided there is enough sunshine in those locations).

The common lilac and the Chinese lilac also make excellent hedges and can be used similarly. Do not underestimate the old-fashion lilacs that grandmother grew. Their blossoms may not be as showy as some of the new hybrids, but their fragrance will win you over.

Dwarf lilacs are useful for foundation plantings and are often most practical for small yards. The dwarf Korean or the little-leaf lilac is one you may use to frame your house, perhaps accompanied by low-growing evergreen plants. The dwarfs also work well in lining the driveway or walk, and even perform well as a specimen in a very small yard.

The Himalayan, Hungarian, and large-leaf lilacs all make handsome specimens. Plant them where you will not obscure windows and in sunny, front yard locations where their beauty will show. They grow much too tall (up to 12 feet) to be easily used as foundation plantings although, like other lilacs, they can be pruned.

The large blossoms of the French hybrids make them well worth the extra cost of purchasing them.

They also make ideal specimen plants.

The Japanese tree lilac makes a handsome specimen. It can grow up to 30 feet tall. (Be sure to read in this chapter about its specific needs.) The Preston (sometimes called *Canadian lilac*) can be trained to tree form (growing to 15 feet) or as a tall shrub. This lilac makes a very hardy, late season blooming specimen. The nodding and Peking lilacs are two other tall-growing lilacs, up to 10 or 12 feet, which will show off your yard. Except for its lack of fragrance, the Peking lilac is also attractive.

Most lilacs can be used as single plants or hedges, depending upon how you choose to plant them. Lilac hedges provide friendly screens between you and your neighbors. You will love these plants no matter how you use them.

Planting

Young transplants from the nursery will be the type of material most people will set out. Growing lilacs from seed or from home cuttings is not recommended. Seeds take too long to mature and hybrids will not reproduce from seed, but revert back to their original strains. Home propagation may not produce virus-free plants. It is however, usually safe to transplant cuttings of trouble-free plants to another part of your yard.

Spring planting is recommended for northern growers, and fall planting is favored for those who live in milder areas of the country. In the spring, plant lilacs before the buds open. Plant lilacs in the fall after the leaves have dropped but before the ground freezes. Whatever season you plant, the object is to allow new roots to develop and get a head start before the plant leafs out.

A sunny location with good air circulation is the place for your lilacs. Never plant lilacs in the shade or in places where they will not receive at least half of a day's sun. Such lilacs rarely flower and are soon plagued with mildew problems.

In planting lilacs, dig a hole big enough to accommodate the roots without twisting or breaking them. Work peat moss, composted manure, and garden lime into the hole. (Be careful to not use quicklime, because it may burn young roots.) You want to develop a good root system to hasten the establishment of the shrub.

Place plants 2 to 3 inches deeper than they grew in the nursery. You can tell this by looking at the crown area (just above the roots). The bark will look different where it has been underground. Some nurseries will save you the bother by painting a mark so you know automatically at what level of depth your plant should go. Be careful to not set the plant too deep, or you may kill it. When the hole is filled in, tamp down the soil, and water the area thoroughly. Allow the water to drain in, then fill any exposed areas where the water washed away soil, and tamp down gently again. Unless planning a lilac hedge, the plants should not be spaced any closer than 6 feet between them.

Pruning

Be careful to not overprune lilacs. Let the plant develop several branches from its base, instead of only one or two. This will allow you to remove old stems that become too tall or are attacked by insects or disease and still have flowering wood.

Pruning is unnecessary for the first three to four years. Thereafter, restrict pruning to eliminate weaker wood from the center of the bush. This will help to prevent the plant from becoming a thicket. Prune shortly after the flowers have faded or early in the spring. Prune bushes to open them up to air circulation and sunlight. Never prune in late summer, fall, or winter. Late pruning can result in the removal of flower buds and serious winter injury.

Old bushes with wild growth may need a system called *renewal pruning*. The purpose of this type of pruning is to "renew" the flowering wood. In such cases, remove about one-third of the height of the plant until the old wood has been cut down to a level, equal position. Cut out the skinny wood and select those branches that will bear the best clusters. Keep the plant uniform so that it does not develop uneven growth. Remove flowers shortly after they have died. This will help to insure vigorous growth for the rest of the season and abundant blooms for next year.

Some lilacs sucker and others do not. Remove

suckers unless you want your plant to become a thicket. These suckers can be transplanted to other areas of your yard where they will soon develop into new shrubs, or you can give them away.

PESTS

A number of insects and diseases attack lilacs, but only a few cause serious injury.

Powdery mildew is the most common disease. It usually appears in late summer, giving leaves a white, dusty appearance. You can control it by dusting leaves with sulfur as soon as you spot it, or use a copper-sulfate fungicide, such as Bourdeaux mixture, on a regular basis until the disease is no longer present.

Oystershell scale and *San Jose scale* pierce the bark and suck sap from the plant, which causes great injury to the flower-bearing stems. Control scale by removing them from the bark with a dull instrument. Be careful not to injure the plant. A dormant oil spray is helpful in controlling scales, as is the introduction of a predatory insect, such as the ladybug.

Lilac borers are insects that bore into the wood, sometimes leaving small amounts of sawdust as evidence of their presence. The larvae are creamy-white caterpillars about 3/4-inch long. They are usually found on the old branches, but sometimes go after the new branches. They are especially damaging to grafted plants. A serious infestation of borers can affect the entire bush, causing leaves to wilt and stems to break off. You may have to remove branches that are heavily infested. Kill borers by probing their holes with a wire. Mothballs can be crushed and placed around the soil of the shrub to discourage borers.

Chapter 21

Azaleas and Rhododendrons

Azaleas and rhododendrons are among the most popular garden plants, and their brightly colored, pleasantly scented flowers are prized for both indoor and outdoor floral display. These two acid-loving species require special care but are very rewarding.

Azaleas and rhododendrons both belong to the genus *Rhododendron*. There are wild species native to the United States and Europe, but garden varieties are mostly hybrids. Some Europeans make jelly out of the flower of the tree rhododendron (*Rhododendron arboreum*), but most plant parts within this genus are poisonous. An oil used as a healing salve in Italy called *Olio di marmotta* is extracted from the buds of some European species.

Azaleas are very similar to rhododendrons, except they have a finer leaf texture and generally grow smaller than rhododendrons. Azalea leaves are quite small and delicate.

Rhododendron leaves are much larger and much coarser. Some are deciduous and other types are broadleaf evergreens. The broadleaf evergreen varieties are usually most popular. They retain their leaves all year around. The leaves of some of the rhododendrons change color from green to maroon with the advent of cold weather.

Garden varieties are mostly hybrid cultivars that took years of breeding from the finer selections. Much of this extensive work with azaleas and rhododendrons was done in England, where the flowers are treasured. Now most of these excellent selections are available for gardeners in this country. People who live in the north will want to grow the hardiest hybrids available.

Azaleas and rhododendrons are available in a rainbow of blossom colors. Their clear, vibrant colors truly produce a very showy flower. These flowers will bring spring beauty and class to your home, garden, and neighborhood.

CULTURE

Azaleas and rhododendrons have the same cultural requirements. They are high-maintenance plants that will require special care and love to develop into prize garden specimens. Most garden soil is not suitable. These plants require a moist, acid soil.

Check your soil's pH levels before planting either azaleas or rhododendrons. If necessary, as it probably will be, add *aluminum sulfate* or *ferrous sulfate* to acidify your soil. Follow the instructions on the label of whatever product you are using.

The addition of peat moss will be beneficial. Some people like to use half peat moss and half soil for a rich, organic planting medium. Keep plants well-watered throughout the growing season, into the fall until about one week before the ground freezes. Do not water plants after the ground has frozen.

The broadleaf evergreen species will usually arrive balled and burlapped or in a container. These plants are difficult to transplant, because they are in a stage of active growth at the time you transplant them. Extra care must be used in the planting operation and in maintenance of plants so that you do not lose them. The roots are held together by either the container or the ball of dirt and burlap that is tightly wrapped around them. Gently loosen this or remove the container. If possible, try to not lose any of the dirt wrapped around the roots, and be careful to not injure roots when you transplant them.

Set roots down gently into the hole. Be sure that each hole will be large enough to accommodate the plant without cramping. Make certain that the hole is not too big, either. Tamp soil firmly around each plant. Water thoroughly. After the water is allowed to drain, add more dirt to the areas where it may have washed away.

Always plant so that there is a shallow depression in a ring around the plant to catch natural rainfall. Use mulch of straw or shredded leaves to help keep weeds down and conserve soil moisture. Water plants on a weekly basis, more often during periods of dry weather. Keep the soil around the base of each plant moist, but not wet, to the touch.

Each year, you should add a little ferrous sulfate and manure in the spring. Place it in a circle around the base of each plant. (Do not touch the plant with fresh manure.) Toss a few shovelsful of dirt over the manure and water in thoroughly.

These acid-loving plants are very sensitive to the soil pH level. It must be acidic enough, or they cannot extract the iron they need from the soil. Iron-deficient plants develop a disease called iron chlorosis. The only remedy for this disorder is to acidify the soil to see that the plant receives the iron it needs.

There are foliar fertilizers that contain iron. These feed plants through their leaves and can go to work almost immediately. If you have a plant with yellowing leaves (a symptom of iron chlorosis), you may want to use one of these foliar fertilizers. Incidentally, yellowing leaves can also be a symptom of drought or nitrogen deficiency, so you will want to check out the problem first.

TYPES

Azaleas and rhododendrons are available in all shapes and sizes, from dwarf bushes to treelike forms. Whatever form you choose, be sure that it will be hardy in your area. There are many excellent varieties. Check with your nursery to see which ones you will want. For people who live in the north, try one of the following hardy strains:

Molle hybrid azaleas (*Rhododendron* x *kosteranum*) have a spreading form. It requires moist, acid soil and does best in filtered shade. This species bears flowers in the spring that are of yellow and orange hues. Its foliage turns red in the fall.

The PJM hybrid rhododendron (*Rhododendron* x *hybrida* var. *pjm*) has a round form. It needs a moist, acid soil and grows best in shady areas. The PJM rhododendron has profuse lavender flowers in the spring. A hardy broadleaf evergreen, its leaves turn purple in the fall.

Chapter 22
Gardenias and Camellias

Gardenias and camellias are among the two most beautiful plants southern gardens can display. They are not sufficiently hardy in most northern areas, but they can be grown indoors where winters are severe.

Gardenias. Gardenias, also called *Cape jasmine* in some areas, is an evergreen garden shrub that grows in southern states as far north as the coastal plains area of Virginia. Its white flowers appear over a period of several months, mostly in May and June.

The common gardenia (*Gardenia jasminoides*) is the most widely planted of the species. Another species (*Gardenia veitchi*) flowers more freely in the winter and is popular for houseplants and greenhouse culture.

The gardenia is valued not only as an ornamental shrub, but is also one of the most desired cut flowers in the south. Its dark-green leaves contrast with the bright white blossoms, and its heavy fragrance fills the room. It also has better keeping qualities than many other flowers. It is an excellent flower for florists.

Most of the florist's gardenias in the north are actually from outdoor gardenias grown in the south and shipped northward. The largest volume is usually sent out around Memorial Day, but shipments continue as long as there are flowers available. There is a large market for gardenias as a cut flower, and you could plant yours with this in mind. There are many growers supplying the market, however, so the competition is sometimes fierce.

Culture. Gardenias are strictly a southern ornamental. They are not sufficiently winter hardy to survive outdoors in the north. If grown in the north, they will have to overwinter indoors and therefore should be restricted to container plantings. In the south, they can be used lavishly to decorate any landscape.

Gardenias usually arrive from the nursery balled and burlapped. That is, with their roots wrapped up in a ball of soil and protected with burlap to hold the soil together. It is important that the plants are handled extra gently to avoid disturbing the soil around the roots. When laid into the planting hole, remove the burlap very carefully, so you disturb the root system as little as possible. Do not just yank it off, or you may seriously injure the plant. (Handle the plant as you would a baby. You do not just yank a diaper off of an infant—you tenderly remove it, keeping the infant in a secure place where it cannot fall. Use this same treatment for your gardenia plants.)

Plant gardenias in rich, but well-drained soil. They prefer a slightly acid soil, so peat moss should be added at planting time. Water plants to keep the soil moist, but not drenched, at all times. Prune the branches to encourage the development of flowering shoots.

If conditions are favorable, a few flowers can be expected the second season. The plants are in their prime during the third, fourth, and fifth seasons. When they become older, they tend to produce small buds with little foliage and appear leggy. Prune to shorten the older wood and fertilize heavily to encourage robust growth. This will help to lengthen the productive life of the gardenias for several years.

The flowers will keep for several weeks if, after being cut, they are stored in a cool room. They do not last very long if they are exposed to the open sun and warm temperatures.

The best time to cut flowers is when they are fully open. They can be removed with or without some of the foliage attached to the flower stem. Be careful not to bruise the petals of the flower blossom, because this causes it to turn brown.

Use. Gardenias are beautiful as single specimens and accent plants. When planted *en masse*, they can be used to form a lovely low-growing flowering hedge for a border along a path or to separate areas in the landscape. Keep in mind that although the plants are usually in bloom the heaviest in May and June, they will blossom during other times as well. One flower can fill the air with intoxicating perfume, which alone makes it worth the planting.

Even when the plant is not in flower, the shiny dark-green leaves are quite attractive. The plants grow up to 5 feet tall and perform best in a partially shaded location.

Camellias. Camellias are among the most beautiful of flowering shrubs. They bloom at those times when few other plants do—in late fall, winter, and early spring. These are evergreen shrubs that do best when planted in filtered shade.

Camellias are not sufficiently winter hardy for northern areas. If growing them in the north, they should be grown in containers that can be taken inside during winter months. Some camellia species are hardy enough to grow as far north as Long Island, New York, when given adequate winter protection. The hardiest species can withstand winter temperatures to 10° F; you can grow camellias anywhere you can protect them from temperatures lower than 10° F and prevent their roots from freezing.

Camellias prefer light shade. They are shallow rooted and favor a loose, rich loam soil that is slightly acid and has lots of humus. Camellias do not tolerate poorly drained soils, where water is left standing for prolonged periods of time. Heavy clay soils will need to have plenty of organic matter mixed in to lighten them before they are suitable for planting to camellias.

Cultivars. Camellias are available in a wide range of colors: red, pink, white, and combinations of these. There are three species that are commonly cultivated in the United States. These are *Camellia japonica, Camellia sasanqua,* and *Camellia reticulata.*

Camellia japonica is the hardiest of the three species and the best for planting along the Atlantic coast into the Washington, D.C. area. It can be grown farther north with winter protection (to Long Island, New York). This species has dark glossy leaves and blooms from late winter through spring.

Camellia sasanqua also has glossy leaves but is hardy only as far north as the nation's capital. It blooms in October and November.

Camellia reticulata is the most tender of the species. Although it can be grown outdoors in southern California and in the deep south, it should be grown only in containers in other parts of the country, so that it can be taken inside during the winter. This species has dull green leaves and blooms in the spring.

Selecting Plants. Before you purchase any plants, check to see which species is hardy in your area. Your county agent can usually supply you with that information if it is not readily available in your garden catalog.

Most nurseries sell camellias balled and burlapped. (This is simply a burlap wrapped ball of soil around the roots.) Some nurseries sell plants in containers, and mail-order nurseries will sell bare root plants to save on shipping charges. Buy balled and burlapped or container grown plants whenever you can, because they are easier to establish and will more readily adapt successfully than will bare root plants.

Buy 2-year-old plants. They are better to work with and will bloom quicker than 1-year-old or young seedlings. Two-year-old plants will be 18 to 24 inches tall. Purchase healthy plants only. If you buy plants from a local garden center, look them over carefully. Inspect for wounds or scars near the base of the main stem. Wounded areas may become cankerous and cause early plant death. It is important to remember, however, that grafted plants may have a swollen area near their base; this is not a sign of poor health.

When selecting plants from a group, pick only those that are well-branched from the ground up. Select those that have the best form and the greenest and freshest foliage. By choosing plants with the greatest number of healthy leaves, you will be getting those that most likely have the best root systems as well.

Do not be misled by the size of containers. A vigorous plant growing in a gallon can is better than a poor plant growing in a 5-gallon can; the vigorous plant will likely outgrow the poor one in a single season.

Planting. Fall is the best time to plant camellias. In Virginia, spring planting is also satisfactory and sometimes preferred. Try to select a site that will provide at least a half-day's shade during the summer, some shade in winter, and protection from winter winds. Camellias usually work well planted on the north side of buildings or under tall pine trees. Remember: camellias are a southern shrub and should not be planted in northern states out-of-doors.

A fully mature camellia can spread from 8 to 10 feet in diameter. Plan for this future growth when you are setting out plants. Set camellias at least 3 feet away from buildings. If you are planting a camellia hedge, set plants 5 to 7 feet apart to prevent crowding. The plants will quickly fill in any gaps and provide a compact hedge.

On well-drained soils, you can simply dig a hole to set your camellia. On heavy soils and those that drain poorly, however, another system called *mounding* is used.

Mounding. Dig the hole about twice the size of the width and depth of the rootball. Refill the hole slightly more than half full with good soil or well-composted cow manure. Be sure to only use composted manure, because fresh manure can burn plant roots. Tamp the soil with your feet to provide a firm base for the plant.

If the roots of the plant are balled and burlapped, you may remove the burlap before setting the plant in the hole. If you accidentally broke the rootball, or the removal of the burlap causes the soil to fall apart, you can cut the twine and fold back or cut off exposed parts of the burlap after setting the plant in the hole.

If the plant is in a container, cut away the sides of the container with metal shears and remove the rootball carefully. Do not knock the rootball out from the can; you are likely to injure roots if you do.

Place the plant into the hole and pack the soil around the plant forming a mound around the plant made up of soil and peat moss. Water the plant in thoroughly. Water at the base of the mound in a circle around the plant. Do not apply too much pressure, or you will undo the mound that you made. Allow the water to drain in.

Culture. A mulch is usually applied immediately after planting. It should be regularly maintained. Mulching reduces fluctuations in soil temperatures, helps to prevent weed growth, and conserves soil moisture. Peat moss, pine needles, and *oakleaf mold* (decaying oak leaves) make excellent mulches. Be sure that water can penetrate through the mulch and that it is not so thick that it acts like a thatched roof, or the plant will suffer from drought stress. Plastic mulches are not advisable. If using oak leaves, shred them first. You can shred oak leaves by using a shredder, or running a power lawn mower over them several times. A 2-inch deep mulch is as deep as you will want for summer. In winter, the mulch can be as deep as 4 inches, depending upon how cold it gets in the area.

In the humid regions of the southeast and south, normal rainfall usually provides enough moisture for mulched camellias. In the southwest and California, plants will need to be irrigated. Water at weekly intervals; during droughts, water more frequently. When watering, soak the ground thoroughly. It is especially important to water plants during the time of bud set and when plants are in full bloom.

A common problem, especially when using chemical fertilizers, is overfertilization. If plants are overfertilized, it promotes a loose open growth that spoils the compact habit of the plant. Overfeeding can also cause the plants to be more susceptible to winter injury.

Camellias are effective as specimens or when planted in groups of three or more. It rivals roses, in warm winter climates, for beauty.

Chapter 23

Shade Trees

During the summer, nothing can be appreciated more than a nice shade tree to sit under, take an afternoon siesta or just escape from the heat.

Too often, when people buy a lot and start to build a new home, they tear out all the existing trees. In doing so, they remove more than a source of just beauty. Established trees help to hold the soil in place. They keep moisture in the ground and, in the case of deciduous trees, add fertility to the soil with their fallen leaves. If at all possible, it is a good idea to plan so that you can save as much of the natural vegetation (trees and shrubs) as possible. This will create a more rewarding landscape than trying to start completely from scratch.

The tree you choose to provide shade for your yard is a selection to which you want to give careful thought. Shade trees usually grow quite large: some reach as high as 80 feet at maturity. You will want to determine what space you have and whether you have room for more than one shade tree if you should want to plant more. Remember, you will not want your entire yard under shade, or your other landscape plants may have difficulty growing. When

planting a shade tree, think in terms of the tree at its mature height and width. That way, you will allow it plenty of space to grow and develop.

Where you set your tree will depend upon your individual needs. Most people opt for a shade tree in their backyard, which is a nice place for outdoor dining and summer picnics. Shade trees in the front yard were more popular in the days when yards were bigger. Today, smaller trees called *lawn trees* are more practical for most front yards. Lawn trees do not become so large, and they have replaced the old-fashioned shade tree in many modern home landscapes.

DECIDUOUS TREES

Deciduous trees provide the best shade trees, especially those with large tops. A deciduous tree will cool an area during the summer with its large canopy but allow the sun to warm the area during the winter, when all its leaves have fallen.

Conifers and columnar-shaped trees are not as effective at providing shade. Although they may cast some shade, it is quite close to the trunk. Even with the removal of the lower limbs, they are not as effective as deciduous shade trees.

There are differing degrees of shade. Some trees, such as maples, cast a heavy shade, while other trees, such as honeylocust, cast a light, filtered shade. The heavier the shade cast, the cooler it will be under the tree, and the more attention you will have to pay to the planting of shade-tolerant species in the immediate vicinity of the tree.

Some shade trees produce flowers, but most shade trees are chosen for other characteristics. An example of a flowering shade tree is the magnolia. A few shade trees produce seeds or fruits, which can be considered a maintenance nuisance. Sometimes these seeds or fruits have foul odors when they decay. If you do not want to be bothered with seeds, it is best to plant only the male cultivars of species. With trees that bear both sexes, it may be desirable to consider planting a different type of tree altogether.

Shade trees do not all grow at the same rate. Usually, deciduous trees that grow fastest have soft wood and are more likely to be injured by severe storms. Conversely, slow-growing trees generally have hard wood and are more durable under the stress of inclement weather. There are exceptions. For example, white and green ash grow moderately fast, yet both have hard durable wood. They are also quite attractive in the landscape and usually provide fall color as well. If a quick shade is desired, a fast-growing tree is most practical to plant.

Note: according to strictly botanical classification, all deciduous trees are *hardwoods*, and all coniferous trees are *softwoods*. Deciduous trees that grow fast produce a softer hardwood than do those that mature slowly. Conversely, a slow-growing conifer can produce a hard softwood.

LOCATION

After you have decided on the features you want in a shade tree, do not forget to check it for hardiness. Any tree that is incompatible with your climate— that includes the amount of yearly rainfall as well as the average winter cold temperature reading— will not likely survive for very long.

The area where you choose to place your tree is important. The roots of many trees grow near the soil surface. If they are planted too close to walks or driveways, they can upheave the pavement. Tree roots can also interfere with sewer lines and clog drainage pipes. Shade trees should never be placed too close to power or telephone lines.

Some of the popular shade trees of yesteryear are not practical today. Dutch elm disease is so widespread in the United States that it is rapidly depleting the graceful American elms that once lined the streets of cities and small towns. It is not worth the heartache to plant an American elm tree. If you must plant an elm, try one of the European new hybrids that are much more resistant to the dreaded Dutch elm disease.

Shade trees have differently shaped *canopies*. The pendulant branches of the weeping birch, or the ascending branches of the white oak, offer a sharp contrast in form. The choice of the shade tree you select will do much to establish the theme of your landscape. Idyllic scenes can be created with weeping birch or weeping willow, whereas oaks tend to create a more woodsy feel to a place.

Whatever tree you finally decide upon, you will find a shade tree to be an enduring and endearing friend. It will soon become a symbol of home and, in its own special way, a part of the family.

SHADE SPECIES

The best trees are those that will cast a heavy shade, but you may want a shade tree that casts a filtered shade. The tree you choose depends upon how much shade you desire and what other plants are growing in your yard.

With the aid of heavy earth moving equipment, nurserymen can move and transplant trees of huge size . . . up to 60 feet and more. The cost is enormous, however, and you will probably want to plant trees that are less than 10 to 12 feet tall. They may take longer to develop, but the cost is reasonable and their chance of survival is greater.

Planting time varies with locality, but usually deciduous trees are best moved in early spring while trees are dormant (before new growth) and in mid-autumn when leaves begin to fall.

Once you have determined what type of shade tree you will plant, where it will go, and what its cultural requirements are, you must test your soil and see what modification in pH level, fertility, and consistency must be made. (For tips on preparing soil, see Chapter 5, Deciduous Hedges.)

Dig a hole that is much larger than the spread of roots. Loosen the soil remaining in the hole and work in organic materials, fertilizers, and pH correctives well.

If you are planting a bare-rooted tree, make sure the roots do not dry out for even a short period of time. Keep them wrapped in wet newspapers or burlap and plant as soon as possible. Before setting the tree in its hole, use a sharp knife to cut off any dead or broken roots.

Make a slight mound of earth in the hole and place the tree upright on it. Spread the roots out in the way they grew naturally. If roots are badly tangled, soak them in water to untangle them.

If you are planting a balled and burlapped tree, set it directly into the hole and cut away the twine and burlap that covers the root ball, being careful not to dislodge the tree from position. Remove as much burlap as possible, especially any that will protrude above ground. It will act as a wick and dry the roots. Any burlap left deep in the ground will merely rot away.

Be sure to set the tree in at the same depth at which it grew (Fig. 23-1). Never plant a tree deeper than 2 inches over its original depth. (If it is necessary to change the depth at which a tree is planted because of changes in the grade of the lawn, you can either make a *raised bed* (if lawn level is lowered) edged in rock or concrete, or a *tree well* (if level is raised) lined with rock or concrete.) These structures should be about half the diameter of the full spread of branches.

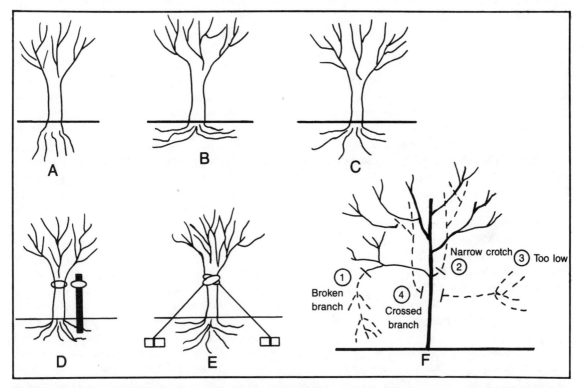

Fig. 23-1. Trees must be planted at the correct depth, staked, and pruned carefully if they are to thrive: (A) too shallow; (B) too deep; (C) correct depth; (D) tree correctly staked; (E) tree supported by "dead men" and guide lines; (F) correct pruning to remove narrow crotches, broken, crowded, and low limbs.

Fill the hole with shovelsful of good soil. Work it between and around roots. When hole is about three-quarters filled, tamp the soil down firmly with your feet or with a blunt implement. The remainder of the hole should now be filled with water once or twice and allowed to absorb it before completing the filling. Make a saucerlike depression, edged with a ridge of soil, around the base of the tree to catch rainwater.

If the tree is tall and in an exposed area, you may want to stake or secure it. Drive three heavy stakes into the undisturbed earth beyond the hole. Run guy wires from around the trunk of the tree to the stakes and secure. Where the wire comes in contact with the tree, it should be run through a piece of hose or padded with burlap to prevent bark injury.

A single large stake driven deep into the ground beside the tree and secured to it can also be used. Likewise, two heavy pieces of log can be buried in the ground beyond the tree's branch span and guy wires run from these "dead men" to the tree for support.

After the tree is staked, wrap the trunk with burlap or special tree wrap to protect it from sun scald, splitting, and insects. Keep the tree well watered and apply a mulch to conserve moisture.

You should prune newly planted trees to remove dead, diseased, or injured branches. Remove any straggly or unattractive branches, but do not shorten the main trunk. This pruning will not hurt the tree, because the roots were probably cut when the tree was dug up, and they cannot supply the demands of the full load of branches. Pruning the branches allows the roots to redevelop and strengthen. Up to one-third of the branches can be removed in this *compensatory pruning*.

Pruning cuts over 1 inch in diameter should be painted with *tree wound paint*. This is commercially available or you can mix your own out of sulphur and leaded paint.

Most shade trees are pruned to grow with a single main trunk or *leader*. Others have either *modified leaders* (one trunk and two main branches) or *open centers* (more than one trunk). For all three types, make sure that no unwanted side shoots or water sprouts develop along central branches and main crotches and that no suckers begin to grow from the base of the tree.

Crossing branches, broken or diseased branches, and narrow crotches that could break should be removed to keep the tree neat. Encourage main branches to grow so that air and light can penetrate. Most shade trees will not need more than periodical light pruning to clean them up in early spring and fall.

Ash

Trees of the Fraxinus genus make ideal shade trees because of their moderately fast growth and sturdy structure. Ash trees produce medium to heavy shade.

Arizona Ash. It is not sufficiently hardy for the north. Arizona ash (*Fraxinus velutina*) is a moderately fast-growing tree that reaches about 40 feet. It is best suited for the southwest, and northern California. It has a round canopy.

Arizona ash is highly drought-resistant and will even grow in parts of the desert. This is an excellent ash tree for those in warmer climates who desire an attractive shade tree.

Green Ash. This species produces male and female flowers on separate trees. The female flowers bear seeds that can become a maintenance problem. Plant only male cultivars to avoid this problem. The green ash (*Fraxinus pennsylvanica*) grows moderately fast to 40 feet or more. It produces maplelike leaves that are apple-green in color throughout the summer. During the fall, the leaves turn to golden yellow.

Plant in any well-drained soil. Green ash favors a rich, moist soil, but it is more drought-tolerant than white ash and will grow in dry areas where white ash would suffer badly. Green ash has a straight trunk and round-to-oval canopy. It is an excellent shade tree, providing fall color as well as summer shade. There are a couple of excellent cultivars: *Marshall's Seedless* is seedless with dark glossy foliage and brilliant yellow fall color. *Summit* has a columnar form. It is useful for screens along driveways. It has a fine-textured foliage and, again, a yellow fall color.

White Ash. If you are an especially fastidious person, this tree may annoy you, because it has the habit of shedding twigs and bark. The white ash (*Fraxinus americana*) is a rapidly growing tree that can reach over 90 feet tall. The canopy of the white ash tends to vary somewhat in shape, but it is mostly round.

Plant in any well-drained soil. White ash does not hold up well under drought stress and must be watered during dry spells. This tree favors a rich, moist soil.

Birch

Birch trees are a graceful additions to any landscape. Their slender trunks and shimmering green leaves add a touch of unspoiled natural beauty to a well-manicured lawn.

Cutleaf European Birch. The cutleaf European birch (*Betula pendula* var. *gracilis*) is a tall weeping form of birch. It very much resembles the paper birch, except for its smaller leaves and weeping character (Fig. 23-2). The leaves look as if they were shredded, hence the name "cutleaf."

The cutleaf European birch favors cool, moist soil. It is as hardy as the paper birch and can be grown in the far north. It does better in the north than in southern climates where its bark may not turn white. Keep the soil around its base damp, not wet, to the touch. A summer mulch to conserve moisture is recommended.

The cutleaf European birch can be set anywhere a weeping-type tree is desired. It is very graceful and makes a spectacular addition to any landscape. You must remember to protect its bark from rodent damage, however.

Japanese White Birch. The Japanese white birch (*Betula platyphylla japonica*) can grow to a height of 40 feet, although it usually does not get that tall. It has forest-green leaves and a pyramidal shape. The bark turns paper-white and provides an excellent color contrast to its green foliage.

The Japanese white birch is a superior new strain of birch that can adapt to a wider temperature range than ordinary paper birch. It is very hardy. It was developed at the University of Wisconsin-

Fig. 23-2. Cutleaf weeping birch. Courtesy Stark Bro's Nurseries & Orchards Co.

Madison to be highly resistant to the bronze birch borer (among its other traits).

Plant in any well-drained soil. It favors a slightly acidic woodsy soil. Leafmold or peat moss should be added to the planting site.

This is a rapid-growing species. Water on a regular, weekly basis. During extremely dry weather, water more often. Do not water plants daily, or they may never develop a good deep root system—you could also create drainage problems. Soak the area around the base when watering. Do not sprinkle, because growing trees need plenty of water. Water only during the growing season. Do not water trees after the ground freezes.

Paper Birch. Birch trees are very graceful and cast a filtered shade. They are more practical for the north, because the paper birch may not develop the white color of its bark when grown in the south and warmer climates.

Paper birch (*Betula papyrifera*) is perhaps the most famous of the birches. It is distinguished by its peeling, white bark. While the tree is young, it has light brown bark, but as the tree ages, its bark turns white and makes a very ornamental display. It usually takes about two or three years for the bark to turn white.

Paper birch is the tree some American Indian tribes used to make canoes. It can be found growing wild throughout the northern woods of the United States and Canada. It has dark green leaves in the summer, changing to golden-yellow in the fall.

Paper birch favors cool, moist soil and does not grow well in dry soils. Plenty of peat moss should be added to the planting site. Remember, this is a species that is native to woodlands. A moist, woodsy soil, rich in organic matter, is best. Paper birch is most attractive when planted in clumps of three.

The bark of these trees needs to be protected from gnawing mice and rabbits, especially during the winter. Mice can do a great deal of damage, sometimes girdling the tree and killing it. Either commercial tree wrap or aluminum foil can be effective deterrents to rodents. They are also effective in protecting trunks from the *bronze birch borer,* which will deface and even kill trees if infestation is heavy.

Plant in clumps of three for best effect. It can be grown as a single specimen, but looks so much more dramatic when it is grown in clumps. All birches are very attractive trees, and you will never regret planting this species.

River Birch. The river birch (*Betula nigra*) is not planted as widely as it deserves to be. Its bark never turns white, but instead is pinkish-brown and peeling. This is the most fascinating feature about this species. You really have to see one in a landscape to appreciate its beauty.

River birches are moderate growers with a vase-shaped canopy. They produce a good summer shade. The foliage is green throughout the summer. This tree can sometimes be found in the wild, growing near rivers and streams.

River branches are very intolerant of alkaline soils. They like a moist, acid soil. Check your soil's pH before planting this species. This tree tolerates poorly drained soils very well. It actually favors a wet soil, but will grow surprisingly well in dry soils, provided it receives irrigation. Water plants on a weekly basis for best growth. Soak the areas under the branch span, not just at the trunk.

Maple

All species of the genus Acer make splendid shade trees. Although most noted for their unequalled fall display of fiery foliage, the maples are sturdy, attractive, medium sized shade trees that blend in well in any landscape scheme.

Amur Maple. Amur maple (*Acer ginnala*) produces a low tree anywhere from 15 to 30 feet in height at maturity. It is a wide-spreading tree with a round canopy and quite hardy for northern areas. The tree favors a sunny location, but will grow under partial shade. It produces a red, inedible fruit. The fall foliage is red. Amur maples take up space, so be sure to give them plenty of room when planting.

Amur maples have the same cultural habits as the other maples. During periods of drought, it should be watered. Its leaves will wilt if it gets too dry, but it is not as fussy about soils as many of the other maples.

The Amur maple is useful for border shrubs, because it has a shrubby growth that can be maintained by pruning. It is also effective as a single specimen.

Box Elder. The box elder (*Acer negundo*) is practical everywhere in the Middle West. It is so prevalent that some consider it a "weed tree," because one of its good traits is that it grows like a weed. This tree is very easy to grow.

It is sometimes used for street plantings, but is really requires maintenance to keep it well-trimmed and the area under it clean of seed pods and other debris. Its large leaves provide a dense shade.

Red Maple. The red maple (*Acer rubra*) is a very hardy tree and fairly fast growing. It has smooth gray bark and yellow, orange, or red fall foliage. Although the tree is neat in appearance and quite attractive throughout the year, it is in its best display in the fall landscape.

Red maple is slightly hardier than the sugar maple and much faster growing. It tends to favor a moist, acidic soil. It is one of the few trees that can actually tolerate poor soil drainage. They can be planted anywhere that sugar maples are. There are several excellent cultivars on the market. Some of the best are *Schlesingeri*, which has red-orange fall foliage; *Bowhall* has orange fall color; and *Autumn Flame*, which colors up to a rich scarlet early in the season.

Silver Maple. The silver maple (*Acer saccharinum*) is a fast-growing tree with a vase shape. It has fine-textured leaves that usually color up a bright yellow in the fall. In some cases, there may be no fall color, usually when trees are planted in the shade or have been given too much fertilizer late in the season.

Silver maples favor moist soil. They are quite tolerant of poor drainage conditions, but if you have serious drainage problems, they should be corrected before you plant this or any tree. Contact your county agricultural agent for assistance with any soil problems you may encounter.

Silver maples are so-called *soft maples,* in contrast to sugar maples and other *hard maples.* This is because they are very weak-wooded.

Silver maples tend to have large roots that extrude from the surface of the soil. These roots may present landscape problems, not only because of the aesthetics of the roots' appearance, but also due to the fact that the roots will disrupt property fixtures like sewer pipes, sidewalks, etc. For this reason, they are best used as shade trees and planted at a distance from any buildings or property fixtures.

The silver maple is so fast-growing that it is ideal for providing quick shade. When planted in full sun, it provides a spectacular fall color. Mix with other maples for an unforgettable fall landscape. Among the best of the silver maple cultivars is *Silver Queen,* a seedless variety. Another top silver maple is *Wierei,* a cutleaf cultivar. It has finer-textured leaves. For a pyramid-shape variety, try *Pyramidale.* This cultivar will add the often desired pyramidal shape-type tree to those landscapes where this look is most practical. Under silver maples, use a groundcover to hide barren areas and extruding roots. (See Chapter 17, Groundcovers.)

Sugar Maple. The best trees for the home landscape are those that belong to the maple family. They will tolerate a wide range of climates and soil conditions and are available in different sizes from small to large trees. All maples have dense canopies, and many are famous for the bright colors of their fall foliage.

The sugar maple (*Acer saccharum*) is the best example. It is a fairly slow growing tree with an almost round canopy. Sugar maples are most famous for two things: their fall foliage colors, and as a source of natural maple sugar and syrup. The leaves of sugar maple turn bright orange or scarlet in the fall.

Sugar maple is salt-sensitive and should not be planted in seaside locations or areas where salt injury may occur. This includes near city streets and sidewalks, where salt may be used heavily in winter deicing programs. Sugar maples are also quite sensitive to air pollutants. Most urban gardens are not ideal locations for these trees.

Sugar maples do best when set out in rich soil and full sun. If they do not receive adequate sunlight, their leaves will not color up as well in the fall.

The sugar maple is an excellent shade tree. It can be grown as a single specimen or set in a row—provided that you have a big enough yard, because they grow quite large. You must rake up their leaves in the fall, but they will provide you with plenty of compost material for next spring's garden.

One of the best cultivars of sugar maple is *Green Mountain*, from Vermont. It has scorch-resistant, leathery leaves. Because the leaves play an important role in the beauty of the sugar maple, these two traits are an improvement over the regular sugar maple.

Oak

The members of the Quercus genus are unrivaled as shade trees—provided that you have the space and the time. Given room to spread out and decades to mature, the oaks add a timeless beauty and sense of permanence to any home landscape.

Pin Oak. Pin oak got its name from the hardness of its wood, which was used to make "pins" (nails) for ships and buildings during colonial times. The pin oak (*Quercus palustris*) grows tall and straight and is one of the most ornamental oaks. It has a fine straight trunk and a round canopy. This tree is prone to having pendulous lower branches. Sometimes these lower branches are pruned off to improve the appearance of the tree.

The pin oak has red fall foliage. It is very slow-growing but forms a tall stately tree that casts a heavy cool shade during the summer.

The pin oak is very susceptible to iron chlorosis. Check your soil's pH before planting. You will have to be certain that it is acidic enough for your tree. This tree favors a moister soil than is normally required for oak trees. Add peat moss to the planting site.

This is a lovely tree for home and street plantings. Pin oaks make handsome, long-lived trees. They are very hardy and practical for northern gardeners who cannot grow other ornamental shade trees. Because it grows so slowly, you can even plant this tree in your front lawn.

Red Oak. The red oak (*Quercus borealis*) grows to about 100 feet. It bears the typical acorns that are associated with oaks. Some people consider acorns a litter problem, and they can be a nuisance if you like to run barefoot in the shade.

Red oak leaves turn scarlet in the fall. The color is not as striking as that of the scarlet oak, however. This is a good tree for urban areas, because it seems able to adapt well to the city environment. The red oak has a pyramidal shape when young, but changes to a dense, round canopy as it ages. It casts an excellent shade. It is best in large back yards.

The red oak favors a slightly acid soil. Water young trees on a weekly basis, more often during dry weather. Water by soaking the area under the branch span thoroughly.

Scarlet Oak. Oak trees offer some of the best shade. Their majestic canopies produce a heavy, cool shade in the summer. In autumn, their leaves provide fall color, and although not as spectacular as the maples, oaks still afford a sign of the changing seasons. During the winter, their dark silhouettes present an interesting contrast to the frozen landscape. In springtime, new leaves appear in shades of pink to red and green; they are almost as colorful as in the fall.

The scarlet oak (*Quercus coccinea*) grows to 50 feet. It has an open, spreading canopy. An excellent shade tree, its foliage is forest-green throughout the summer and changes to a brilliant scarlet during the fall. This is one of the best Quercus species for fall color.

Oak leaves are an excellent source of material for your compost bin. Gather leaves from your neighbors if they are foolish enough to bag them and throw them away. The leaves biodegrade into rich garden humus.

The scarlet oak requires a slightly acid soil that is well-drained. It is not a rapid grower, so give it time. This tree is most practical for backyards, unless you are fortunate enough to own a large front yard.

Other Shade Trees

There are innumerable other species of trees that can be used as fine shade producers. Leaf through garden catalogs and reference books to find the one you want. Be sure to pay attention to the tree's range of hardiness, its cultural requirements, upkeep, growth habits, foliage color, and shape.

Honeylocust. Common honeylocust trees have wicked thorns. For most people, especially those with small children, it is best to plant only the thornless cultivars. Honeylocust (*Gleditsia triacanthos*) is a fast-growing shade tree that reaches up to 70 feet in some areas. It has a vase shape and very fine textured foliage. The delicate, fernlike leaves cast a filtered shade, allowing grass to grow

Fig. 23-3. Thornless honeylocust. Courtesy of Paul & Alvalina Nandory.

perhaps the most popular of the thornless honeylocust trees. It produces yellow new foliage and the tips of the old foliage are yellow. This makes the tree look as if it is continuously in flower. *Ruby Lace* is the same as Sunburst, except that it produces ruby-red new growth. The thornless honeylocust is very practical for city gardeners, who want some shade but prefer a filtered shade. It is easy to grow and very beautiful. The delicate leaves will quickly decay into your lawn so there is no litter problem or fall raking to do.

Littleleaf Linden. The littleleaf linden (*Tilia cordata*) is a tall tree with a pyramidal shape. Growing up to 80 feet, this tree has heart-shaped leaves. It is an excellent tree for urban sites, because it tolerates city conditions very well.

The littleleaf linden is a cousin to the European linden or lime tree, *Tilia vulgaris,* the tree that lines the famous Berlin thoroughfare, Unter Den Linden, which is German for "Under the Lindens."

This tree has a dense canopy and casts a cool shade. It has yellow fall foliage. A cultivar of the littleleaf linden worth considering is *Chancellor.* Also worthy of consideration is the cultivar *Greenspire.*

Littleleaf linden favors a rich, moist soil. Young trees often have a poor branch structure and may require training. (The exception to this is with the cultivar *Greenspire.*) To learn to train branches, call your county agent. He or she can examine your tree and show you which branches need training and also what tools you will need. Note: if you mess up, it will affect the appearance of your tree, so it is important to get expert help before you try to train branches.

Be sure that your tree receives sufficient water. Do not just sprinkle when watering; soak the area under the branch span of the tree. A mulch will help to conserve soil moisture.

A beautiful shade tree, it is also an ideal boulevard tree. Check with your city streets department or city forester to see if you can plant this tree along your street.

right up to its trunk. It is very hardy. The honeylocust is extremely tolerant of urban conditions and an excellent tree for city lots and streets (Fig. 23-3).

Male and female flowers are borne on separate plants. The female flowers produce seed pods that can be something of a litter problem. If you wish to avoid them, plant only the male cultivars. Most people plant varieties of the thornless honeylocust, (*Gleditsia triacanthos inermis*). It will produce a thornfree tree. Some exciting varieties you may wish to try are: *Imperial,* which has a round canopy. It is podless, low-growing and somewhat flattened on top. It is a very attractive shade tree. *Shademaster* has a somewhat irregular top. It tends to be a cross between a vase-shaped and round canopy. It is podless and, as it ages, tends to form more of a vase-shaped canopy. *Skyline* is podless and has a very brilliant golden-yellow fall foliage. *Sunburst* is

Chapter 24

Lawn Trees

Every yard, no matter how small, should have a tree, but if you have a small yard, a large tree is impractical. It will take up too much room, produce too much shade, and interfere with other plants that you want to grow. The solution is a lawn tree—a small ornamental tree that will provide just the right amount of shade without overpowering either your landscape design or other plantings.

TRAITS

There are several features that make up a good lawn tree. The most important is size. A lawn tree should never grow higher than 30 feet at maturity. For most homes, 15 to 20 feet is ideal, but anything over 30 feet tends to be too large.

Flowers and Fruits

Another important trait to consider is the flowering and/or fruiting habit of the tree. Although it is not necessary to have a flowering tree, remember that your lawn tree is most often planted in the front yard. A showy tree that offers an interesting flowering or fruiting display is well worth considering. It may even be the focal point of your landscape.

Texture

Other than flowering, foliage texture is a feature of which you will want to take note. Fine-textured trees are generally more ornamental than coarse textured (large-leaf) trees. How the tree blends in with the rest of your landscape is important. You will want it to harmonize with your other plantings.

Remember when selecting your lawn tree that its sole purpose is to add ornamental interest to your yard. You are not choosing it for shade or for wood, only for beauty. It will be worth your time to study several species of trees and imagine how each might fit into your landscape plan. For tips on planting lawn trees, refer to Chapter 23, Shade Trees.

SPECIES

The trees listed in this chapter are not all-inclusive. There are many fine species not mentioned, but those listed are among the finest, easy-to-grow, and popular species for the home lawn. Exotic trees are fine, if you understand their cultural requirements and they suit your climate, but the novice should stick to something that he or she can grow successfully.

Bristlecone Pine. Bristlecone pine (*Pinus aristata*) is an unusual, picturesque plant that forms a small, twisted tree whose branches seem to curve and bend without any direction. This tree is often used as a Bonsai, because of its fine-textured foliage, apple-green color, and dwarf growth habit. It grows to about 20 feet in height, usually much less. This is a slow-growing species. Bristlecone pine is one of the oldest plants known in existence. Records show these plants were around as long as 4,000 years ago.

Bristlecone pine likes a well-drained, slightly acidic soil. It is not too fussy about sites, but it will not thrive in poorly drained soils. Full sun is best for this species, so find a sunny spot in your yard for this tree. Although it will grow in semishady areas, it is best to avoid heavy shade.

Ordinary care is all that is needed to raise this easy-to-grow species. Water it about once a week, soaking the area around its base. Keep weeds out of the vicinity of the tree and cut tall grasses. Apply manure in the spring, spreading it evenly in a circle around the base of the tree. Do not touch the trunk with fresh manure. Cover fresh manure with a few shovels full of dirt.

Prune the tree if you want to shape it. You can stake this tree, but most people let it grow naturally.

This little lawn tree will be a conversation piece. Because it looks so different and unusual, it is a show stealer and tends to distract attention. It is useful in a sunny area where you want people to focus on something other than what else may be in the corner.

Corkscrew Willow. Corkscrew willow (*Salix matsudana* var. *tortuosa*) grows to about 12 feet in height, often less. It has an upright growth habit. The main feature of this tree, which makes it such an interesting ornamental, is the contorted, twisting branches, twigs, and trunk. These features are especially obvious during the winter. The silhouette it creates against the wintry sky is quite memorable.

During the summer, it has long, slender, glossy, green leaves. The leaves tend to sway with the slightest breeze, producing a very graceful effect. The flowers of the corkscrew willow are silvery *catkins* that appear in the spring. Some people like to use them for indoor floral arrangements, but they are not especially showy by themselves.

The corkscrew willow likes a rich, moist soil. It is very tolerant of wet spots and poor soil drainage. It even prefers such areas. It does not like dry, sandy soil. Add plenty of organic matter to the planting site to improve both its fertility and water-holding capacity for this species.

Water the corkscrew willow on a weekly basis, more often if there is much dry weather. Soak the ground around the base of the tree thoroughly each time you water. Determine when to water by touching the ground. If it is dry, water. Keep the ground moist, not wet, to the touch. A mulch is helpful in conserving soil moisture.

Scab and/or canker diseases can sometimes be a problem. Control these diseases by spraying your tree with Bourdeaux mixture in early spring.

Eastern Redbud. The redbud is grown primarily for its spring floral display. It is, however, attractive during the summer and in the fall when its leaves change color. The eastern redbud (*Cercis canadensis*) grows to about 20 feet in height. It is a small tree that covers itself with purplish-pink blossoms in the spring. It tends to have a spreading habit, with somewhat horizontal growth of the branches.

Eastern redbud has yellow fall foliage. These plants are very hardy.

People who live in the west will want a different species, the western redbud, *Cercis occidentalis*. This is a redbud for locations like California. It is very similar to the eastern redbud, except it is better adapted to warmer climates. The western redbud does not have as impressive a fall display as the eastern redbud.)

Redbuds are easy to grow. Select one best adapted to your area. It will grow in most types of soil, provided the site is well-drained. Redbuds seem to do well in sun or shade, a somewhat unusual trait, as most flowering trees definitely favor full sun.

Their flowers usually appear before new leaves in the spring, making the tree a cloud of purplish-pink. Sometimes it has blossoms and leaves at the same time. The redbud in bloom will be a focal point in your yard in the springtime, and again in the autumn when its leaves start to turn yellow.

European Mountain Ash. The European mountain ash (*Sorbus aucuparia*) is a highly ornamental tree that rarely grows over 25 feet tall. It has dense, fernlike leaves, a long straight trunk, and fine texture. In the spring, it bears clusters of white blossoms. In the summer, the plant abounds with clusters of reddish-orange berries that stand out in colorful contrast to the delicate green foliage. Birds love these berries, and you can make jelly from them. In the fall, leaves turn red and gold.

The European mountain ash is hardy and seems to thrive almost anywhere. They may have some difficulty growing in the semiarid regions of the West, unless given irrigation.

Plant where your tree can receive full sun. The production of flowers and berries and the fall color will all be better when trees are set out in sunny areas. Although an ideal lawn tree, this species has a dense canopy and can also be considered an excellent small shade tree.

Globe Willow. The globe willow (*Salix globosa*) is good in urban areas, where it seems able to take the pollution-abuse that is so common in many cities.

The globe willow derives its name from the almost round or globular shape of its canopy. For such a small tree, the dense, leafy branches spread over quite a wide area. It is a fast-growing tree and an excellent choice for people who live in the semiarid regions of the West, because it holds up to drought and summer heat so well. It is also quite hardy in regard to cold temperatures. It grows to about 20 feet in height.

Although very tolerant of drought, this species favors a rich, moist soil. It is more tolerant of dry spells than many other willows, however. Water trees as often as is needed. Usually about once a week is best. Do not water any plant every day, or you can cause its roots to grow too shallow, and it will be dependent upon you for survival. Do not be stingy with the water when you irrigate. Soak the area.

To sustain its rapid growth, water and fertilize your tree. Animal manure in the spring is a great booster, adding vital organic matter to the soil as it decomposes. Spread the manure evenly around the tree and cover fresh manure with dirt. Do not allow fresh manure to touch the tree's trunk.

To control scab and/or canker diseases that may become a problem, spray the tree early in the spring with Bourdeaux mixture. This is a copper-sulfate based fungicide—an old formula, but one of the safest, and still the best for most people.

This tree needs plenty of space. It can be planted in a row with 4 feet between each tree for windbreaks, or use it as a garden specimen.

Japanese Maple. The Japanese maple (*Acer palmatum*) grows to about 20 feet in height, sometimes a little taller. This is a naturally small tree with a wide, spreading canopy. Most Japanese maples have red foliage throughout the summer. (There are exceptions.) These red leaves create an attractive contrast with regular garden greenery. This species also offers fall color, as its leaves turn a brilliant scarlet in autumn. There are many fine selections of Japanese maple. Here are a couple that you may wish to try:

The species *Acer palmatum septemlobum* var. *osakazuki* has one of the best fall foliage colors—a very bright red. Your yard will look aflame with one of these in it. The cultivar *Dissectum*, offers a different type of foliage. Its leaves are finer textured than most Japanese maples, with an almost shredded appearance. They are also a different color. This is one of the above-mentioned exceptions to the normally red summer foliage. This cultivar has light, apple-green leaves throughout the summer. During the fall, its leaves turn a golden-yellow.

Always plant Japanese maples in full sun. This is necessary to achieve the best fall color. When planted under heavy shade, the tree's foliage color will not be as brilliant.

This species likes a rich, moist soil. If you have dry soil, add plenty of peat moss or other organic matter to improve it before planting. Peat moss works well for that purpose. It can be added at planting time and will improve the soil's water-holding capacity. A summer mulch to help retain soil moisture is also helpful.

Prune only to remove diseased or dead wood. You can prune to remove straggly growth, but remember that part of the beauty of this tree is its loose, open growth. A favorite for oriental-theme gardens, these trees look nice in any sunny location.

Newport Plum. The Newport plum (*Prunus newport*) grows to about 15 feet in height. It is sometimes called the *purple-leaf plum*, because of its reddish-purple leaves. It maintains its purplish foliage throughout the summer and is primarily grown for its unusual foliage color.

The Newport plum bears pinkish flowers in the spring, which show up nicely against the reddish-purple background foliage. Sometimes it is in bloom before the leaves emerge.

The Newport plum can be grown as either a tall shrub or tree. It is very attractive when grown in tree form. To grow in this manner, simply remove the lower branches. It is best to train plants when young. Do not try to make a tree out of a full-grown bush. It will be an ugly specimen, distorted by the cuts that you make. If it is already growing as a tall shrub, let it continue to do so.

The Newport plum requires a sunny location in order to develop its best leaf color. It favors a well-drained sandy loam. A slightly acidic soil is best.

Stimulate new growth to obtain the best coloring. The new foliage is always the most vivid. Just take off a few inches on the outer rims of the tree. This will shape the tree and also stimulate new leaf production. Do not be careless when pruning. If you cut off too much you can dwarf the tree.

The Newport plum is most often used as a contrasting focal point in conjunction with green-leaf plants.

Pagoda Dogwood. A good tree for use in an urban location, the pagoda dogwood (*Cornus alternifolia)* is a large spreading shrub, best trained as a small tree. It is small, so it does not take up much space, and it stands up well to common city pollutants. This species is very hardy and is found growing as far north as Saint Paul, Minnesota. It grows up to 12 feet tall, sometimes a little taller.

It has a horizontal branching habit that is very graceful, especially in the spring, when white clusters of flowers appear. The pagoda dogwood has small dark blue berries during the summer. The leaves change color in the autumn from green to maroon.

This plant likes shady locations and a cool, moist soil. It must not be planted in areas where it will be exposed to hot, drying winds. Water it each week, more often when the weather is very dry.

Pagoda dogwood has an oriental flavor to it. It is very useful in creating Japanese or Chinese gardens and is sure to be a conversation piece at any garden party.

Red Leaf Plum. The red leaf plum (*Prunus x cistena)* is a naturally dwarf species most noted for its red leaves, which give the tree its summer color (Fig. 24-1). It grows to about 8 feet in height. It can be trained as a shrub or as a dwarf tree,

Fig. 24-1. Redleaf plum. Courtesy Denver Water Department, Xeriscape Conservation Garden.

depending upon your personal preference. To induce the red leaf plum to grow in tree form, cut off its lower branches.

The red colored leaves contrast delightfully with the regular garden greenery surrounding it. There is no fall color with the red leaf plum, but it tends to darken slightly after the first frost. To obtain the best leaf color, plant in full sun. Provide a slightly acidic, well-drained soil. Also to obtain the best color display, the red leaf plum should be pruned back each spring. Trim off about one-third of the growth evenly over the entire canopy. This stimulates the production of new foliage. The new leaves are always the brightest red. Do not cut back too much, or you may stunt the tree's growth. Be sure you cut evenly all around the plant, otherwise you will create an imbalanced or "lopsided" growth.

Water plants once a week. Soak the ground thoroughly when you water; do not merely sprinkle. Aim water under the branch span, not just at the trunk. Remember, roots are growing under the branch span.

This tree is ideal for sunny lawns. It stays a dwarf, so it can be grown in almost any yard without fear of it becoming too large. Interplant among your garden greenery for contrast.

Rose Tree of China. The rose tree of China (*Prunus triloba*) makes a spectacular early spring display before it leafs out. It is covered with delicate, double rose-pink flowers that herald the season. It is very showy and will be the focal point of your yard when in bloom.

It grows to about 8 feet and is a natural dwarf that can be grown in either shrub or tree form. To grow in tree form, simply prune off the lower branches.

The rose tree of China favors full sun. It is a miniature tree and can fit into the smallest of yards. It grows well in all types of soils, except those that are poorly drained. A sandy loam seems to be ideal.

Although grown for its spring floral display, it makes a neat little tree the rest of the year as well. Do not prune this plant unless you absolutely have to. If you cut it back, you may dwarf it. Because this is already a dwarf, you will not want it to get much smaller. Although it may be tempting to cut off

branches for indoor display, do not fall prey to this temptation. This plant must not be used for cut flowers. To do so will dwarf the tree. Go outside if you want to enjoy this plant, or set it within view of a favorite window.

Water plants once a week—more often when dry weather prevails. Be especially generous with water during blooming time. A summer mulch is a helpful way to conserve moisture.

The rose tree of China is small enough to plant several. If grown as a shrub, it makes an attractive, albeit open, hedge. When grown in tree form, plants are usually used as single specimens.

Russian Olive. The Russian olive (Elaeagnus angustifolia) is a fast growing tree. Under favorable conditions, nursery transplants can reach 4 to 5 feet the first year and 8 to 12 feet the second year. (Under dry conditions, as found in the Great Plains, you can expect to achieve about half this rate of growth.) An open, shrublike tree, it grows to 20 feet. When it is irrigated or planted in places with abundant moisture, it can grow taller. Its branches spread as wide as the tree is tall—sometimes more so.

The Russian olive has silver leaves that are long and narrow. It provides an interesting contrast when the tree is set out amongst green leaf trees and evergreens. It bears small, fragrant yellow flowers in the spring. Later on, these turn into pea-size silver berries. There is also a pink- or brown-fruited variety that has larger fruit and may be considered more ornamental by some. Birds prefer the silver-fruited variety.

Russian olives are usually multitrunked trees, with several trunks. The unpruned tree has five or six stems starting near the ground. If you remove all but one of these trunks and keep it free of lower branches, you can grow a larger tree.

The Russian olive thrives throughout most of the United States. It is especially suited to the western states, where it tolerates temperatures from −50° F to 115° F. In salt tolerance, it is surpassed only by the salt cedar and a few other salt-tolerant plants. Plants do not tolerate acid soils, however. They are very drought-resistant.

The Russian olive can be used to border property lines or provide windbreaks. It is especially attractive because of is weeping leaves. For an easy-to-care-for tree, highly tolerant of city conditions and neglect, the Russian olive is a very good choice in the landscape.

White Fringe Tree. The foliage of the white fringe tree (*Chinoanthus virginicus*) is extremely attractive. Bright green most of the summer, the leaves change to a buttercup yellow in the fall. It grows to about 15 feet.

This tree is *dioecious* (male and female flowers are borne on separate trees). When both sexes are present, this tree can produce edible, blue fruits that resemble small plums. Only the female trees bear fruit: if you consider the fruits a litter problem, plant only male trees.

The white fringe is very easy to grow. It likes a sunny location and seems to grow well on dry, sandy soils. It may be necessary to stake young transplants the first few years to help them grow upright. Simply tie the trunk to a stake placed in the ground. Use a soft string and check it each spring to see that it is not so tight that it girdles the tree. Once the tree has gained some size, these stakes can be removed.

To prevent problems with borer insects, wrap trunks with aluminum foil. Carefully check the wrap each spring to see that nothing is living inside the wrap.

Chapter 25

Flowering Crabapples

The hardy, easy-to-grow flowering crabapple is a must in any spring landscape. Flowering crabs come in a size and shape to suit any taste, from dwarf to standard, and from informally spreading to formally columnar.

Flowering crabapples belong to the *Malus* genus. Most are hybrids and there are many species. They are among our finest ornamental trees. Not many plants can offer so many all-season values as flowering crabs.

In the spring, the showy and sometimes fragrant blossoms make their annual debut, usually in April and May in the north, earlier in the south. The time of bloom tends to vary from year to year depending upon temperature and other weather-related factors. Some species and cultivars will bloom earlier than others. By careful selection of plants, you can have sequential bloom for a month or more. Individual trees will usually be in bloom for only a couple of weeks.

WHAT IS A CRABAPPLE?

A crabapple is any member of the apple family with fruits (usually tart) 2 inches or smaller in diameter. Any fruit larger is simply an apple. Crabapple fruits vary in size from 1/4 to 2 inches in diameter. Fruit colors range from bright red to purple, and from bright orange to yellow and green. Some fruits begin to color in August, although in many varieties the fruit does not reach full color until September or October.

Most flowering crabs are small trees, with some less than 20 feet in height; others may grow 30 to 40 feet or more. Common types are round and dense, but growth forms vary from columnar to pendulous. Each form of crabapple lends a distinctive character to the landscape, and the twisted limbs of older trees can add a picturesque beauty to the winter scene.

POPULARITY

There are many reasons for the tremendous popularity of flowering crabs: their interest during all seasons, their variety of sizes and forms, their low-maintenance requirements, and their adaptibility to most sites—to name a few.

Even before your crabapple tree has started to bloom in the spring, the beauty of its buds is of interest. Even those with white blossoms show a flash of pink or red in the bud. Colors of open blossoms may range from white to dark, purplish-red, with many varieties of pink in between. The majority of crabapples have single flowers, but there are a few with semidouble and double blossoms, with the latter bearing few fruits, if any.

In the summer, crabapples have attractive leaves. Some have a reddish or bronze leaf color, at least on their new growth, others are crimson, and many are green. Most crabapple trees do not provide much fall color. Whatever fruits remain are ornamental and provide winter food for birds. Sometimes these fruits can present a litter problem in your yard, but unless you have dozens of trees, you can merely rake them up.

Crabapples can be used to provide shade and supply a background mass of green to tie a house into a landscape. They can take the place of larger shade trees and are ideal for small urban lots where large shade trees may be too bulky to fit into the landscape effectively.

The diminutive size of individual flowers and fruits may be appreciated at close range in the home landscape, yet the combined flowers produce a showy beauty that is also appreciated at a distance. When one of these trees is planted in the corner of a garden, it is the focal point. Its striking beauty accentuates the landscape. In larger yards, these trees can be planted in groups so that their combined effect will be apparent from a considerable distance.

Crabapples are of special significance as street trees, where shade is not important but the aesthetic value of spring and fall color is desirable. The problem of tree limbs growing across power lines, common in street tree plantings, does not occur with this low-growing species. Many neighborhoods and communities have lined their streets with flowering crabs of various types.

CULTURE

Flowering crabapples adapt to a wide range of soil conditions. They grow best in soil that is well-drained. Flowering crabs are very tolerant of urban conditions. Although they can withstand conditions in the narrow strip between street and sidewalk, most types should be planted a little farther back from the sidewalk, in the lawn area. This is especially advised for those who live in northern cities where salt is used to deice streets and sidewalks in the winter. Excess levels of salt can build up in the soil and can injure your lawn and other landscape plants, including your flowering crabs. If possible, use sand as a substitute for salt.

Planting

When dormant trees arrive from the nursery, every effort should be made to keep the roots from drying out before the trees are planted. Immerse roots in a bucket of water and let soak for an hour or two before setting the young trees out. If you do not have a large enough bucket, rinse out a trash can. Be sure to wash it out thoroughly so that there are no remnants of garbage or noxious odors before you fill it with water and set roots in it.

Dig the planting hole wide and deep so that the roots can be accommodated without cramping. Spread roots out evenly in the hole so that the tree is balanced. Plant the tree at about the same depth as it grew in the nursery. Some nurseries will mark that depth with a painted line. If your nursery did not, simply look at the crown area and plant with common sense. Do not bury your tree, and do not allow roots to be exposed.

Fill the hole with the best topsoil available. Usually, it is helpful to add peat moss and composted manure to the planting hole. If you add manure, use only well-rotted manure, as fresh manure will injure and even kill plant roots.

After the hole is about two-thirds full, fill it in with water. Let the water drain, then add the remaining soil. Tamp it down and water the plant again. Once water has drained, fill in any gaps with soil and tamp down firmly. There must be no gaps or air pockets left in the hole. It is best to leave a slight saucerlike depression around the base of each tree. This will help collect rainwater.

Mulch newly planted trees to help conserve moisture and keep weeds under control. Watering the plant on a weekly basis is vital to the tree's survival during the first season's growth. When you water, soak the entire area around the base thoroughly. Do not just sprinkle. Wait until the soil has been allowed to dry before watering again. During dry periods, additional waterings may be necessary. It is important to get the tree well established the first year for it to survive.

Some people like to buy flowering crabs that are already at their flowering stage. These large trees create an "instant" landscape. They are much more expensive than the younger transplants and require greater care in handling. These trees come balled and burlapped. Do not attempt to plant these trees alone. The bare-root younger transplants are probably the best route to take for most people, but if you do try the larger trees, remember they are in an active state of growth and need really delicate treatment. They can be planted the same way as bare-root trees. Be careful when removing burlap that the ball of soil held next to the roots does not all fall apart.

Pruning

Prune crabapples lightly, if at all. Occasionally, you may need to thin out the tops. This should be done by cutting back a few of the smaller branches to the crotch. Heavy cuts of 1 inch and more are to be avoided, because they may induce the growth of *water sprouts*. (Water sprouts are leafless suckers that arise from the branches. They sap the strength of the tree.) Suckers that arise from the base of the trunk can be a problem with some varieties of flowering crabs and must be pruned to the ground each season.

PESTS

On occasion, insects such as aphids, leafhoppers, tent caterpillars, scale, and sometimes borers, can be troublesome. They can all be controlled quite effectively.

Aphids will likely be the most common pests. They can be controlled by ladybugs. To control aphids, leafhoppers, and scale, spray plants with a solution of water and the shavings of a bar of gentle face soap, such as Ivory, on a regular basis or as the need arises. A dormant oil spray will also help to eliminate scale. Tent caterpillars can be gotten rid of by removing the egg clusters from the branches and burning them. Eliminate borer damage by covering trunks with a protective wrap, either a commercial wrap or just plain aluminum foil will do.

The bark of flowering crabapples is a favorite wintertime food for rabbits. They feed on the bark of trees and can kill trees by girdling them. Rabbits usually do not bother the trunks of older trees, but will chew the bark off the trunks and exposed lower limbs of young trees, reaching above the snow cover. Cover trunks and lower limbs with aluminum foil to prevent rabbit damage.

Mice damage flowering crabs by root and/or trunk girdling during the winter months. If severe damage occurs, the tree may die. The problem is most severe where mice work under the protection of a groundcover, a heavy layer of mulch, or snow cover. To reduce mouse damage, wrap trunks with aluminum foil to protect them. Place mousetraps in strategic locations along mouse runways.

Diseases

Certain flowering crabapples can be rendered unsightly or severely injured by one or all four common diseases: *apple scab, fire blight, cedar apple rust,* and *powdery mildew*. Some varieties are more or less resistant to one or all of these diseases.

Three of these common diseases, apple scab, cedar apple rust, and powdery mildew, are fungal diseases. They can all be controlled by a few simple measures:

☐ Plant in full sunlight, with good air circulation.

☐ Avoid planting near junipers, cedars, and plants that are alternate hosts to a disease.

☐ If a disease is common to your area, try planting a resistant variety.

☐ Treat with weekly sprayings of Bourdeaux mixture until the symptoms are no longer present.

Fire blight is a bacterial disease. The only cure is to prune off and burn infected branches, and to plant resistant varieties.

Chapter 26

Other Flowering Trees

Nothing enhances the beauty of your landscape more than a large flowering tree in full bloom. The attraction of flowers is universal and few can resist their charm. Many species of trees bear flowers, but some trees are more noteworthy for their flowering characteristics than others. The trees with the showiest display of blooms are in most demand.

There are many points to consider about a tree's flowering habit, including size of bloom, color, and fragrance. These have to be weighed when considering where the tree will fit into the total picture of your landscape. The size of individual blooms may not be important if the tree grows its flowers in clusters. Clusters of what would otherwise be small flowers can have very dramatic effects. Color is a factor that depends in part upon personal preferences and partly upon the color scheme in your garden. For example, if your landscape is heavy in yellow with yellow-foliaged plants, flowers, etc., a red-flowered tree may look somewhat out-of-place. On the other hand, it may be what you need to add contrast.

TIMING

The time of the flowering itself may be of importance. Many people like to plan their landscape so that there is always something blossoming (or interesting) at all times throughout the growing season. Selecting trees that bloom at different times offers different points of interest to visitors. That involves wise planning. Too often, landscapes are filled with only spring-blooming plants, which for two or three weeks fill the yard with great beauty, only to turn to a monotonous green the rest of the season. That is the result of poor, or nonexistant, planning.

When selecting a tree for your yard, take your time. Figure out your tree needs. Try to imagine what each tree would look like in your landscape. Will it harmonize with other shrubs? A tree that bears large, showy flowers will be something that you will treasure year after year.

SPECIES

There are many excellent species of flowering trees. Your nursery catalog is a good place to look to see what you might like. Remember that plant hardiness is the critical factor in survival. Do not plant trees that are not sufficiently winter-hardy in your area. It will be a waste of your time, labor, and money.

Cockspur Hawthorn. The cockspur hawthorn (*Crataegus crus-galli*) will encourage birds to come to your yard to eat its attractive fruits. It forms a small tree, 20 feet or more, with a spreading canopy. It bears flowers in the spring, about the same time as crabapples. The cockspur hawthorn has long, very sharp thorns. There is a thornless species that you may wish to try—*Crataegus crusgalli inermis*. It is identical to the regular cockspur hawthorn except it is thornless.

It is an excellent tree for urban areas. It has persistent fruits that hang on even into the early winter. The fruits are small, brick-red in color. Cockspur hawthorn has an orange to red fall color, and the same cultural requirements as other hawthorns.

The thornless variety is usually preferred, but if you have a problem with neighborhood youngsters climbing your trees, plant the variety with thorns. No child will ever climb that tree!

Downy Hawthorn. The downy hawthorn (*Crataegus mollis*) bears fruits that can be used for jelly. These large red fruits look like small apples, or crabapples, and have a very tart taste. The fruits tend to ripen earlier than most.

Downy hawthorns have green leaves during the summer with showy, red fruits. During the fall, the leaves turn yellow.

Downy hawthorns like a heavy soil. Add plenty of peat moss to the planting site. Water these trees on a regular, weekly basis. Wet the ground thoroughly; do not sprinkle. This species tends to grow rather slowly so don't let that worry you. It is only its natural growth habit. They need a sunny location with good air circulation.

Avoid planting near apples, crabs, junipers, and cedars, as they can host diseases that can invade your hawthorn.

This is an excellent species for providing color throughout the seasons for front or back yards. It does have thorns, so be very careful when working near it, watering, cutting grass, or pruning. If you get too close, you can get scratched up quite badly.

Flowering Dogwood. The flowering dogwood (*Cornus florida*) is a delightful small tree growing to 20 feet in height. It is a spring-flowering species that bears large white bracts in early spring.

For a pink-flowering version, try (*Cornus florida* var. *rubra*). There is a red-flowering cultivar of this species called *Cherokee Chief*. This red-flowering cultivar does not usually get as tall as its parent, growing to about 15 feet.

These three trees look great when planted individually or mixed to produce a sensational splash of color in the spring landscape. Dogwoods are among the first trees to bloom in the spring. For woodland gardens or among naturalized daffodils, they are ideal.

An unusual feature about the flowering dogwood is that the real flowers are quite small and insignificant, but the colorful bracts, which most people call the flowers, are really petallike leaves, similar to those of the poinsettia.

Dogwood trees like a shady location and a cool moist soil. Plant in an area with filtered, but not heavy shade. Some sunlight is desired for best leaf coloring.

A good woodsy soil is best. Add plenty of peat moss to the planting site. Dogwoods are found growing in the wild around the edges of woodlands and in clearings where some sunlight can penetrate through. If grown in full sun, be sure to keep the plant well-watered. A mulch is recommended to prevent moisture loss from the soil.

Dogwood trees are very easy to grow and require only minimal care. They may have trouble flowering if grown in the deep south, however, as they seem to require some winter chill for their leaf coloring. They may not be sufficiently winter hardy for the far north. If grown in areas with severe winters, plant them in a sheltered location.

Golden Chain Tree. The golden chain tree (*Laburnum anagroides*) will actually enrichen your soil. A small deciduous tree that grows to a height of 20 feet, it has buttercup yellow flowers in the early summer. The blooms hang in racemes, (like grape clusters) some about 1 1/2 feet long. The tree is somewhat coarse, with large leaves, but its floral display makes it a worthwhile tree for all but the most formal of landscapes. A better selection of this tree is the hybrid *Laburnum* x *vossii*. The flowers of this hybrid are longer than the common golden chain tree.

This tree is a member of the legume (bean) family. It does not tolerate acidic soil, so check your soil's pH before planting. An alkaline soil is best. If necessary, add garden lime to the planting site.

Water on a regular weekly basis. It likes a moist location: the soil must not be soggy, but it should feel damp.

The golden chain tree is very easy to grow, but they are not sufficiently hardy north of Southern Illinois. Do not plant this tree if you live in North Dakota or Wyoming. A lovely tree for the lawn or backyard, it's sure to be a favorite for those with a suitable climate.

Japanese Flowering Cherry. If you ever visited Washington, D.C. in April, you were probably impressed by the breathtaking loveliness of the Japanese cherry trees, and you may have pictured them in your own yard.

The Japanese flowering cherry, (*Prunus serrulata*) can grow up to 20 feet in height depending upon the cultivar. This tree is planted primarily because of its spring flowers, which are very showy. Japanese cherries bloom while they are very young, often only a year or two after planting.

The most popular cultivar is *Kanzan*, sometimes spelled "Kwanzan" in nursery catalogs. This species produces double, deep-pink blossoms in the spring. The flowers are large and abundant, and they cover the entire tree when in full bloom. For a white-flowering variety, try the cultivar *Mount Fuji*.

Japanese flowering cherry trees favor a slightly acidic soil. A sandy loam will be most suitable. The tree will not perform well on poorly drained soils.

The Japanese flowering cherry is not sufficiently hardy for most northern climes. Check with your country agricultural agent to see if they can be grown in your area if you live north or Washington, D.C.

The weeping growth habit of the *weeping Japanese cherry* (*Prunus subhirtella*) lends grace to your landscape throughout the entire year, although it is primarily grown for its spectacular spring floral display. Even in the midst of winter, the barren weeping branches may remind you of the coming spring, when they will once again be loaded with beautiful blossoms. Plant it in a location where all can admire its beauty.

Lavalle Hawthorn. If you live in a city, the Lavalle hawthorn (*Crataegus* x *lavallei*) may be just right for you. Lavalle hawthorn has an upright branching habit. It flowers in the springtime and, like other hawthorns, it does have thorns.

The foliage of the Lavalle hawthorn is very glossy and attractive as it reflects the summer sun. During summer, the leaves are green; during the fall, the leaves turn to a bronzy-red. Be careful of its thorns when working around the tree, because you can get cut up if you forget about them.

The hawthorn should always be planted in full sun and in heavy soil. It needs plenty of space, because it likes good air circulation around it. This species is a slow grower that is helped by an application of manure in the spring. Spread the manure evenly around the base of the tree in a circle.

It is best to keep the area surrounding the tree supplied with plenty of moisture. Do not, however, drown the tree. If you water every day you can cause soil drainage problems.

Warning: like other hawthorns, do not plant this tree near apples, cedars, or junipers. (This includes crabapple trees.) These species can be alternate hosts to diseases that attack each other. Look at your neighbor's yard to see that he or she does not have any plant that might threaten your hawthorn.

Saucer Magnolia. The saucer magnolia (*Magnolia* x *soulangeana*) is one of the first plants to bloom in the spring, with large cup-shaped flowers, pink on the outside and white on the inside and edges. The blossoms appear even before the leaves, so this tree is spectacular when in full bloom. This tree usually does not reach more than 15 feet in height. The leaves are large and somewhat coarse.

The saucer magnolia is the most popular magnolia grown in the United States. One reason for its popularity is its hardiness, but it may not be sufficiently winter hardy in some northern areas. (Where you live is sometimes more important than your latitude. For example, the Great Lakes serve to temper the climate in that region, so Michigan and the eastern half of Wisconsin are warmer than Minnesota and other states in the same latitude.

Plants that grow in a port city like Sturgeon Bay, Wisconsin, will not grow in an inland city like Minot, South Dakota.) Saucer magnolias are not fully hardy in many areas of the north. They should be planted in protected sites that allow plenty of sun but will shelter the plants from strong winds.

Saucer magnolias favor full sun. They should not be planted under heavy shade. They also like a rich, moist soil; to ensure that the plant's needs are met, it is beneficial to add manure in the spring. Spread manure evenly in a circle around the base of the tree. Do not touch the tree with fresh manure.

Water your tree at least once a week. Soak the area under the branch span of the tree when watering. Do not just sprinkle. Mulch the area under the tree to control weeds and lessen moisture loss to evaporation.

Usually one tree is all that you will want, because this is a demanding tree and you will have to baby it, especially if you live in the north.

Star Magnolia. The star magnolia (*Magnolia stellata*) is a very showy ornamental, especially in the early spring when its large white star-shaped blossoms waft their delicate fragrance in the breeze. During the rest of the year, it will tend to blend in with the other shrubs.

The star magnolia grows into a small tree, almost shrublike in appearance. This species is slightly hardier than the saucer magnolia, but in northern areas, it will need a sheltered location to protect the flowers from spring frosts.

Star magnolia favors full sun: do not plant it under heavy shade. It should be set in a place with good air circulation. It requires a fertile, moist soil and may not grow as well on dry soils. It is important that plenty of moisture be available for good growth and spring bloom. Water plants at least once a week. Soak the area under the branch span; do not just sprinkle.

Mulch trees in summer to conserve soil moisture. A winter mulch is recommended in colder areas. It should be at least 3 to 4 inches thick and spread evenly in a circle around the base of the plant. Straw or leaf composts work nicely.

Because this is a small tree, more than one can often fit into a yard. Where the climate is right, the star magnolia will give you a "jump" on spring.

Toba Hawthorn. If you have heavy clay soil, you might consider including Toba hawthorn (*Crataegus x toba*) in your landscape plans. A naturally dwarf hawthorn tree that grows to about 15 feet in height, it has glossy green foliage. In the spring, Toba hawthorn is covered with richly fragrant double-pink flowers. It blooms about the same time as crabapples.

This plant bears tiny red fruits that attract birds and are quite ornamental. Sometimes the fruits fall off the tree and litter the yard, but they are so small that they "melt" into the grass. There is no major clean-up problem when growing this tree.

This tree will fit into yards that are too poorly drained for flowering crabs, but not so wet as to prevent this species from thriving. A very practical ornamental tree for the right location.

Washington Hawthorn. The Washington hawthorn (*Crataegus phaenopyrum*) is very tolerant of urban conditions and can often be seen in city parks and yards. It is the latest blooming of all the hawthorns. It grows to about 30 feet in height, making it a large tree (as hawthorns go) and one of the most widely planted.

The Washington hawthorn has an upright growth habit. It bears small persistent fruits. The ability of the fruits to hang onto the tree means that there is less of a "litter" problem with this tree. The fruits are borne in clusters and are orange-red in color. It has orange fall foliage and very long, sharp thorns.

The Washington hawthorn attracts birds. Plant in a heavy soil, or add organic matter to your soil. Sandy soil can benefit from the addition of some clay soil to it. The Washington hawthorn must have full sun. It needs plenty of room around it to provide for good air circulation.

The Washington hawthorn tends to grow slightly faster than most hawthorns. This means that if you set out a young transplant, you will not have so long to wait before you have a flowering tree. Sometimes it only takes two or three years.

This tree is useful as a focal point, but you will not want to play ball near it. Pity the poor soul who tries to recover the ball under its thorny branches!

Chapter 27

Trees for Home Woodlots

There are many ways to heat your home, but wood remains one of the cheapest and most efficient means of producing home heating and hot water. Unlike natural or bottled gas, oil, electricity, coal, and kerosene, wood is a renewable resource, and a home woodlot can give you independence from the rising prices of other energy sources.

WOOD VERSUS ALL OTHERS

Electricity is probably the most expensive and inefficient way to heat a home. It makes you totally dependent upon the supplier for all your needs (Fig. 27-1). Should power lines be downed during some subzero night, your family could literally freeze to death if electricity is your sole source of heat and energy.

Natural gas prices fluctuate. Usually cheaper than electricity or oil, they are limited to only those areas connected to their lines. Rural customers have to use propane gas, stored on their property in tanks. An empty gas tank on a cold winter's night is no picnic, either.

Home heating oil has shot up in price during the past decade, even though prices vary in different parts of the country. Fossil and nuclear fuels are irreplaceable—once they are used up, they are gone forever (except for the radiation left behind from nuclear wastes). Wood can be constantly replenished, but must be nurtured and managed.

The wood you grow yourself is almost certain to be your cheapest fuel. Firewood is becoming more competitive in price with other high-priced fuels. If you cannot save money, it defeats the purpose of having a woodstove.

WOODSTOVES

Before you rush out and buy a woodstove, there are several things you should think about.

Wood heat is dirty. Most woodstoves will allow a little smoke to escape inside the house from time to time. Even when undetectable otherwise, it adds to the dust level in the house. A basement is the ideal place for a woodstove. That way you can have central heating and also keep most of the soot

Fig. 27-1. A home woodlot provides beauty and independence.

downstairs and away from your fine furniture.

Woodstoves are time-consuming. A woodstove will not run itself. Somebody has to cut the wood, stack the wood, bring in the wood, and somebody had to feed the fire to keep it going. That "somebody" may all be the same person, or you can split those responsibilities among other family members.

Some wood stoves are better than others. A cast-iron stove is stronger than one made from a single layer of blue steel. It is safer to be around and there is less danger of producing too hot a fire. Some of the double layer, furnace-type stoves are also safe, but much more expensive than the single layer units. Buy a good stove! Above all, avoid the type that looks like they could be opened with a can opener. Do not take chances with your family's lives.

MAINTENANCE

Chimneys have to be cleaned each year. Chimney sweeps did this in olden days. Unless you can afford to hire a chimney sweep (if you can find one), you will have to do this dirty job yourself.

Pick a summer day, when you will not need a fire. Put on old worn clothes that you do not mind ruining because they will be once you get to work cleaning out the soot from those stove pipes and chimneys.

If you do not clean out these pipes and chimneys, several things can happen, all bad. The fire may not burn because of insufficient air flow and lack of oxygen, thus causing much smoke and dust in your rooms. Or, worst of all, you could have an extremely hot blaze that can burn down your entire home by causing the soot or kreosote in the chimney to catch fire.

TERMS YOU SHOULD KNOW

Firewood is measured in units called *cords*. This is a cubic measure: one cord is equal to a stack of wood that is 4 feet high, by 4 feet wide, by 8 feet long. A *short cord* consists of wood cut in shorter than 4-foot lengths.

The average home woodstove uses four to five cords of wood for each season. Wood is likely to be used during chilly nights in the early fall and during the day later in the season, throughout winter, and the early spring. Only rarely will the woodstove be on during summertime. Figure on one cord of wood to last one month. Five cords takes you from November to March. During the coldest months, you may burn more wood and, conversely, during warmer weather less wood is used. It is only important to take the early morning and nighttime chill off on many days in the fall and spring.

Energy released from wood or other fuels is most often measured in terms of Btu (British thermal units). The Btu tells you how much energy is released when you burn a particular type of wood. Many times, especially during the fall, garden magazines have articles about the Btu values of various firewoods. They may even list the Btu values for comparison. It is likely, however, that such listings may be misleading. Most people probably do not understand what they are reading, and the Btu value of a particular firewood is by no means the best criteria in determining whether or not you should grow that particular type of tree. For example, oak has a high Btu rating, because it is a hardwood and burns a hot fire. It takes several years to grow however, and, because it grows so slowly, it is not practical for people who rely on wood for heat. A wood with a low Btu rating, such as cottonwood or hybrid populars, will produce more wood in a shorter period of time.

SPECIES

Will trees grow in your area? Remember your climate. In areas of Nebraska, you may need artificial irrigation to grow practically any tree at all, because the natural rainfall is so light that it may not sustain tree life by itself. Pioneers in those areas made their homes out of sod and "buffalo chips" because of a shortage of lumber.

When growing trees for the home woodlot, remember that dry wood burns better and more safely than green wood. Dry wood has been cut and allowed to *season* for several months. Green wood is freshly cut wood that still has the green living tissue in its *cambrium* (inner bark). Green wood burns slow and is almost impossible to use for starting a fire. (For information on proper planting and pruning techniques, see Chapter 23, Shade Trees.)

Cottonwood. The cottonwood (*Populus deltoides)* can be found growing in more areas with different climates than any other tree in the United States. It grows almost anywhere and is extremely easy to propagate. This drought-resistant species can weather the coldest of winters. Although cottonwoods can reach 80 feet in height, they rarely do because they are usually cut before they get to that size.

Cottonwood produces soft wood that is useful for firewood or pulpwood for the paper industry. Its fast growth rate can provide firewood in only three or four years after planting, making it ideal for the home woodlot.

This tree is very easy to reproduce. Cut a twig in the springtime and stick it in moist ground. Within a few days, it will develop roots and a new tree has formed! Only the female trees produce "cotton" (a white cottonlike material that will litter your yard). To avoid this litter, plant only male trees. Try a cottonless strain such as *Siouxland.*

For fastest growth, water your trees on a regular, weekly basis. Soak the area under the branch span thoroughly. Do not sprinkle. If you use commercial fertilizers, a timed-release pellet when planting is quite effective. Otherwise, apply manure in the spring. Do not allow fresh manure to touch the trunk. Spread manure evenly in a circle around the base of the tree and cover it with dirt.

It is essential that all weeds and grasses be removed from around the base of young cuttings or transplants. It is preferable to keep the immediate area free of vegetation, or at least, cut the grass and remove the weeds regularly so that they do not inhibit the tree's growth or strangle it. Mulch the area under the tree with straw or leaves during the summer to help inhibit weeds. Although cottonwoods make lovely shade trees, they are ideal for raising firewood in a hurry. Plant trees about 4 to 6 feet apart for firewood production.

Douglas Fir. The Douglas fir presents a very attractive appearance with its pyramidal growth and soft, blue-green needlelike leaves. Sometimes people will grow it as an ornamental for a few years and harvest it when it starts to get so big that it dwarfs the other landscape plantings.

Pseudotsuga menziensii grows up to 200 feet tall, so this giant tree will get too big for anyone with a small yard, although most people harvest it before it gets that big. It produces a very high quality wood that is used in the lumber industry for building construction.

Douglas fir favors full sun for fastest growth. It also likes a light, well-drained soil. Avoid clay and poorly drained soils. They will give you problems.

This fast-growing species needs plenty of water for best growth. Water on a weekly basis, more often during dry weather. Always soak the area under the branch span. Do not just sprinkle.

Place timed-release fertilizer pellets in the planting hole or apply manure after planting. Cut tall grasses and weeds from around the trees to give them room.

If you grow your own, they make nice Christmas trees, and you may have extras to sell or give away. It should be sheared to keep its pyramidal shape when grown for Christmas tree use. Douglas fir makes good wood for the home woodlot and, if you have the space, you could grow your own lumber.

Eastern White Pine. The Eastern white pine (*Pinus strobus)* is among the most beautiful of the coniferous trees (Fig. 27-2). It is a vigorous, fast-growing tree, sometimes growing as much as 3 to 4 feet in a single season. The white pine is a lumber tree. The wood is white, easy to work with, and a prize among the timber species. It was once the major timber tree in America, but has been replaced by other species—most notably the Douglas fir of

Fig. 27-2. White pine is among the most beautiful of the coniferous trees.

the western United States.

White pine is very easy to grow. It favors a light, sandy well-drained soil and a sunny location. Remember when planting white pines that they grow quite large, so do not crowd them too closely unless you are trying to form a windbreak or screen.

Weeds must be controlled so that they do not smother young transplants. A mulch will be helpful in inhibiting weed growth.

Visitors will stop and admire a white pine tree, because it is so pretty. The long slender needles are even soft to the touch. It is truly one of the most beautiful trees, almost too pretty to cut up for wood. But if it gets cold enough and these are your only trees—well, you make the decision.

Hybrid Poplars. Commercial paper companies use much poplar for paper production. There are many species in the genus *Populus* that have been bred by the forestry department and paper industries to produce fast growth. Most of these are soft wooded trees that will grow at an incredible rate.

Many nurseries offer these new hybrids. Some offer them as unrooted cuttings that are easy to root by sticking into moist ground. Keep the area free of tall grasses and weeds, and keep the ground moist. The cutting, with a little care, watering, weeding, and fertilzier, will rapidly develop into a nice young tree. Its fast growth will surprise and delight you, because poplars are among the fastest growing of the temperature zone trees.

Nurseries also offer rooted cuttings for more difficult, poor soil areas. These rooted cuttings tend to transplant well, and for those who have the money, larger size transplants can be purchased. These are the best buy for people who are growing trees for shade, windbreaks, or need wood in a hurry.

Some of the poplar species are better for producing firewood than others. Some grow so that if you do not cut down the entire tree, they come back from stumps to regenerate themselves. This way, you can take several cuttings of firewood from the same planting. Check with your nursery to see what hybrid poplars they offer. These are probably the best trees for the home woodlot.

Ponderosa Pine. The ponderosa pine (*Pinus ponderosa*) is a giant tree. It rapidly grows to 175 feet in height with quite a wide spread. This species is one of the "yellow pines," so-called by lumbermen because of the light golden color of its timber. It is an important tree in the lumber industry because its wood is of high quality and is used for building materials. It has dark green foliage and scaled bark.

For fastest growth, plant ponderosa pine in full sun. It favors a slightly acidic soil. If you have heavy soils, try to lighten them by the addition of organic matter, such as peat moss or leaf mold.

A fast growing species like ponderosa pine requires plenty of water. Soak the area under the tree each week, more often during periods of dry weather or if the tree looks like it needs it. A mulch is a helpful way to conserve moisture.

Ponderosa pine responds well to fertilizer. Use timed-release pellet at planting time, or apply manure after planting. Do not touch the tree with fresh manure.

This species is suitable for the home woodlot. It produces a high quality wood that is useful for building materials and construction. (If you have the

Fig. 27-3. Red pine can be found growing in the wild up into Canada. It is one of the hardiest pines.

room, you could grow your own lumber). Ponderosa pine can be used in windbreaks or naturalized in the woodland garden.

Red Pine. Red pine (*Pinus resinosa*) can be found growing in the wild up into Canada. It is one of the hardiest pines. An attractive tree, this species usually has a straight trunk with reddish bark (Fig. 27-3). It can grow to heights of 50 feet. The typical needlelike leaves take on a yellowish-green color during winter.

The red pine favors full sun. It is one of the best evergreens to grow on dry sandy soils. To save money, gather young plants from the woods. If you gather from the wild, be certain that you are not violating any laws or trespassing on private property. Many people think of the wilderness as if it were all part of the public domain, but for the most part, this is not the case. Most wooded areas are privately owned.

Use of timed-release fertilizer pellets are beneficial to help young trees get off to a rapid start. You can use manure. Fresh manure must not touch the young transplant and should be covered with dirt.

Red pine favors a slightly acidic soil. Be sure to water trees on a weekly basis, at least for the first two years, until they become well-established.

Plant trees 6 to 8 feet apart if used for windbreak purposes. Stagger trees, rather than planting them in a straight line when used as screens or windbreaks. Plant in a straight line when growing firewood.

Chapter 28

Patio Fruits

A nice feature about container-grown plants is that you can move the plants indoors during the winter. This allows you to grow fruits that normally would not be sufficiently winter hardy in your area. It also gives you the opportunity to decorate your indoor landscape by bringing summer inside, with fruit plants adding a touch of color and a possible nibble to brighten the drab winter months.

Patio plantings require specific types of fruits. Miniature fruit trees are available for container growing, and these small trees are ideal for the home patio (Fig. 28-1). They are usually preferable to dwarfs for the patio, because they are even smaller, yet many provide full-size fruit. (Some may not, so be sure to check with your nursery.)

The ease of moving your plants makes it possible to rearrange them as well. When you are weary of one patio setting, you can change your plants around almost as easily as you move your outdoor furniture.

There are many other types of fruits that can be grown in containers as well as miniature trees— small, fruiting bushes and vines are also practical.

Fruit plants that grow too large are best avoided. You may have to change the containers of large plants several times to prevent the roots from becoming bound-up as they grow. The fruits you elect to plant will depend entirely upon your personal preference.

Miniature Fruit Trees. There are many ways to obtain the dwarf characteristics so desired in fruit trees. Nearly everyone is familiar with the Japanese art of *bonsai,* but what many do not realize is that bonsai specimens are simply regular trees kept small by *root pruning.* It is a complicated art, and amateurs should study well before attempting it on their own. A bonsai subject removed from its container and planted in the garden (provided that it is hardy enough to grow in that climate) will turn into a regular size tree in rapid time. Bonsai is one way to dwarf trees.

More commonly, people purchase trees that are *grafted dwarfs.* This is easiest and most practical. These trees are dwarfed by use of select *dwarf rootstocks.* These rootstocks give the tree its dwarf nature. Depending upon the tree and the rootstock

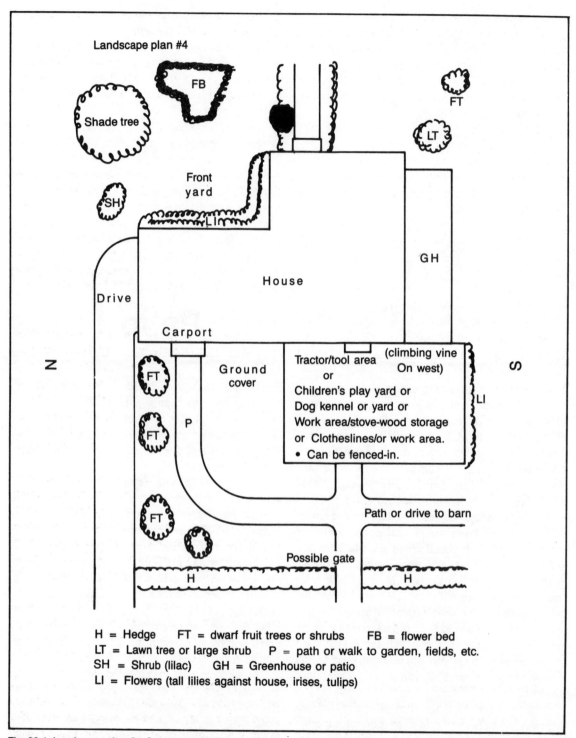

Fig. 28-1. Landscape plan #4. Courtesy of Marion Michaels.

used, you can get some fairly small trees.

There is another strain of dwarfs that produce the *miniature* fruit trees. These trees rarely grow taller than 7 feet, yet many produce full size fruit. Sometimes called *genetic dwarfs,* these plants are the result of extensive breeding, as well as the use of rootstocks and grafting.

Most genetic dwarfs are capable of *self-pollinating,* which makes them even more valuable because it takes only one tree to bear fruit. These trees are quite expensive, more so than regular dwarfs. Check with your nursery to see what genetic dwarfs they may offer.

Patio Apple. The apple is probably the world's favorite fruit. *Malus pumila*, a miniature apple tree, is ideal for the patio garden. Most miniature trees grow to about 6 feet in height. It bears lightly-scented white blossoms in the spring and fruits in late summer and fall.

Usually, the apples from these trees are yellow, but they tend to take on a reddish blush when grown in colder climates. They are sweet-flavored and of a good size, like regular apples. The apples are firm and keep well.

Apples are a little more difficult to maintain than most fruits because of the large number of insects they attract. These pests damage not only the foliage, but the fruits themselves. If you plan on growing any apple trees, including these miniature types, you will have to devote considerable attention to them. Your "picture-perfect" apples will require much effort on your part. If time is a scarce commodity for you, you may wish to consider growing a fruit other than apples.

Patio Apricot. Apricots are one of the most beautiful trees. The apricot (*Prunus armenica*) has fine-textured leaves, which makes it attractive even when not in bloom or with fruit. In the early spring, their delicate pink flowers abound. During summer, their fruits develop and later ripen to a deep golden color. The golden fruits offer great contrast to the dark green leaves.

The patio apricot is a genetic dwarf that grows only about 6 to 7 feet tall. Self-pollinating, this is ideal for the home patio. It bears medium to large fruits, luscious in color as well as taste. The fruits

are firm, but juicy, and develop their sweetest taste when grown in full sunlight.

People in northern areas will want to plant these trees in containers that can be moved inside during the winter. Be sure that containers are properly drained and at least 30 inches in diameter and 2 feet deep.

Patio Nectarine. The patio nectarine (*Prunus persica* var. *nucifera*) is best suited to the western half of the country. It tends to have more disease problems when grown in the humid areas east of the Mississippi. The nectarine is identical to the peach except for one trait—it has no "fuzz." Apparently, fuzzy skin acts to protect fruits from the rot organisms that thrive in humid areas; these same rot organisms are rare in the semiarid regions of the West. For this reason, peaches should be grown in the east and nectarines in the west. (Of course, you can grow nectarines in the east, they will just require more care.)

The varieties available will be labeled according to what each nursery decides to call them. The same plant can have several common names. Check with your nursery to see if they offer these genetic dwarfs. Most miniature nectarines grow to about 5 feet, with beautiful blossoms in the spring and large freestone fruits in late summer. (Not all bear large fruit. Double-check the nursery catalog to see if yours will.)

The patio nectarine has the same requirements as that of the peach. If grown in eastern states, precautions should be taken to protect the fruit. These are simple: remember to take the tree inside during rainy weather; and always water the tree at the base, never over the foliage and fruits, because it may encourage the growth of rot organisms, various molds, and fungi.

Northern growers should plant these trees in containers that can be moved indoors during inclement weather. Out west, you will not have to worry as much, but you must provide winter protection in states where the winters are severe.

Patio Peach. The ideal peach (*Prunus persica*) for the patio garden is a genetic dwarf. The cultivars come under different names, depending upon the nursery. Most are tiny trees that grow about 5 feet.

In spring, this peach will be covered with pink blossoms. During the summer, it bears a crop of full-size, large freestone peaches of high eating quality. People who live in peach-growing areas can enjoy this plant anywhere in their yard. Those who live in cold areas will want to plant their peach trees in containers.

Always use a container that is large enough to successfully accommodate your tree. Containers should be at least 30 inches in diameter and 2 feet deep. The roots should not be crowded. For best growth, a sterile planting medium should be used.

Ordinary soil should be avoided, because it may contain nematodes or other pests. Sterile planting mediums are available commercially, or you can sterilize your soil with steam or by baking it in a hot oven. It is easiest to simply buy a prepackaged sterile medium.

Your container must have good drainage. People forget about the importance of water drainage. Plants grown in containers can easily become waterlogged if the drainage is not adequate. This is a leading cause of plant death for container grown plants.

Chapter 29

Fruit Trees

Although all fruit trees can add beauty to a home, some types are better suited to landscape purposes than others. Most people want low-maintenance plants, because not many people have a lot of time these days to spend on yardwork or the money to hire a gardener. A landscape that can provide maximum appeal and minimum labor is best suited to most people.

All tree fruits require more labor than non-fruiting trees. Pie cherries are among the least time-consuming, and apples will probably take the most time and labor to grow successfully. Of course, you will have to make decisions about what to plant based on your own needs and desires. It is a good idea to keep in mind the amount of time and work you will want to do when considering which fruits to plant.

Before you plant any fruit tree, be certain that you will have the time to care for it properly. A neglected fruit tree is not lovely to look at and frequently dies. The fruit trees that you select should fit into your landscape theme and should integrate with your other plants. For an attractive landscape, you must achieve balance among your plantings.

SEASONAL CHANGES

Almost all fruit trees are deciduous. They experience seasonal changes, and these changes can be an exciting part of your landscape. Plan your other plantings to best take advantage of the different stages of your fruit trees.

The Flowering Stage

A fruit tree in flower is a thing of great beauty, but there are some things you should know. The flowers should not be infested with insects, or it can ruin the display. Bees are good; caterpillars and chewing insects are not. Also, during the flowering stage, be sure that you have another fruit tree (a different variety of the same species) nearby to cross-pollinate the plant. If you do not, your tree may not bear fruit.

The Summer Foliage Stage

The summer leaf display should be pleasing. Leaves

that are chewed by bugs, shrunken, discolored, or malformed from drought stress or neglect will not make an attractive sight. The regular care of weeding, watering, and fertilizing, will not be enough. Special attention must be paid to rid insect pests, when necessary. Yellowing and shrunken leaves often indicate drought stress, but can also be indicative of nutritional deficiencies. For a small fee, your county extension service can do a leaf analysis test to determine nutritional deficiencies, if any.

The Fruit Stage

Nobody likes the looks of blemished or deformed fruits, but keeping your fruits blemish-free will be no small task. You may not be able to have them all picture-perfect, but you will want as many as possible to be perfect, especially if you are fond of giving tours of your home grounds. Deformed or bug-infested fruits will leave an ugly impression, and you want your guests to be enchanted, not repulsed by your landscape.

The Fall Foliage

Some fruit trees provide bright colors during the fall, others do not. If most of your plants are designed for a fall landscape, you may not mind that your fruit trees are unimpressive, because there will be so many other things to look at. In some cases, a fruit tree may be all you have for fall color. You may wish to add a couple of other shrubs to complement the tree under those circumstances. A burning bush is a nice item for fall foliage.

Winter

In winter, your work is not over. Anyone who lives in areas of heavy snow will have to see that their tree is protected from ice damage, sun scald, and other winter injuries. Select a site where there is no salt run-off from salt used to deice paths and driveways. Try using sand instead. In late winter, just towards the edge of the spring, a dormant oil spray should be applied to most fruit trees to protect them from insect pests.

Fig. 29-1. Dwarf apple trees. Courtesy Stark Bro's Nurseries & Orchards Co.

Fig. 29-2. The Juneberry is one of the most beautiful ornamentals.

DWARFS

The dwarf varieties are usually better landscape plants than are standard size trees, but there are exceptions. An old apple, for instance, can provide shade and cast an interesting winter silhouette of contorted branches. If you are starting out, however, you will probably want to plant dwarfs. The most important reason to choose dwarfs is because they are less trouble to take care of and easier to maintain. They are also more likely to fit into the proportion of today's modern homes, with their sleek, low ranch styles and smaller yards.

Dwarfs fit in almost anywhere and you can grow more different kinds of your favorite fruits in the same amount of space that it would take to grow one regular tree. Remember to always select a sunny location. Some fruits, such as sour cherries, are shade-tolerant, but most fruits require full sun. They should be set only in areas where they will have good air circulation. Avoid windy sites where strong gusts are likely to knock fruits off the trees, and avoid frost pockets, where cold spring air settles. Such sites are likely to prevent the tree from ever fruiting, because the frost will kill flower blossoms and prevent fruit set (Fig. 29-1).

Usually, it is best to plant fruit trees in pairs of two different varieties within the same species. Do not plant only one tree or you may never have any fruit.

FRUIT TYPES

Apples seem to be the most popular fruit, but use your imagination. Pears, peaches, nectarines, cherries—both sweet and sour—can all be used effectively in the home landscape. Do not forget unusual and native fruits. The juneberry is one of the most beautiful ornamentals, and it can be grown as a shrub or small tree (Fig. 29-2). Early in spring, often before leafing out, it will be covered with clouds of fleecy-white blossoms. In summer, it bears delicious fruits that look and taste much like blueberries and make a scrumptious pie. In fall, the foliage changes color to be a "show-off" in your fall landscape. That's not all—juneberries are hardy as far north as Alaska!

Mulberries are another fruit that really deserve greater use in the home landscape. Some people do not like the litter of the fallen fruits, which can stain driveways and sidewalks. If you are not all that fussy, or do not plant your mulberry trees too close to sidewalks and other man-made structures that might be stained from fallen fruits, you are sure to enjoy the tree and especially its fruit.

Check your garden catalog to see what types of fruit trees they offer. Do not be afraid to experiment with an unusual or native variety and, of course, select your favorite fruits. Fruit trees can be a practical and beautiful way to decorate your yard and improve your family's nutrition as well.

For information on planting and pruning fruit trees, see Chapter 23, Shade Trees.

Chapter 30

Small Fruits

Tree fruits are not practical for everyone, because some people do not have the room to grow them. Others do not have the time to care for them, and many people do not have the patience to wait for their plants to bear fruits. For these and other reasons, small fruits can be a landscape solution (Fig. 30-1).

Small fruits offer many advantages: they are quick to bear: some yield fruit the very same year that they are planted; most small fruits are easy to grow; and small fruits offer a diversity of plants that can fit into the smallest of yards or into indoor containers for people who have no yard space at all.

Not all small fruits are practical. Grapes, for example, should be avoided. They will require too much for most people, and they have a complicated pruning system that is difficult to learn to do properly. Improperly pruned grapes may have poor yields, or not bear fruit at all.

Integrating Fruits. It is an entirely different task to integrate fruits into your landscape than it is to plant a separate fruit garden. It requires more thought on your part to make the design work, and

more imagination. Do not overlook standards like strawberry barrels or pyramids. They can be attractive, but try a few novel ideas, too. For example, climbing strawberries can be grown against a wall with the support of a wire trellis. They would provide a dual purpose; both as a vine and a producer of edible fruits. The *Fort Laramie* cultivar is an everbearer that can be trained to climb.

Small fruits can be set in rock gardens or other landscape structures that you build. A gazebo surrounded by blueberry bushes is inviting. The blueberry blossoms will look nice in spring, the fruits in summer, and the leaves in the fall.

Blueberries can also be used as hedge plants. Substitute a blueberry hedge for a regular hedge: you will have both beauty and luscious fruits for pies and eating fresh (Fig. 30-2).

Blueberries. Blueberries require special culture to grow successfully. They need a highly acidic soil, so plenty of peat moss should be included in the planting medium. Check your soil's pH before planting blueberries. You will probably have to increase the acidic levels. Aluminum sulfate or

Fig. 30-1. It is an entirely different task to integrate fruits into your landscape than it is to plant a separate fruit garden. Courtesy of Paul & Alvalina Nandory.

ferrous sulfate can be added to make soil more acidic. Ferrous sulfate is probably the best acidifier.

Many gardeners have trouble raising blueberries. Southerners should try planting one of the "rabbiteye" varieties that are best suited to southern climates. Northerners can grow the regular highbush types, but people who live where winters are severe (from central Wisconsin northward) should try one of the new half-high hybrids such as the cultivar *Tophat*. These plants will not grow as large as regular highbush blueberries, so they are less likely to suffer frost damage or winterkill.

Blueberries offer seasonal color. In the spring, they usually bear white to pink, bell-shaped flowers. In early summer, they have glossy green foliage, and later they bear blueberries. Those luscious fruits are delightful in pies, muffins, and fresh off the bush. In the fall, blueberry foliage turns a bright crimsom before it drops. (Incidentally, the bushes do not lose their leaves when taken indoors for the winter, but continue to grow as they normally would during the regular growing season.)

Currants and Gooseberries. Current and/or gooseberry hedges can be used in soil that is not acidic enough for blueberry hedges. These are such easy-to-grow species that you really cannot lose when you plant them. They are ideal for people with busy schedules, and for people who want all the joy of a beautiful landscape, but not the work. Currants and gooseberries can be neglected and still bear fruit.

The plants are especially attractive in the summer when their berries, which are usually borne quite abundantly, add color contrast to their green leaves. Currants may be even more outstanding than gooseberries because the bright red color of their fruits makes them a natural ornamental. These berries make a scrumptious jelly, and gooseberry pie is a treat your whole family will enjoy.

Rhubarb. There is nothing particularly clever or unique in a flower bed planted inside an old automobile tire (enameled white or not). A rhubarb plant set in such an arrangement, however, could be both novel and very practical. In northern climates, rhubarb is often one of the earliest greening plants, with broad, albeit poisonous, showy, leaves. It also serves the very useful task of providing fresh "fruit" for pies or sauces months before most fruits are ready, even about a month earlier than strawberries. The extremely tart, rich flavor of rhubarb lends itself beautifully to pies. In fact, in some areas of the United States, rhubarb is commonly referred to as *pieplant*.

Rhubarb should not be used beyond the early part of July. After that time, the stalks should be allowed to grow and replenish their strength for winter. July will also be a good time for the flowers you have set around each rhubarb plant to bloom. Annual flowers like petunias will provide a colorful ring around the broad green of the rhubarb.

If your yard allows the space and your garage overflows with tires, you may want to use more than one such rhubarb/floral arrangement. Three tires or so, set in a relatively close proximity or in some specific design around the yard, could be a very effective part of your landscape plan.

Strawberries. For most landscape purposes, the everbearing varieties are more practical than the

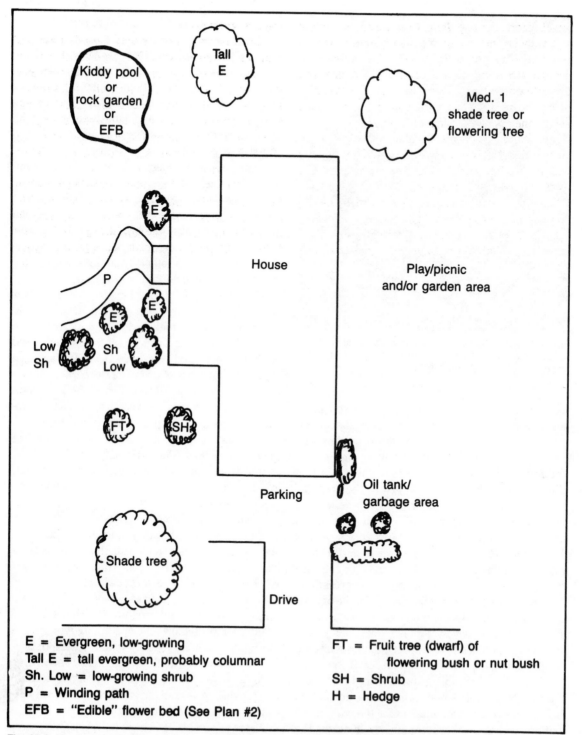

Kiddy pool
or
rock garden
or
EFB

Tall
E

Med. 1
shade tree or
flowering tree

E

House

Play/picnic
and/or garden area

P

Low
Sh

E

Sh
Low

FT

SH

Oil tank/
garbage area

H

Parking

Shade tree

Drive

E = Evergreen, low-growing
Tall E = tall evergreen, probably columnar
Sh. Low = low-growing shrub
P = Winding path
EFB = "Edible" flower bed (See Plan #2)

FT = Fruit tree (dwarf) of
flowering bush or nut bush
SH = Shrub
H = Hedge

Fig. 30-2. Landscape plan #5. Courtesy of Marion Michaels.

Junebearers. For one thing, they are not as prolific at producing new runners. Also, plants grown in containers do not usually have the problem of drought-stress that attacks other plants (unless you forget to water them). There are many fine varieties of everbearers. Check with your nursery to see which ones are best adapted to your area.

For bordering sidewalks and garden paths, try a runnerless cultivar such as *Alpine*. These plants will not produce runners, so they always stay put right where you set them out. They are usually a little more expensive than regular strawberries and do not produce as large a fruit, but they will never get out-of-bounds when planted in an area. Even when not in fruit, their foliage makes a neat and attractive groundcover.

Strawberry plants are very easy to grow, and they can fit into any yard. For those people who do not have a yard, strawberries are ideal for container-growing indoors. The only problem with growing strawberries indoors in containers is that the fruits are so delicious you may never grow enough to satisfy you. Try to avoid the temptation of eating them all fresh, and wait until you have enough berries for shortcake.

Another nice feature about growing strawberries is that it is a nice way to get young children interested in gardening. Your kids will become enthusiastic horticulturists at an early age if you start them growing this practical and delicious fruit.

Sources

You will be able to obtain a wider selection of landscape plants if you order from a mail-order nursery, rather than from a local nursery. Most local garden centers, like any other retail business, maintain a limited inventory on hand. Usually this inventory consists of plants they sell most. You will end up with all the same plants that your neighbors have, if you are not careful.

Mail-order companies generally service the entire nation or a large portion of it. They maintain a wider selection of plant materials and are most likely to be able to supply you with exactly the plants you want. Most reputable firms offer a limited guarantee on the plants they sell.

The following is a list of mail-order firms that sell landscape plants. It is not exhaustive, but gives you several sources of reputable dealers. Your county agent can provide you with a list of local firms or nurseries in your area.

With each address is included information on what the company specializes in and cost, if any, of its catalog or price list. Nurseries may offer additional items that are not listed so be sure to check the individual catalogs.

Abundant Life Seed Foundation
P.O. Box 772
Port Townsend, WA 98368

Organic & untreated seeds, wildflowers, trees. All open-pollinated. $2 for one-year subscription and catalog. This includes four quarterly newsletters. The cost for Canadians is $3 in U.S. currency.

Adams Country Nursery, Inc.
P.O. Box 108
Aspers, PA 17304

Fruit trees. Free catalog.

Agway, Inc.
RD 4 Zeager Rd.
Elizabethtown, Pa 17022

Ahrens Strawberry Nursery
Route 1
Huntingburg, IN 47542

Small fruits. Free catalog.

Altman Specialty Plants
553 Buena Creek Road
San Marcos, CA 92069

Succulents. Catalog $1.

Armstrong Nurseries, Inc.
P.O. Box 4060
Ontario, CA 91761

Roses and fruit trees. Free catalog.

Beersheba Wildflower Gardens
P.O. Box 551
Beersheba Springs, TN 37305

Wildflowers east of the Mississippi. Free catalog.

Bluestone Perennials
7237 Middle Ridge Road
Madison, OH 44057

Perennial flowers, ground covers. Free catalog.

Bountiful Ridge Nurseries, Inc.
Box 250
Princess Anne, MD 21853

Tree and small fruits, ornamentals. Free catalog.

W. Atlee Burpee
300 Park Avenue
Warminster, PA 18974

Flowers, fruits, ornamentals. Free catalog.

D.V. Burrell Seed Growers Co.
P.O. Box 150
Rocky Ford, CO 81067

Flower seeds. Free catalog.

Carrol Gardens
444 E. Main
Westminster, MD 21157

Perennials, rock garden plants, evergreens. Free catalog.

Conley's Garden Center
Boothbay Harbor, ME 04538

Hardy wildflowers, ferns, native perennials, groundcovers. Catalog $1.50.

De Jager Bulbs, Inc.
188 Ashbury Street
South Hamilton, MA 01982

Flower bulbs. Catalog $1.50.

Esp Wildflowers
P.O. Box 5125
El Monte, CA 91734

Wildflower seeds in bulk. Free catalog.

Farmer Seed & Nursery
818 N.W. 4th St.
Faribault, MN 55021

Ornamentals, tree and small fruits, perennials, shade trees. Free catalog.

Henry Field Seed & Nursery Co.
2176 Oak Street
Shenandoah, IA 51602

Fruits, ornamentals. Free catalog.

Gardens of the Blue Ridge
P.O. Box 10
Pineola, NC 28662

Hardy native herbaceous perennials of North Carolina. Catalog $1.

Garden Place
6780 Heisley Road
Mentor, OH 44060

Perennials. Catalog $1.

The Garden Spot
4032 Rosewood Drive
Columbia, SC 29205

Ivy plants. Send self-addressed stamped envelope for price list.

Green Horizons
500 Thompson Drive
Kerrville, TX 78028

Texas wildflowers. Newsletter $7.50.

Greer Gardens
1280 Goodpasture Island Road
Eugene, OR 97401

Rhododendrons and azaleas. Catalog $2.

Hastings
P.O. Box 4274
Atlanta, GA 30302

Ornamentals, flowers, and fruits for the south. Free catalog.

Inter-State Nurseries, Inc.
Hamburg, IA 51640

Roses, perennials, trees, shrubs, fruits. Free catalog.

J.W. Jung Seed Co.
Randolph, WI 53956

Ornamentals, fruits. Free catalog.

Krider Nurseries
Middlebury, In 46540

Roses, ornamentals, perennials, fruits. Free catalog.

224

Lawyer Nursery
Rt. 2 Box 95
Plains, MT

Hardy seedlings, ornamentals, conifers. Free price list.

Mellinger's Inc.
2310 W. South Range Road
North Lima, OH 44452

Ornamentals, shade trees, fruits, flowers, wildflowers. Free catalog.

J.E. Miller Nursery
5060 W. Lake Road
Canandaigua, NY 14424

Tree and small fruits, ornamentals. Free catalog.

Neosho Nurseries
900 North College
Neosho, MO 64850

Evergreens, shade trees, roses, ornamentals. Free catalog.

Plants of the Southwest
1570 Pacheco Street
Santa Fe, NM 87501

Native plants, wildflowers, and grass seeds. Catalog $1.

Prairie Ridge Nursery
RR2 9738 Overland Road
Mt. Horeb, WI 53572

Native southwestern Wisconsin prairie seeds and plants. Catalog 50¢.

Putney Nursery
Rt. 5
Putney, VT 05346

Hardy wildflowers, ferns, and perennials. Free catalog.

Roses of Yesterday and Tommorrow
802 Brown's Valley Rd.
Watsonville, CA 95076

Old and rare roses. Catalog $1.50.

Savage Farms Nursery
P.O. Box 125
McMinnville, TN 37110

Flowering trees and shrubs, evergreens, wildflowers, shade trees. Free catalog.

Stark Bros. Nurseries & Orchards Co.
Louisiana, MO 63353

Dwarf and regular fruit trees, small fruits, ornamentals, roses. Free catalog.

Stern's Nurseries, Inc.
Geneva, NY 14456

Small fruits, flowers, and shrubs. Free price list.

Vanbourgondien Bros.
245 Farmingdale Rd. Rt 109
Babylon, NY 11702

Flower bulbs, perennials, and ornamentals. Free catalog.

Waynesboro Nurseries
Box 987
Waynesboro, VA 22980

Ornamentals, shade and flowering trees, small and tree fruits, evergreens. Free catalog.

Wayside Gardens
Hodges, SC 29695

Perennials, groundcovers, trees. Catalog $1.

White Flower Farm
Route 63
Litchfield, CT 06759

Perennials, ornamentals. Catalog $5

Index

Index

229

OTHER POPULAR TAB BOOKS OF INTEREST

44 Terrific Woodworking Plans & Projects (No. 1762—$12.50 paper; $21.95 hard)

How to Repair Briggs & Stratton Engines—2nd Edition (No. 1687—$8.95 paper; $15.95 hard)

Security for You and Your Home . . . A Complete Handbook (No. 1680—$17.50 paper; $29.95 hard)

46 Step-by-Step Wooden Toy Projects (No. 1675—$9.95 paper; $17.95 hard)

The Kite Building & Kite Flying Handbook, with 42 Kite Plans (No. 1669—$15.50 paper)

Building Better Beds (No. 1664—$14.50 paper; $19.95 hard)

Organic Vegetable Gardening (No. 1660—$16.50 paper; $25.95 hard)

The Woodturning Handbook, with Projects (No. 1655—$14.50 paper; $21.95 hard)

Clock Making for the Woodworker (No. 1648—$11.50 paper; $16.95 hard)

Steel Homes (No. 1641—$15.50 paper; $21.95 hard)

The Homeowner's Illustrated Guide to Concrete (No. 1626—$15.50 paper; $24.95 hard)

Kerosene Heaters (No. 1598—$10.25 paper; $16.95 hard)

Clocks—Construction, Maintenance and Repair (No. 1569—$13.50 paper; $18.95 hard)

The Underground Home Answer Book (No. 1562—$11.50 paper; $16.95 hard)

Airbrushing (No. 1555—$20.50 paper)

Basic Blueprint Reading for Practical Applications (No. 1546—$13.50 paper; $18.95 hard)

Central Heating and Air Conditioning Repair Guide—2nd Edition (No. 1520—$13.50 paper; $18.95 hard)

The Complete Book of Fences (No. 1508—$12.95 paper; $19.95 hard)

How to Sharpen Anything (No. 1463—$12.95 paper; $19.95 hard)

Building a Log Home from Scratch or Kit (No. 1458—$12.50 paper; $17.95 hard)

Build It with Plywood: 88 Furniture Projects (No. 1430—$13.50 paper; $18.95 hard)

The GIANT Book of Metalworking Projects (No. 1357—$12.95 paper; $19.95 hard)

The Welder's Bible (No. 1244—$13.95 paper)

The GIANT Handbook of Food-Preserving Basics (No. 1727—$13.50 paper; $17.95 hard)

Ventilation: Your Secret Key to an Energy-Efficient Home (No. 1681—$8.95 paper; $15.95 hard)

Tuning and Repairing Your Own Piano (No. 1678—$12.50 paper)

Superinsulated, Truss-Frame House Construction (No. 1674—$15.50 paper; $21.95 hard)

Raising Animals for Fun and Profit (No. 1666—$13.50 paper; $18.95 hard)

Practical Herb Gardening . . . with Recipes (No. 1661—$11.95 paper; $15.95 hard)

Effective Lighting for Home and Business (No. 1658—$13.50 paper; $18.95 hard)

Constructing and Maintaining Your Well and Septic System (No. 1654—$12.50 paper; $17.95 hard)

Maps and Compasses: A User's Handbook (No. 1644—$9.25 paper; $15.95 hard)

Woodcarving, with Projects (No. 1639—$11.50 paper; $16.95 hard)

Sign Carving (No. 1601—$13.50 paper; $19.95 hard)

Mastering Household Electrical Wiring (No. 1587—$13.50 paper; $19.95 hard)

Cave Exploring (No. 1566—$10.25 paper; $16.95 hard)

The Radio Control Hobbyist's Handbook (No. 1561—$19.50 paper)

Be Your Own Contractor: The Affordable Way to Home Ownership (No. 1554—$12.50 paper; $17.95 hard)

Beekeeping—An Illustrated Handbook (No. 1524—$10.95 paper; $15.95 hard)

101 Model Railroad Layouts (No. 1514—$11.50 paper; $17.95 hard)

53 Space-Saving, Built-In Furniture Projects (No. 1504—$17.50 paper)

The Home Brewer's Handbook (No. 1461—$10.25 paper; $16.95 hard)

Constructing Outdoor Furniture, with 99 Projects (No. 1454—$15.50 paper)

Draw Your Own House Plans (No. 1381—$14.50 paper; $19.95 hard)

The Fiberglass Repair & Construction Handbook (No. 1297—$11.50 paper; $17.95 hard)

TAB TAB BOOKS Inc.

Blue Ridge Summit, Pa. 17214

Send for FREE TAB Catalog describing over 750 current titles in print.